PHENOMENOLOGY AND TREATMENT OF PSYCHIATRIC EMERGENCIES

Phenomenology and Treatment of
PSYCHIATRIC EMERGENCIES

Edited by

Betsy S. Comstock, M.D.
William E. Fann, M.D.
Alex D. Pokorny, M.D.
Robert L. Williams, M.D.

Department of Psychiatry
Baylor College of Medicine
Houston, Texas

SP MEDICAL & SCIENTIFIC BOOKS
a division of Spectrum Publications, Inc.
New York

SPECTRUM PUBLICATIONS, INC.
175-20 Wexford Terrace
Jamaica, NY 11432

Library of Congress Cataloging in Publication Data
Main entry under title:

Phenomenology and treatment of psychiatric emergencies.

    Bibliography: p.
    Includes index.
    1. Crisis intervention (Psychiatry). 2. Victims of crimes. 3. Phenomenological psychology. I. Comstock, Betsy S. [DNLM: 1. Crisis intervention. 2. Mental health services—United States. WM 401 P541]
RC480.6.P48   1983   616.89'025   83-12563
ISBN 0-89335-182-2

Printed in the United States of America.

Contributors

Gail M. Barton M.D. • Associate Professor of Psychiatry, University of Michigan, Ann Arbor, Michigan

Betsy S. Comstock, M.D. • Associate Professor of Psychiatry, Baylor College of Medicine, Houston, Texas

Martin J. Drell, M.D. • Assistant Professor of Psychiatry and Associate Director, Child and Adolescent Psychiatric Clinic, Baylor College of Medicine, Houston, Texas

Beverly J. Fauman, M.D. • Assistant Professor of Psychiatry, Wayne State University, Detroit Michigan

Michael A. Fauman, M.D. • Assistant Professor of Psychiatry, Wayne State University, Detroit, Michigan

Charles M. Gaitz, M.D. • Clinical Professor of Psychiatry and Head, Gerontology Section, Texas Research Institute of Mental Sciences (TRIMS), Houston, Texas

Donald G. Langsley, M.D. • Executive Vice-President, American Board of Medical Specialties, Evanston, Illinois

Paul A. McClelland, M.D. • Director of Consultation–Liaison Psychiatry, University of Maryland, Baltimore, Maryland

Perry Ottenberg, M.D. • Chairman, American Psychiatric Association Committee on Emerging Issues, Philadelphia, Pennsylvania

Alex D. Pokorny, M.D. • Professor and Vice-Chairman of Psychiatry, Baylor College of Medicine, Houston, Texas

Pedro Ruiz, M.D. • Professor of Psychiatry, Baylor College of Medicine, Houston, Texas

Larry B. Silver, M.D. • Deputy Director, National Institute of Mental Health, Rockville, Maryland

Edward Silverman, Ph.D. • Assistant Professor of Psychology, Department of Psychiatry, Baylor College of Medicine, Houston, Texas

Andrew Edmund Slaby, M.D., Ph.D., M.P.H. • Professor of Psychiatry and Human Behavior; Psychiatrist-in-Chief, Rhode Island Hospital, Providence, Rhode Island

Stephen M. Soreff, M.D. • Chief, Emergency Psychiatry and Consultation, Maine Medical Center, Portland, Maine

Jay D. Tarnow, M.D. • Clinical Associate Professor of Psychiatry, University of Texas Health Science Center; Director, Child Guidance Center, Houston, Texas

Contents

SPECIAL POPULATIONS AND PROBLEMS

Introduction

BETSY S. COMSTOCK
WILLIAM E. FANN
ALEX D. POKORNY
ROBERT L. WILLIAMS

Psychiatric emergencies are complex events always involving several people. At the minimum, a person identified as patient experiences sufficient personal distress or inflicts sufficient distress on others that a service provider is sought to reduce the suffering. The essential elements, then, are a patient's psychic pain or behavioral disturbance and relevant intervention, urgently sought and promptly provided, by a helping person. Many people may be involved in the same distress or disturbance, and a team of professionals may intervene utilizing a program organized in advance for that purpose, or a single distressed person may seek crisis care from an individual professional.

The chapters in this book consider the circumstances in which psychiatric emergencies can occur and the clinical techniques which experienced professionals have found useful in their practical management. The orientation is toward the psychiatric emergency as it is encountered in general medical emergency programs. Nevertheless, most of what is written here is easily transferable to psychiatric crisis clinics operating outside the structure and facilities of hospitals and to psychiatric emergencies wherever they occur. The book is addressed first to medical personnel: psychiatrists, psychiatric residents, medical students, and emergency medicine physicians, as well as physicians in general and specialty practice who inevitably will be called upon to manage the acute stage of a psychiatric emergency at some point in their careers. The book is also addressed to the nonmedical personnel who function prominently in crisis intervention work, to psychologists, social workers, and to administrative and clerical staff who are often the first institutional representatives confronted by a patient in acute distress. It is addressed

1

directly to nurses, and particularly to psychiatric nurses and their assistants who have provided the major staffing and much of the leadership in existing emergency psychiatry programs. Parts of the book may also be useful to volunteers in community crisis programs of the "Hotline" model. However, the primary orientation is toward the needs of professionals concerned with managing and resolving the psychiatric emergency in its many forms.

The care-delivery systems are complex, involving as they do several professional disciplines, a sequence of interrelated tasks, and a work-setting or program which has critical boundaries not only with other medical departments but also with the network of service agencies in the community. The patient-problem dyad is similarly complex, involving not only patient and present illness, but also their impact on all the important others in the patient's life, and their emergence in a field where family concerns, educational and occupational effects, legal considerations, and economic factors all enter the equation.

THE WORK SETTING

Emergency psychiatry is a medical discipline, a specialized approach to diagnosable problems which are encountered in a specific setting, the hospital emergency center. Often similar or identical problems are treated in other settings with different programatic orientations. However, the present discussion is focused specifically on emergency psychiatry and on the work setting found in hospital emergency departments. Generalization and transfer of the discussion to non-hospital settings is left to the reader. With this in mind, certain predictable aspects of work in an emergency center deserve comment.

The most troublesome aspect of emergency medical programs is the variability of the work load. Staffing must be planned to meet peak work loads in a safe and productive way. Yet staffing which is appropriate for the occasional high volume period will seem excessive and wasteful during slack times. No amount of busy work, extra in-service training, or general morale-tending efforts can entirely undo the damage to staff consequent to idleness. But even more difficult to manage is the erosion of staff morale by work demands when too many patients with too frightening problems arrive too fast. In very large programs a more nearly steady state can be achieved and to a limited extent it may be possible to anticipate volume: e.g. busy Saturday nights compared to slow week-day mornings. However, the work load will remain unforeseeable, and thus beyond the control of the program administrators.

Emergency psychiatry work places a number of special demands on staff members. A willingness to take risks is necessary. In more conventional psychiatric treatment approaches there are opportunities for trial and error, exploration and reconsideration, revision of treatment approach, and correction of errors. Revisions and corrections are based on observations of progress and on response from patients about the impact of treatment efforts. But emergency interventions usually are one time efforts involving a sequence of evaluation, therapeutic intervention, and referral out. Response is limited or absent and there are no opportunities for corrections over time. Therefore, interventions and referrals must be made on the basis of first evaluations, with positive conviction related to current best effort and despite the lack of guidance derived from tracking the patient's progress over time. The staff must tolerate the risk-taking required, and must also be prepared to forego the gratification of seeing the beneficial results of the work done. Even in programs structured to allow return visits, and despite the occasional information provided by other agencies after referrals, the majority of patients are lost to follow up. The usefulness of specific interventions is hard to evaluate and the satisfaction of seeing a task completed is rarely available.

The emergency program staff must tolerate a considerable amount of stress in the environment. Emergency care centers are collection points for an extraordinary volume of human suffering. The anxieties and strains associated with persistent urgency of need, alarm related to unexpected difficulties, fearfulness about outcome, closeness of death, and presence of pain pervade the atmosphere. The general emergency center staff is required to remain effective, responsive, and sympathetic. However, certain psychological defenses are marshalled which protect the staff from becoming overwhelmed by the presence of human suffering. American film and television viewing audiences are familiar with a burlesque of these defenses in the field hospital staff of M.A.S.H. The uses and usefulness of humor, depersonalization, dehumanization, isolation of affect, intellectualization, and more humor are apparent. In the psychiatric emergency, however, staff members are required to add empathy to effectiveness, responsiveness and sympathy. To a degree, the protective defenses must be surrendered. The emotions of the staff member in contact with those of the patient become a part of the evaluation and treatment mechanism. The cost in emotional demand made on the staff is much increased. Protection of personal boundaries and preservation of personal well being are essential, but these must be accomplished without distancing and isolating the patients. Preservation of empathy in the presence of psychic pain without experiencing excessive personal distress is difficult. Fewer individuals can accomplish this than can function effectively in medical settings which allow greater psychological distance from patients.

To the other stressful factors must be added apprehension about personal danger. Injuries to staff members in emergency centers are reassuringly infrequent. However, emergency psychiatry personnel must deal with patients whose mental illness may make them dangerous. Uncooperativeness, belliger-ence, agitation, and combativeness are encountered and must be controlled. Patients are in fact seeking external controls by such presentations. One of the most difficult judgements which must be made is whether physical restraint is necessary in reponse to a non-verbal request for control. Both the needs of the patient and the safety of the staff must be considered. Staff members must have reasonable assurance of personal safety. They also must be personally willing to tolerate the risk of working in a situtation where assaultive behavior may emerge, remaining alert without being excessively preoccupied with that possibility.

Because of the limited opportunity for seeing the positive results of work done, and because of the necessity for a positive attitude in spite of the stressful environment, emergency psychiatry personnel require what has been called "outrageous optimism." The story is told of a little boy found in a shed shovelling aside a pile of manure. When asked why he wanted to do that he answered, "I know with this much manure here, there is bound to be a pony somewhere." The ideal emergency psychiatry staff member not only believes there is a pony somewhere, but also thinks that the manure can be useful for making a garden.

In addition to variability of the work load and special issues related to staff personality, the emergency center presents other differences when com-pared to conventional health care settings. One difference relates to the variability of problems to be confronted. "If you're ever going to see a case of _____ disorder, you'll see it in the emergency center." The blank may be Munchausen's disease or Giles de la Tourette's syndrome or hemiballismus or rapidly dissecting aortic aneurysm. "There is no telling what's going to happen in the emergency center." "Expect the unexpected." The unspoken refrain is, "Will I know what to do when the unexpected happens?" In other work settings there is a clear understanding of what actions staff will need to perform, but not in the emergency center. Expecting the unexpected implies being ready to do the unrehearsed.

Finally, the nature of psychiatric emergencies provides patients and pathology unusual to routine practice. People often seek psychiatric help in an emergency care clinic because they feel out of control or others consider them out of control. In no other setting is there likely to be a comparable incidence of dyscontrol, impulsive behavior, and fear of loss of control. In addition, because acute psychotic reactions regularly lead to emergency center visits, there is a high level of primary process exposure. Related to these two factors are consequent behavioral disturbances. It becomes possible to judge the ambiance of an emergency psychiatry setting on the basis of what may be called the "primary process density." The flux of staff and patient apprehension constitutes a gestalt which is derived from the special problems of very disturbed patients. When it becomes distinct, "something in the air," behavioral disturbance on the part of impulsive patients can be predicted. Staff perceptions of "something brewing" seem in fact to be derived from such a gestalt. These perceptions deserve attention and specific action to reduce patient apprehension, provide assurances that the staff is prepared to exert control in emergent situations, and exploration of the various sources of the "something" which is brewing.

Emergency psychiatry patients, irrespective of their diagnosis, are involved in situations in which ego resources are reduced. As such, they often are not able to cooperate sufficiently in their own care. They frequently are not thinking logically, and cannot be engaged by a rational approach to their problems. Even if they are capable of being cooperative and rational, they may be sufficiently overcome by a sense of personal ineffectiveness and hopelessness that active efforts are impossible. In such cases the need for rapid intervention is thwarted by the very illness which occasions the need.

In summary, the emergency setting provides rather unique problems for psychiatric work. The work load is variable. The staff members are required to take risks in initiating treatment without available feedback or opportunity for correcting ineffective efforts. The work setting presents a high level of human suffering with demand for empathic responsiveness despite anxiety producing situations. A high level of personal optimism is essential. There is risk of personal danger from combative patients, and of feeling inadequate when there are unexpected events requiring unrehearsed responses. Patients interact with one another, combining primary process productions with fears of loss of control, and increasing the chances for behavioral disturbances for which staff must remain appropriately alert but not excessively apprehensive. Patient capacity for cooperation in planned interventions may be sufficiently impaired that treatment efforts repeatedly are frustrated. In short, the work is demanding and the setting unique.

DEFINITIONS

One definition of psychiatric emergency already has been suggested, that is, that it is a complex event involving two or more people where one, the patient, either experiences personal distress or inflicts distress on others, and the other, a psychiatric professional, endeavors to intervene promptly to reduce the distress. This implies that the distress is somehow the result of the patient's mental illness and that the level of distress is sufficient to call for emergency actions. The essential elements are a mentally ill patient, a situation characterized by distress, the judgement that remedial action is needed urgently, and a responding psychiatric professional. Far more complex descriptions could be built on these four essentials, emphasizing the possible involvement of more than one person in the crisis events, better defining the kinds of distress encountered, clarifying the judgements made about urgency, and elaborating a complex treatment team response. Just such elaboration will be explicit in the chapters of this volume.

A different approach to the definition of psychiatric emergency can be built upon the concept of the human personality as determined and controlled by various ego functions. Personal boundaries are established through perceptions of what is self and what is not-self. Reality testing allows for repeated affirmation of the sameness over time of various not-self perceptions and for validation of these through communication about them with others. Internal or intrapsychic events come under the control of other ego functions so that overwhelming emotions such as storms of rage, paralysing fear, or devastating guilt and remorse are checked by various defensive patterns. A psychiatric emergency then can be conceived as any life event or brief state of being where ego mechanisms fail in the presence of disrupting and anxiety provoking circumstances, resulting in loss of reality testing, failure of personal boundaries, intolerable emotional extremes, or inappropriate behavioral responses. To these must be added the judgement that the extent of ego impairment is sufficient or the abruptness of the failure so impressive as to demand immediate intervention. Often this is a subjective judgement on the part of the mentally ill person. It can as well be a judgement made by concerned others.

One objection to the definition of psychiatric emergency in purely intra-psychic terms is that it does not take into account either the importance of precipitating events or the reverberations of the ego failure on the network of personal systems in which every individual more or less continuously interacts. This rather ponderous phrase reduces to the interpersonal business of the patient plus all his or her concerns in social systems: living arrangements, job, schooling, finances, commercial, and legal affairs.

In addition, it seems illogical to build a definition which leaves out the service delivery system. Without an intervention the psychiatric emergency would be better described as a personal catastrophe. When the nature of interventions is examined it is even more evident that a strictly intrapsychic description serves poorly. Interventions depend heavily on a systems approach which takes into account the whole network of personal affairs in social systems.

INTERVENTIONS

Interventions in a psychiatric emergency may focus on any one, several, or all of the components identified in the definitions suggested here.

Intrapsychic interventions are of two types: those which aim at structural change in the patient to eliminate some area of vulnerability or to generate new capacity for future functioning, and those which aim at reinforcing existing personality structure to add temporary support until the crisis is over. It is a rather uncritically accepted convention that the former requires too much time to be relevant in emergencies and that the latter is the appropriate emergency modality. In fact, there are exceptions to this generalization. Recognition of this should encourage emergency personnel to think in terms of the psychodynamics of every emergency presentation, and to attempt exploratory and interpretive work when a patient manifests self observing capacity, curiosity about psychological processes, and willingness for change. It happens in some instances that a crisis event engenders a state of defensive instability with severe anxiety or symptom elaboration which occasions an emergency visit, but such that the very failure of defenses makes underlying conflicts more accessible than they could be otherwise. Such situations may in fact constitute nodal points in personality development, times when there is substantial potential for growth, and when the psychiatric service provider should encourage self exploration and improved insight.

Interventions which are aimed chiefly at strengthening or supporting existing structures can be classified as (1) anxiety reducing by promoting ventilation of distress, by pharmacologic intervention, or by reassurance, (2) ego lending, in which a therapist's capacity to dissipate emotional turmoil or to construct a rational sequence for evaluating behavioral alternatives is placed briefly at the disposal of the patient, and (3) defense facilitation, in which a customary defense is "set up" such as through provision of tasks requiring neatness and precision for a depressed compulsive personality, or acceptance of the role of nondestructive projection object for a decompensating paranoid. These techniques together provide a major segment of the crisis intervention armamentarium.

Attention to precipitating events often provides the basis for a different kind of intervention. A necessary part of every patient evaluation is seeking answers to the question, "Why now?"

If it can be determined that an otherwise stable adjustment of a successfully employed, 59-year-old house painter who has mild organic brain syndrome is interrupted by trips out of town organized by his wife, then the trips can be stopped. The painter can be spared the recurrent "emergencies" characterized by confusional states and belligerence. In the calm interval which will follow it will be necessary to investigate the etiology of his early organic brain syndrome. But all that is required for correcting the crisis decompensation is recognition and removal of the precipitating factor.

Interventions at the level of interpersonal process constitute another major segment of the crisis intervention armamentarium. A combined exploration and intervention process can proceed through a general sequence. (1) Define the crisis in its extension beyond the index patient, identifying the important others involved and the nature of their involvement, (2) identify the communication patterns among the people involved and search for difficulties in communication; (3) explore the psychopathology of others and attempt to learn how it is activated in relation to the patient's pathology; (4) utilize all available cooperation from important others, both for identifying patterns of interlocking dysfunctional states or psychopathology and for discovering and rehearsing more adaptive kinds of behavior.

Involvement of the index patient in a network of social systems provides the basis for another major category of interventions, namely environmental manipulation. The evaluation process should include details of living arrangements, money problems, occupational or school adjustment, and any legal difficulties. Social interventions aimed at relieving stress or at accomplishing some purpose in which the patient's efforts had been frustrated often produces resolution of a crisis. It is important to consider both the etiologic impact of social factors and also the secondary encumbrances of the illness by the reactions of the social systems to the illness. The evaluation also must support a decision that the patient's autonomous function will or will not be reduced by interventions aimed at solving environmental dilemmas.

Evaluation and referral constitute another major segment of work done in emergency programs. It seems useful to point out that this is not crisis intervention but is an inevitable part of emergency psychiatry. This is true because any program staffed 24-hours per day will attract patients seeking psychotherapy or social service, who are not involved in emergency problems, but who do not know how to gain access to the service delivery system. Emergency programs may constitute an expensive route for such entry and if initial evaluation makes this clear, then a prompt referral should be undertaken without the error of trying to establish short term emergency intervention goals. In addition, referral is necessary for continuing many efforts begun as emergency interventions.

In summary, psychiatric emergencies can be thought of as having the components, (1) precipitating circumstances, (2) intrapsychic vulnerability manifest by some breakdown of ego function, (3) interpersonal reverberations, often involving interlocking psychopathology of others, and (4) ongoing involvement within the environmental network of economic, legal, educational or occupational systems. Corresponding interventions can be directed to any one or several of these components with goals of (1) eliminating precipitating pressure, (2) promoting growth of new personality structures to overcome intrapsychic vulnerability, or promoting temporary support of exisiting defenses, (3) correction of adversive patterns of interpersonal interactions, (4) environmental manipulation to reduce secondary stresses which otherwise would be either adding to or developing in reaction to the emergency. Evaluation and referral for nonemergency treatment should be added to complete the list of types of work done in emergency psychiatry programs.

EVALUATION

The work of patient evaluation occurs before treatment planning and activation of treatment efforts can be undertaken. Three special problems in evaluation are specific to the emergency setting. The first is the problem that some cases present without identifiable crisis and it becomes necessary not to find out what is wrong but to find why the patient presents himself or herself without something wrong. The second problem is that patients often are excessively disabled with respect to cooperative participation in evaluation interviews. The third is the time limitation imposed on the process, requiring that a useful amount of data be obtained quite rapidly and that staff members make compromise decisions to proceed in the absence of information which might be available after some delay.

"No-crisis" presentations are perplexing and sometimes baffling. Patients present stating they need to talk to someone, asking for a psychiatrist, or stating they were told they could get help in the emergency program. When their story is heard, however, it may suggest a psychiatric diagnosis but not any current problem justifying the emergency visit. One possibility is that the patient wants some specific service but is unsure how to obtain it. He or she is withholding information, hoping to gain through exposure a better understanding of the program objectives and expectations of patients. Another possibility is that the decision for seeking help was made by another person, not present, and that the identified patient does not know the reasons and does not share the conviction that an emergency exists. A third possibility, mentioned earlier, is that the patient does not understand how to gain access to nonemergency treatment programs and in fact is only seeking referral.

Whether a crisis is conspicuous or absent it is worthwhile early in the evaluation to explore why the patient has come at the present time rather than any other time. Other relevant questions include who is really in trouble, at what point in time was the decision reached to seek emergency help, what were the related circumstances, and who made the decision.

Issues related to interview technique and special skills relevant to rapid evaluation are discussed in other chapters. A systematic approach for organization of information will be explored here.

Psychiatric emergencies have been described as complex events involving several components already discussed. As events they can be thought of as having a definite history, as beginning at a point in time prior to which some nonemergency status existed. The crisis events can be traced from their beginning up to the time of the evaluation. Precisely because issues related to time are of critical importance in an emergency, the account is best organized along a time-line. The pre-crisis time should be explored to establish both the patient's usual coping style and the immediately preceding living circumstances. Precipitating events and influences should be recorded in detail. Progressive changes in the patient and in his or her circumstances in the interval from onset of the crisis to the time of the evaluation should be understood chronologically. All related interpersonal links should be identified and explored. The hopes and expectations both of the identified patient and of the important others should be stated.

Observational data need to be recorded in detail since that data may afford a very different picture of the patient than can be obtained from historical data. However, the cross-sectional nature of current observations always must be kept in mind. In times of crisis, patients show very fluid status. Psychological defenses shift rapidly, symptoms flare, and recede. Opportunities for sequential observations are limited in emergency care. Consequently, any conclusions based on one-time observations must be made with awareness of the time sequence of the patient's illness.

TREATMENT PLANNING

The time limit of emergency settings are such that treatment planning rarely occurs as an isolated effort. Evaluation and intervention may proceed during the same interview. However, a formal decision process with articulation of treatment goals and selection of techniques for intervention can keep the emergency effort appropriately and realistically focused. If this effort is bypassed the work can become chaotic and ineffective.

Setting treatment goals requires acceptance by staff members of the reality that an emergency program offers the briefest of therapy encounters. These encounters are intense and highly meaningful, but they are brief.

Treatment plans need to be specific to the presenting problems. Just as it is frustrating and injurious to try to do too much, it also is ludicrous to try to do the wrong thing. A young man presenting with homosexual panic needs to have his anxiety reduced. He does not need to have his sexual preference settled for all time.

Only after treatment goals have been identified is it possible to select intervention techniques. These techniques already have been discussed in a general way and are elaborated for particular problem areas in later chapters. It is at this point in emergency work that staff teamwork is most essential. The various professional disciplines relevant to emergency psychiatry diverge along lines of different expertise in interventions. The team leader must take responsibility for designating who is to do what and for assuring that information developed during the evaluation is communicated in a precise and useful way.

SUMMARY

This volume presents a series of invited papers on topics of major importance for the practice of emergency psychiatry. The overview in this chapter has provided a definition of emergency psychiatry as a subspecialty in which patients with mental illness causing severe or urgent disturbances are treated. Specialized techniques are required for implementing in an orderly way the needed patient evaluations, goal-setting, treatment planning, and emergency interventions. Unique qualities of emergency psychiatry are the urgency with which the work must be done, the severe time limits placed on emergency interventions, the stress experienced by the staff, and the limitations imposed by the lack of outcome information.

Many of the chapters in this book have been contributed by members of the American Psychiatric Association's Task Force on Psychiatric Emergency Care Issues. This Task Force has prepared a monograph which offers substantial detail in areas covered briefly in this overview chapter [1].

REFERENCES

1. Barton, G.M. and Friedman, D.: Psychiatric Emergency Care: A Task Force Report of the American Psychiatric Association, in press.

Confronting the
Psychiatric
Emergency

1

Crisis Intervention in a Medical Setting

GAIL M. BARTON

Crisis intervention in a medical setting must be done in an orderly, methodical and humanistic manner [1,2]. Of course, organic disease must be ruled out or separated from the emotional crisis for management. The steps are the same as anywhere, although perhaps done with more economy of time in an emergency department. The patient should be interviewed as well as the family, the ambulance attendants, or the police—whoever brought the patient in or complained about a problem behavior [3]. The chief complaint must be clarified as well as the answer to the question, "Why *now*?" [2]. The social and medical history is taken as well as what medications. The mental status exam including appearance, affect, thought content, thought process, capacity for insight, judgment, estimate of intellect, orientation, and recall should all be clearly defined so that a differential diagnosis may be entertained [1]. At that point crisis intervention may be determined to be useful and begun.

Crisis intervention is a form of brief psychotherapy which may be extremely useful in managing an acute stress-filled situation [4–9]. Intervention should be brief, very focused, intensive, and flexibly scheduled to help resolve the crisis [4].

There are discrete steps a therapist can take to assist a person through a crisis [5–10]: (1) confront the danger including its concomitant fear and peril; (2) confront the crisis in small, tolerable aspects; (3) clarify facts surrounding the crisis; (4) establish the patient's capacity to focus on reality; (5) support the patient's capacity to break the situation down into component parts; (6) do not give false assurances; they interrupt problem solving; (7) direct, if necessary, toward more adaptive actions and behaviors; (8) minimize any associated mental phenomena such as fantasies and hallucinations; (9) encourage the patient to take responsibility which is legitimate for the crisis; (10) discourage placing blame; (11) be consistent and supportive; (12) make provisions for every day tasks to be assisted with while the person is in turmoil; (13) provide an environment which is accepting of the associated guilt, fear, and shame accompanying the crisis; (14) preserve the person's dignity and personal identity, (15) enhance the person's awareness that others in the usual environment are helpful; (16) foster interaction with the usual environment; (17) help the person understand that the cry for help is not a confession of weakness, but a natural way to regain equilibrium and even growth; (18) help the person anticipate the future and how to cope with it and suggest further assistance could be available should it be necessary.

For particular categories of patients the crisis intervention approach must be geared toward the presenting features, especially in regard to psychotics, anxiety disorders, grief reactions, and character disorders [1-3,11-14].

PSYCHOTICS

While gathering data it is important to be supportive to both the patient and the family since both are in turmoil and will be needed to cooperate in the treatment process [11]. Compliance with treatment, whether as an inpatient or outpatient, may be contingent upon the beginning therapeutic rapport provided in the initial crisis presentation [1-3,11-14]. An empathetic awareness by the examiner that the psychotic experience is painful may save the patient and family feelings of embarrassment towards it [11]. If the patient is agitated, a security officer nearby and visible can decrease everyone's anxiety about control [3,11]. Tranquilization may be necessary for further control [2,11]. Defining and focusing the problems are helpful. Showing interest in the history, admitting if there is trouble following the patient's train of thought, summarizing what should be done and why, can make a difference in acceptance of the best disposition [1-3,11-13].

With anxiety disorders, crisis intervention by the examiner can help a patient reestablish equilibrium and provide a chance to regain control over feelings and thoughts [3,11]. Ventilation along with stressing strengths can increase the patient's feelings of competence and diminish those of helplessness [10-13]. Providing guidance about what to give high priority, how to organize time, and suggesting an environmental change may bring the anxiety back into bounds [2,11]. The crisis intervention might include anxiolytic medication and should include follow-up visits to establish understanding of the underlying psychological problems which brought on the attack of anxiety [1–3,11–13].

Patients experiencing grief reactions may be greatly assisted by crisis intervention [2,11]. The grief may be triggered by the loss of an individual, a body part, or a significant economic loss such as a job [11,15]. They may present with the overt complaint of a loss or veiled as a depression, phobia, anxiety attack, alcoholic binge, marital discord, or school problem [2,11]. Reactions to the loss are partly personality linked and partly culture bound [2,11,15] Crisis intervention can help verbalize feelings so that the grief can be managed in tolerable segments and more thoroughly than otherwise [2,11,15]. A person who is grieving usually goes through rather discrete phases: intense mental suffering, somatic distress, preoccupation with the image of the deceased, waves of guilt, a loss of warmth in relationships with others, hostile feelings toward others, a change in the pattern of activities of daily living, and even assuming traits of the deceased [15]. Crisis intervention can provide the person or persons with a chance to talk about the deceased, including reviewing their relationship, making overt the angry feelings they have, suggesting that family and friends be mobilized to talk and work out feelings and logistics of future, providing an accepting environment to cry, ventilate, reminisce, and restitute [2,3,11,15]. Sedation is usually not advised since it keeps the grieving from happening [2,11,15].

Personality disorders provide a particularly difficult challenge in the emergency setting, yet can be benefitted by crisis intervention techniques. Borderline personality disorders are prone to brief paranoid episodes, impulsive drinking or drug taking, and self mutilation [11]. They tend to have superficial, transient or dependent relationships and exude hostility and anger without realizing it [1,2,11]. In an emergency facility they require personnel who can see them without becoming enraged or apathetic [3,11]. By exploring the specific events which brought them there and providing structure and limit setting as well as ventilation, they can feel that their crisis has been managed [11,13]. Low dose neuroleptics may decrease their accompanying anxiety, but a short, structured ventilatory visit may be enough [3,11].

The histrionic personality disorder who presents with instability, excitability, and dramatic effect may be faced best by a calm, firm examiner who will encourage these patients to make their own decisions from within their own armamentarium after they have had plenty of time to ventilate and tell their elaborate problems [1,3,11]. Their suicide potential should always be assessed and they should be offered an opportunity to return [1,3,11]. A single dose of a minor tranquilizer may decrease their immediate anxiety if it is severe [1,3,11].

The antisocial personality disorder who presents asking for drugs, housing, or money may become violent when frustrated with not having his needs met [2,11]. Security officers are an important part of the crisis intervention here, as is firm limit setting [2,11]. Medication dispensing is contraindicated in most instances with these individuals [2,11].

SUMMARY

Crisis intervention is an important technique to utilize in a medical setting, especially in the emergency department or with a patient having emotional problems on a medical floor.

When crisis intervention is used the patient is appreciative for regaining control over an emotion that seemed to have taken on a life of its own; the relatives are comfortable that they do not have to feel blamed for forcing another to help; the hospital staff can go on about managing the other aspects of the patient's care; the therapist can have the satisfaction of knowing the skills learned have been well utilized and can be useful from there on to face new crises.

REFERENCES

1. Slaby, A., Lieb, J. and Tancredi, L.: Handbook of Psychiatric Emergencies 2nd Ed., Medical Examination Pub. Co., Inc., Garden City, N.J., 1981.
2. Fauman, B. and Fauman, M.: Emergency Psychiatry for the House Officer, Williams and Wilkins, Baltimore, 1981.
3. Soreff, S.: Management of the Psychiatric Emergency, John Wiley & Sons, N.Y. 1981.
4. Funk, J.: Mental health services to low income persons. Neb Nurse 3:14–16, March 1970.
5. Llinas, J.: Crisis intervention: A technique physicians should master. Mich Med, pp 446–447, Aug. 1976.
6. Schwartz, S.: A review of crisis intervention programs. Psychiat Quarterly 45:498, 1971.
7. Aguilera, D. and Messick, J.: Crisis Intervention: Theory and Methodology, 3rd Ed., C.V. Mosby, St. Louis, Mo., 1976.
8. Caplan, S.: An Approach to Community Mental Health, Grune and Stratton, N.Y. 1961.
9. Mendel, W.: Supportive Care: Theory and Technique, Mara Books, Los Angeles, 1975.
10. Barton, G. and Barton, W.: Community Mental Health in Barton, W. and Barton, G.: Administration in Mental Health: Principles and Practice, Human Sciences Press, N.Y. 1982.
11. Dubin, W., et al: Course in Emergency Psychiatry at American Psychiatric Association Annual Meeting, New Orleans, 1981.
12. Resnick, H. and Ruben, H. (eds.): Emergency Psychiatric Care, Charles Press, Bowie, Md., 1975.
13. Gershon, S. and Bassuk, E.: Psychiatric emergencies: An overview, Am J Psychiat 137:327–328, 1980.
14. Lieb, J., Lipsitch, I., Slaby, A.: The Crisis Team: A Handbook for the Mental Health Professional, Harper and Row, N.Y., 1973.
15. Packard, K.: Grief Reactions, a Presentation at Towsley Center for Continuing Medical Education at the University of Michigan, March 1981.

2

Diagnostic Emergencies

ANDREW EDMUND SLABY

Emergency psychiatry and diagnostic psychiatry have increasingly become areas of particular concern and growth over the past several years. Consumers and health care providers alike are becoming aware that nowhere in the trajectory of mental health services is skill as great and as diversified required as in the delivery of emergency psychiatric services. Patients presenting in crisis demand skills in rapid and focused interviewing, in the differential diagnosis and diagnosis of disorders of mood, thought and behavior. Psychosocial, biological and existential factors converge to determine the presenting symptoms of even the most biologically based aberrations of behavior and this understanding is used by skillful therapists to manage such disorders [1-3]. Individuals, when threatened by either external stressors or internal physiological decompensation, defend themselves unconsciously in a holistic manner to prevent destruction of the integrity of the personality [4].

Providers of emergency psychiatric services must ascertain the degree to which converging sociological, psychological, biological and existential factors alter an individual's functioning, develop a rational biopsychosocial management plan to restore functioning, and, ideally, promote some growth in the individual emerging from crisis [1,5,6]. The objectives of emergency psychiatry are not merely alleviation of anxiety and depression and a return to premorbid functioning, but also personal growth so that an individual will be ultimately stronger as a result of the crisis. Achievement of such goals in an emergency setting requires that clinicians have available to them a variety of psychotherapeutic and sociotherapeutic skills, as well as the knowledge of the differential diagnosis and diagnosis of psychiatric disorders [1,3].

The cornerstone of emergency psychiatric services is diagnostic psychiatry [1-3,7,8]. Diagnosis guides therapeutic choices and provides parameters by which improvement may be measured. Aberrations of mood, thought, and behavior have differential diagnoses much like headache, fever, or seizures. When an individual presents to a neurologist with a headache, the neurologist seeks to find the etiology in order to define the course of management. Headaches associated with visual disturbances, gastrointestinal symptoms, and unilateral in nature (although not always affecting the same side of the head) suggest migraine. This is especially true if there is a history of migraine in the family, especially in the female members. Individuals who have attendant weakness or sensory changes, coupled with severe headaches and nausea, are likely to have an intracranial mass such as an expanding neoplasm. Other causes of headaches include cerebral infections, sinus congestion, visual problems, and muscular tension. So too, when patients present with violent outbursts, dementia, delirium, depression, anxiety, or thought disorders, there is a differential diagnosis composed of a number of organic and so-called "psychogenic" states which may present with the symptom or symptom complex alone or together with other signs and symptoms which guide one to the exact etiology of the disorder [1,2,9-18].

Emergency psychiatric clinicians often collude with their nonpsychiatric colleagues and see themselves as sources of disposition rather than as equal members of a medical team with unique diagnostic skills in disorders of mood, thought and behavior [19,20]. The diagnostic capabilities of a psychiatrist are particularly demanded in an emergency situation where many patients with behavioral disturbances are seen for diagnostic evaluation prior to referral to a secondary care facility, where it will be assumed that the individuals have been adequately worked up for any medical or surgical problems which may present as psychiatric illness.

Diagnostic psychiatry, within and outside of the emergency situation, is a special skill developed by experience gained from the evaluation of numbers of individuals with disorders of behavior. Many individuals who have received medical clearance in emergency rooms are transferred to hospitals, community mental health centers, and clinics staffed with individuals with less supervised exposure to patients with medical and surgical problems presenting as behavioral aberrations and fewer diagnostic resources to ascertain the underlying difficulties. Consequences of such lack of diagnostic sophistication are numerous [19]. Patients who present with impending myocardial infarction, conduction defects of the heart, hypotensive shock, pulmonary emboli, or other medical (or surgical) emergencies with overwhelming anxiety and a sense of impending doom may go unrecognized and referred to a psychiatric service as an anxiety neurosis or incipient psychosis and die if a clinician is unaware of these diagnostic possibilities.

In less extreme instances, individuals are referred for psychiatric treatment of depressions which may be based in a degenerative disease of the nervous system [12]. Failure to identify the underlying etiology may lead clinicians and family to demand alterations in his life which are impossible because of his limited cognitive abilities.

Individuals with migraine equivalents may be mislabeled as schizophrenic and a process of labeling commenced which is destructive to the patient and to his or her family members. If patients with disorders such as encephalitis or a migraine equivalent present as psychotic and are unrecognized, they may be treated as "schizophrenic" and their illnesses run their course and they recover. The "schizophrenia" would be seen as a "good prognostic schizophrenia" given the good premorbid history and the fact that the patient recovered social functioning. The onset, no doubt, would be somewhat acute in a patient with a good premorbid history and occupational functioning. The confusion and strong affective components often seen in migraine or encephalitis would indicate a favorable prognosis for a true schizophrenia. In many instances, there may be no personal or family history of major psychiatric illness, further suggesting a good prognosis. It would therefore be assumed that the patient would recover in a relatively short period of time. If the psychosis lasted less than six months, it would be labeled a schizophreniform psychosis. Medication would probably be prescribed and found effective, since antipsychotic medication is often helpful in the management of an organic mental syndrome. If rapid neuroleptization was used, it would be expected in the instance of the migraine equivalent that it would appear to be quite effective as the illness would go away by itself in a few hours, as would the transient hemiparesis or blindness that is also sometimes seen as a migraine equivalent and diagnosed as conversion hysteria because of its remitting course. The patient's affect may appear flattened after the use of neuroleptics since individuals who are not psychotic who receive antipsychotic medication often appear obtunded. This may cause clinicians observing the patient to feel that the affect was flattened prior to the episode but minimized or denied by the family or friends because of their relationship to the patient and because of an emotional investment in not recognizing that the patient is ill.

Illnesses that present as disorders of mood, thought, or behavior that are characterized by remissions and exacerbations may remit, giving the illusion of a cure, only to recur later in the same or some other form. Temporal lobe epilepsy, multiple sclerosis, migraine equivalents, paroxysmal atrial tachycardia, and mitral valve prolapse [21,22] are examples of such illnesses. If patients with such illnesses are placed in a long-term psychodynamically oriented hospital because of their good prognosis, clinicians may find corroborating evidence for a psychodynamic approach. The patients will do well and usually will return to full functioning. This would be seen as supporting the theory that long-term hospitalization without medication in which intensive psychotherapy is used will help some severely ill psychiatric patients. Briefer hospitalizations (or no hospitalizations without medication in which intensive psychotherapy is used) will help some severely ill psychiatric patients. Briefer hospitalizations or no hospitalizations with intensive or little follow-up, however, would show the same results. In the latter instance, this could be interpreted as supporting the use of brief hospitalization or crisis intervention as an approach to the same spectrum of illnesses.

In instances where medical illnesses are unrecognized and diagnosed as psychiatric illnesses, patients stand not only the risk of not receiving treatment which is more appropriate to the illness and, in some instances, lifesaving but also suffer from a number of social consequences that have been variously referred to by sociologists and anthropologists in the field as labeling or attribution. A person who has been misdiagnosed as having a psychiatric illness may feel that he or she is less able to handle psychological stress and develop a life-long pattern of retreat from situations which may arouse too intense emotion or conflict. Other individuals, including family members, friends, lovers, and employers, may attribute any difficulty the individual has to the fact that they have a mental illness or are a "psychiatric case." Employers may hesitate to promote or hire such individuals because of a fear of another decompensation. Individuals so labeled and their children also may fear genetic transmission of such illnesses as schizophrenia or unipolar or bipolar affective illness which have been proven in adopted-away studies to have forms that are transmitted genetically. Family members may feel considerable guilt for having contributed to the genesis of an illness or in passing on the genes. In some cases, they may blame themselves or others for something which, in fact, they had little or no control over. Psychiatric hospitalization and psychotherapy are not without cost to a patient and their family and considerable debt may accrue for a treatment that is not indicated and without any effect on the actual course of the illness [19].

Medical and surgical illnesses which may present as disorders of mood, thought and behavior are given in Tables 1 through 4. These are abbreviated lists and obviously do not include all medical and surgical problems which may present behaviorally. A more complete discussion of such illness is provided in *Clinical Psychiatric Medicine* [3] co-authored by Drs. Laurence Tancredi, Julian Lieb, and myself. The tables provided here are to heighten clinicians' awareness of the fact that a number of relatively common disorders may present as psychiatric syndromes and are often misdiagnosed. Unfortunately, one cannot diagnose that which one cannot recognize. The commonly held myth that one never sees such problems is inaccurate; clinicians probably have seen instances of most of such illnesses but fail to recognize them because they did not know they existed or did not know how to diagnose them. This problem exists not only for psychologists, social workers, and nurses. Many internists, pediatricians, and surgeons fail to recognize behavioral disturbance as a symptom of an underlying illness which in another form they would diagnose and recognize as within the discipline of their treatment responsibilities.

Clinicians may see a great number of behavioral manifestations of medical and surgical illness, but, if they are unsophisticated in psychiatric diagnosis or without good facilities for diagnostic work-up, may not recognize and diagnose physical illness and proceed to treat an apparent psychological disorder. In a large city hospital with available on-site capacity for emergency electroencephalography one may see instances of psychomotor status (temporal lobe epileptic status) that present as schizophrenic disorders. Individuals presenting in a dream-like state (sometimes referred to as an oneiroid state) as part of temporal lobe epileptic status may be diagnosed as schizophrenic and treated as such without clinicians ever knowing the difference.

Clinicians who work in diagnostic psychiatry, especially in crisis and emergency situations, are impressed by the large number of individuals they see who have medical and surgical disorders presenting as psychiatric disorders which if unrecognized would be seen as good prognostic schizophrenia [1,3,6–10,11]. In most such instances, the patients have a good premorbid history. They have worked steadily at a job for years and have many close and intimate friends. They often have married or had stable spouse equivalents, had children, and maintained commitments to family and friends. When seen in an emergency situation, one would have to say that their illness had a sudden onset without obvious precipitating factors. In addition, they seldom will have a family or personal history of psychiatric illness. This would further indicate "good prognosis." They are sometimes confused and have a strong affective component because of the underlying medical and surgical condition. Both confusion and a strong affective component, again, suggest a good prognosis. Because such illnesses are often brief in duration and remit without medical intervention, as does a temporal lobe epileptic episode or a migraine equivalent, the illnesses go away and the patient is diagnosed as a good prognosis schizophrenia.

Whether there is such a thing as a good prognostic schizophrenia or just a number of medical illnesses which are yet unrecognized presenting with schizophreniform symptoms that go away without major psychiatric intervention or respond to conventional psychiatric treatment is yet to be resolved. Unfortunately, without a clinician who is sophisticated in diagnosis and without the laboratory capacity for immediate diagnostic evaluation, many such individuals have suffered the consequences of labeling and inappropriate treatment with drugs known to have long-term irreversible consequences in some instances (e.g., tardive dyskinesia).

Depression is ubiquitous in the population. It is one of the most common medical illnesses seen. An estimated one out of five people will have the type of depression that will respond to drugs at some point during their lifetime [2,3]. The type of depression which responds to medication usually represents an episode of depression seen as part of unipolar or bipolar affective illness. These depressions, accompanied by vegetative signs, are often referred to as vital depressions or endogenous depressions. Such individuals have sleep disturbance (e.g. difficulty falling asleep, awakening in the middle of the night, early morning awakening or hypersomnia), weight and appetite disturbance (either weight gain or weight loss), decreased sexual interest and a diurnal variation of mood. The majority of depressive episodes that are part of affective illness respond to antidepressant medication and/or electroconvulsive therapy coupled with sociotherapy and psychotherapy provided after the symptoms of the depression have remitted. Untreated, a major depressive episode lasts about nine months to ten months [3].

The signs and symptoms of medical illness (see Table 1) presenting as depression do not differ in kind or intensity from those of the so-called psychological types discussed above [2]. The onset may be more sudden but not always. Suicidal thoughts and behavior may be present, and individuals have suicided with depressions secondary to medical illnesses such an antihypertensive drug toxicity or the profound depression accompanying cessation of amphetamine use [69]. When depression accompanies the use of medication such as steroids (e.g. prednisone) or antihypertensive medication (e.g., propranolol or reserpine), the onset is generally more sudden than with the depressive episodes of unipolar or bipolar affective illness. The symptoms, however, are similar and as profound. Depressions that accompany hypokalemia, degenerative neurological diseases such as Alzheimer's disease [40] or Pick's disease, cerebral neoplasia [76], hypothyroidism or hyperthyroidism, syphilis, or vitamin deficiencies tend to be more insidious in onset and therefore more easily confused with affective illness of the psychogenic type.

Medical illnesses that have depression as a symptom may occur in individuals with a personal or family history of affective illness, further confusing matters. They also may be superimposed on extant diseases such as dementia or present as nonaffective illness such as dementia. In the latter instance, the clinical picture is referred to as pseudodementia. Electroshock and antidepressants would be expected to alleviate the symptoms in such instances. Obversely, what appears to be depression in older people may be an

Table 1.   Medical/Surgical Illness Presenting with Depression

Addison's disease	General paresis
Alcohol intoxication	Hepatic failure
Alzheimer's disease [40]	Hepatitis
Amphetamine and other sympathomimetic withdrawal [69]	Huntington's chorea
	Hyperkalemia
Antihypertensive toxicity (e.g., methyldopa, propranolol, reserpine)	Hyperparathyroidism
	Hyperthyroidism
Arteriosclerosis	Hypoglycemia
Barbiturate intoxication	Hypokalemia
Benzodiazepine intoxication	Hyponatremia
Carbon disulfide intoxication	Hypothyroidism
Carcinoma of the pancreas	Infectious mononucleosis
Cerebral neoplasia	Levodopa intoxication
Cerebral tuberculosis	Multiple sclerosis
Cerebrovascular syphilis	Normal pressure hydrocephalus
Cessation of amphetamine or cocaine use	Occult malignancy [76]
Cirrhosis of the liver	Pernicious anemia
Cushing's syndrome	Pick's disease
Diabetes	Post-viral infection syndrome
Diabetes mellitus	Renal failure
Digitalis toxicity	Steroid toxicity
Distal effects of cancer	Subdural hematoma
Disulfiram intoxication	Thallium intoxication
Encephalitis	

insidious dementia as suggested by a person's lack of response to traditional antidepressant medication or electroshock and his or her inability to engage in sociotherapeutic activities with an almost rigid adherence to routine. Depressions accompanying a dementia may deepen a cognitive deficit.

Hyperthyroidism may be confused with an agitated depression. Most of the other depressions accompanying endocrine disease, however, will tend to resemble more retarded depressions and be confused with insidious onset schizophrenia or, more rarely, dementia. Tuberculosis, syphilis, and pernicious anemia have been historically referred to as the great masqueraders. Syphilis may present as mania, depression, dementia, or schizophrenia. Tubercular meningitis most frequently presents with an insouciance which suggests a retarded depression, schizophrenia, or dementia. Depression is a common symptom of liver disease such as cirrhosis or infectious mononucleosis with accompanying liver problems. Digitalis toxicity is common and may cause a patient to look confused, schizophrenic, or depressed. In such instances, obtaining a serum digoxin level will confirm the diagnosis. Pancreatic carcinoma may present as a profound depression before it is diagnosed, and depression may be seen with a number of other occult cancers [76]. It is not necessary for cancer to enter the brain to cause psychological disturbance. Cancer may cause a person to look depressed by actually invading the brain or as a primary tumor within the brain, or by causing endocrine changes in the body which change the electrolyte balance and make a person look depressed [3]. In other instances, the treatment of cancer with steroids may predispose the individual to infections which can create the appearance of depression. A fungal infection, in rare instances, may occur in the brain because of the treatment. Subdural hematomas are frequently seen in alcoholics or epileptics and may be confused with depression; if appropriate neurosurgical intervention is thereby delayed, permanent alteration in cognitive functioning can ensue.

The differential diagnosis of the patient presenting with violence (see Table 2) includes, in addition to drug toxicity, a number of other infectious, neoplastic, degenerative, and metabolic diseases. Temporal lobe epilepsy may present with the symptoms of other-directed violence. Drugs such as barbiturates, benzodiazepines, and tricyclics [27,34,36,38,45,66,79,83] may cause an individual to be more violent, especially if he has any prior existing organic mental syndrome. Phencyclidine (PCP) and amphetamines cause a person to be violent. In cases of phencyclidine intoxication quite brutal murders have occurred. LSD tends to make a person more benign and less other-directed violent. Migraine equivalents make a person quite upset and sometimes violent.

Alcohol may cause an individual to be violent in a number of ways, including directly through alcoholic intoxication either due to an excess or due to what is referred to as idiopathic alcoholic intoxication in which a small amount of alcohol causes a person to be violent or in other ways alters behavior. In the latter instance, it is felt that a small amount of alcohol causes a behavior to be unleashed in much the same way alcohol lowers a seizure threshold. In some instances, in fact, it is possible to find abnormal electroencephalograms in such individuals. Unfortunately, this is not always true and not all individuals reproduce the changes when given another challenge dose of a small amount of alcohol. Individuals who have been chronic alcohol users may show alcoholic paranoia or alcoholic hallucinosis. In the case of alcoholic paranoia, they may feel that their wife or husband has taken a lover and proceed to be violent with her or him or his or her presumed lover. In the case of alcoholic hallucinosis the hallucinations, be they visual or auditory, may be so violent as to cause the person to try to escape them by jumping out of a window or challenging and attacking the environment. Hypoglycemia is known to make a person look depressed, violent, or in other ways sustain alterations of personality.

Table 2.   Medical/Surgical Illnesses Presenting with Violent Behavior

Alcoholic hallucinosis	Drug withdrawal [26,59]
Alcoholic Intoxication	Hypoglycemia
Alcoholic paranoia	Idiopathic alcoholic intoxication
Amphetamine-induced psychosis	LSD-induced psychosis
Cerebral infections	Migraine equivalent
Cerebral neoplasia	PCP-induced psychosis
Degenerative brain disease	Side-effects of barbiturates, benzodiazepines and
Delirium [30]	tricyclic therapy [27,34,36,38,45,66,79,83]
Delirium tremens	Temporal lobe epilepsy

Thought disorders may be part of a number of medical and surgical illnesses (see Table 3). Only toxicity from amphetamines and other sympathomimetic substances [48] and phencyclidine psychoses [25,67,68,73] truly simulate schizophrenia. They produce a paranoid psychosis with a clear sensorium that is virtually indistinguishable from paranoid schizophrenia. The risk of homicide and suicide, therefore is great. Alcoholic hallucinosis and withdrawal from alcohol and other central nervous system depressants and benzodiazepines look much like schizophrenia. The psychosis accompanying delirium tremens seen with withdrawal from alcohol, barbiturates, meprobamate, and a number of other substances and with fever may precede changes in blood pressure, sweating, tremor, seizures and pulse rate, confusing the diagnosis. All dementias accompanying degenerative brain disease may be accompanied by personality changes or apathy suggestive of schizophrenia. The psychoses seen with Huntington's Chorea [35] and Pick's disease in particular suggest schizophrenia. Interestingly, profound depression, a frequent accompaniment or predecessor of cognitive alterations seen with Huntington's Chorea, may be seen alone without the dementia in some relatives. Both, however, the affected and nonaffected members have an increased suicide rate. Endocrine disease, in particular Addison's disease, hypopituitarism, hyperthyroidism, hypothyroidism, and Cushing's disease may present with symptoms of thought disorder. Cerebrovascular brain disease may present either as depression or schizophrenia. Psychomotor epilepsy, encephalitis, and migraine equivalents are sometimes confused with schizophrenia. Many drugs, including anticonvulsants [44] and disulfiram [65,80] used for the treatment of alcoholism, may cause a psychosis suggestive of schizophrenia. The atropine psychoses that are seen with some antidepressants and neuroleptics may be mistaken for schizophrenia, although confusion seen as part of the symptom picture may be so great as to make its drug etiology quite apparent. Akathesia and atropine psychosis accompanying neuroleptic drug use [42] are sometimes mistaken for an exacerbation of

Table 3. Medical/Surgical Illnesses Presenting with Disordered Thoughts

Addison's disease
Alcoholic hallucinosis
Alcoholic paranoia
Alzheimer's disease
Amantadine-associated psychosis [52]
Amphetamine-induced psychosis [48]
Angel's trumpet intoxication [51]
Anticonvulsant intoxication [44]
Antimalarial toxicity
Antipsychotic medication toxicity
Atropine psychosis [53,62]
Bacterial meningitis
Barbiturate and similar-acting sedative toxicity
Bromide intoxication [33]
Cannabis intoxication
Cerebroarteriosclerosis
Cerebrovascular syphilis [28]
Cimetidine intoxication [24,37]
Cocaine intoxication [74]
Cushing's disease
Delirium after cataract surgery [78]
Delirium tremens
Digitalis toxicity
Disulfiram toxicity [65,80]
Frontal lobe neoplasm
General paresis
Hallucinogen hallucinosis [29,31,43]
Huntington's chorea [35]
Hyperthyroidism
Hypothyroidism
Idiosyncratic alcohol intoxication
Insecticide (organophosphate intoxication)
Isoniazed intoxication
L-Dopa intoxication [32,60]

Lead intoxication
Manganese intoxication
Meningovascular syphilis
Mental subnormality
Meperidine toxicity
Mercury intoxication
Methyldopa (Aldomet) toxicity
Migraine equivalent
Multiple sclerosis
Neuroleptic intoxication [17]
Niacin deficiency
Normal pressure hydrocephalus
Nutmeg intoxication
Panhypopituitarism
Pernicious anemia
Phencyclidine intoxication [25,67,68,73]
Phenelzine-induced psychosis [55,72]
Pick's disease
Porphyria
Postcardiotomy delirium [54]
Schilder's disease
Senile degeneration of the brain
Steroid toxicity
Subdural hematoma [82]
Systemic lupus erythematosus
Temporal lobe epilepsy
Thallium intoxication
Tricyclic antidepressant induced psychosis [61]
Tubercular meningitis
Volatile nitrite toxicity [75]
Wilson's disease (hepatolenticular degeneration)
Withdrawal from barbiturates, benzo-
    diazepines and tricyclic antidepressants

schizophrenia, causing a clinician to increase the dose of psychotropic medication, which actually worsens the problem.

Anxiety may be a harbinger of many diseases (see Table 4), including some quite lethal. Fatal medical and surgical illnesses such as myocardial infarction, pulmonary emboli, septic shock, and shock due to blood loss may present with overwhelming anxiety and a sense of impending doom. The cause of the blood loss may be external trauma or a ruptured spleen, bleeding ulcer, or ruptured esophogeal varices. Potentially fatal cardiac arrhythmias and congestive heart failure also present with extreme anxiety. The symptoms and

Table 4.   Medical Surgical Illnesses Presenting with Anxiety

Alcohol withdrawal	Hypoglycemia
Amphetamine and other sympathomimetic	Hypokalemia
intoxication [48,70]	Impending myocardial infarction
Antipsychotic medication toxicity	Insecticide (organophosphate) intoxication
Atropine psychosis	Internal hemorrhage
Barbiturate and other drug withdrawal	Lead intoxication
[38,39,41,42,45,46,50,56,58,63,64,77,81]	Mitral valve prolapse
Caffeinism [49]	Nonbacterial thrombotic endocarditis [57]
Cannabis intoxication	Non-epileptic temporal lobe disease
Cerebroarteriosclerosis	Other temporal lobe disease
Cocaine intoxication	Paroxysmal atrial tachycardia and other
Encephalitis	cardiac arrhythmias
Glue sniffing	Phencyclidine intoxication
Hallucinogen intoxication	Post-concussion syndrome
Hypertension	Pulmonary embolism
Hyperthyroidism	Subacute bacterial endocarditis
Hyperventilation syndrome	Temporal lobe epilepsy
Hypocalcemia	Thyrotoxicosis

signs of anxiety such as light-headedness, hyperventilation, sweating palms, dry mouth, hyperactivity, tremor, and tachycardia are common in a greater or lesser degree to a number of less immediately life-threatening illnesses such as amphetamine and cocaine toxicity, cerebroarteriosclerosis, essential hypertension, the postconcussion syndrome, thyrotoxicosis, subacute bacterial endocarditis, encephalitis, hypokalemia, and hypocalcemia. Recreational drugs such as marijuana and hallucinogens may cause severe anxiety in individuals predisposed psychologically. Well circumscribed episodes of anxiety are seen with hypoglycemia, pheochromocytoma, temporal lobe epilepsy, transient cardiac arrhythmias, paroxysmal atrial tachycardia, and other transient cardiac arrhythmias and mitral valve prolapse. In the instance of mitral valve prolapse, the anxiety may present as agarophobia (fear of open spaces).

The episodes of anxiety seen with hypoglycemia often occur a fixed number of hours after eating and are relieved by eating. A five hour glucose tolerance curve is important in identifying such individuals. Overindulgence in coffee and other caffeine-containing beverages may cause agitation, restlessness, palpitations, tachycardia, tachypnea, nervousness, anxiety, and tremulousness simulating an anxiety neurosis [49]. Withdrawal from drugs such as barbiturates, alcohol and other central nervous system depressant might be accompanied by anxiety that is of panic proportions [38,39,41,42,45, 46,50,56,58,63,64,77,81].

The anxiety accompanying medical or surgical disorders is generally distinguishable by the suddenness of its onset in individuals who have no past personal or family history of psychiatric illness or treatment. The presence or absence of precipitants may be misleading because a precipitant may lead to a medical or surgical illness just as it does to a psychological illness, depending upon individual vulnerabilities. Individuals respond to stress in different ways, and while some may respond in psychological ways, others may respond in medical or surgical ways which present with psychological symptoms. When people are anxious or depressed and look back over their past lives, they will always be looking at it through anxious or depressed eyes and therefore distort what has occurred in the direction of anxiety and depression.

Diagnostic acumen is always necessary for accurate diagnoses [1]. Clues to the organic nature of problems are obvious if one has a basic understanding of the normal evolution of personality and the epidemiology of mental illness and has a natural respect for the concept that disorders of mood, thought, and behavior have a differential diagnosis [2] just as do other medical or surgical disorders. Individuals who are found to make and sustain meaningful interpersonal relationships over a long period of time should not suddenly become schizophrenic or sustain other severe mental disorder, except perhaps profound depression, which may occur in anyone and increase in frequency with age [3]. On the whole, schizophrenia is an illness of younger people. Onset over the age of 30 with the exception of the paranoid subtype is very unusual. In many instances, there is a usual family history of comparable disorders.

The onset of affective illness, unipolar or bipolar, is usually insidious. One does not usually become profoundly depressed over days. Depression may occur at any age. The incidence increases, however, with each decade of life. The changes in mood, sleep, sexual function, and in appetite tend to occur over weeks or months. There often is a family history of depression, mania, alcoholism, bankruptcy (common in mania), sociopathy, or suicide.

Anxiety when it appears *de novo* in individuals who have otherwise normal personalities and is well circumscribed and without obvious precipitants should make one think of a medical or surgical illness. Even when depressed or anxious, people attribute their changes to a particular event. The cause may be specious. To reiterate, a stress may have given rise to a physical or surgical illness just as it may give rise to a psychological illness depending upon vulnerabilities. In addition, when someone is depressed or anxious, they will look back over their past life and report events with an emphasis on the negative. When they are feeling good they may see their children and lovers as interesting and their marriages and affairs fulfilling. When they feel depressed, they may see their children and lovers as boring and their marriages and affairs without substance. Depressed people, regardless of what is causing the depression, look at the world through blue-tinted glasses. A good marriage may be perceived as shallow, loving children as ungrateful, success in one's occupation as failure, and an individual with usual self-esteem may see him- or herself as worthless or hopeless. An anxious person can see anything as conflictual and anxiety producing. Alleviation of anxiety may make that person look upon the same events as easily manageable.

There is nothing that can replace experience in heightening clinicans' awareness of the great variety of presentations of medical and surgical illnesses as behavioral emergencies. Reading books or hearing lectures is an inadequate substitute for actually identifying illness in an emergency or crisis situation. The more one works in the area of crisis intervention and emergency psychiatry, the more he or she becomes aware of how much that is perceived as psychiatric illness is in fact a psychiatric manifestation of underlying medical or surgical illness.

REFERENCES

1. Slaby, A.E.: Emergency psychiatry: An Update. Hosp Commun Psychiatry, Vol. 32, No. 10, pp 687–698, 1981.
2. Slaby, A.E., Lieb, J., Tancredi, L.R.: Handbook of Psychiatric Emergencies (2nd Ed.). Flushing, New York, Medical Examination Publishing Company, 1981.
3. Slaby, A.E., Tancredi, L.R., Lieb, J.: Clinical Psychiatric Medicine. New York, Harper & Row, 1981.
4. Slaby, A.E.: Medical and Neurological Problems Presenting as Behavioral Emergencies in Topics in Emergency Medicine (In Press).
5. Gerson, S., Bassuk, E.: Psychiatric emergencies: an overview. Am J Psychiatry, 137:1–11, 1980.
6. Goldberg, R.J., Slaby, A.E.: Diagnosing Disorders of Mood, Thought and Behavior. Flushing, New York, Medical Examination Publishing Company, 1981.
7. Fauman, B.S., Fauman, M.A.: Emergency Psychiatry for the Houseofficer. Baltimore, Williams and Wilkins, 1981.
8. Soroff, S.M.: Management of the Psychiatric Emergency. New York, John Wiley & Sons, 1981.
9. Gelenberg, A.J.: The catatonic syndrome. Lancet, 1:1339–1341, 1976.
10. Hall, R.C.W., Gardner, E.R., Stickney, S.K., et al: Physical illness manifesting as psychiatric disease. II. Analysis of a state hospital inpatient population. Arch Gen Psychiatry, 37:989–995, 1980.
11. Hall, R.C.W., Popkin, M.K., Devaul, R.A., et al: Physical illness presenting as psychiatric disease. Arch Gen Psychiatry, 35:1315–1320, 1978.
12. Herridge, C.F.: Physical disorders in psychiatric illness: a study of 209 consecutive admissions. Lancet, 2:949–951, 1960.
13. Jarvik, F., Ruth, V., Matsuyama, S.S.: Organic brain syndrome and aging: a six-year follow-up of surviving twins. Archives of General Psychiatry, 37:280–286, 1980.

14. Johnson, D.A.W.: Evaluation of routine physical examination in psychiatric cases. Practitioner, 200:686–691, 1968.
15. Koranyi, E.K.: Morbidity and rate of undiagnosed physical illness in a psychiatric clinic population. Arch Gen Psychiatry, 36:414–419, 1979.
16. Krauthammer, C., Klerman, G.L.: Secondary mania. Manic syndromes associated with antecedent physical illness or drugs. Arch Gen Psychiatry, 35:1333–1339, 1978.
17. Maguire, C.P., Granville-Grossman, K.L.: Physical illness in psychiatric patients. Br J Psychiatry, 115:1365–1369, 1968.
18. Slaby, A.E., Wyatt, R.J.: Dementia in the Presenium. Springfield, Illinois. Charles C. Thomas, 1974.
19. Van Scheyen, J.D., Van Kammen, D.P.: Clomipramine-induced mania in unipolar depression. Arch Gen Psychiatry, 36:560–565, 1979.
20. Baxter, S., Chodorkoff, B., Underhill, R.: Psychiatric emergencies: dispositional determinants and the validity of the decision to admit. Am J Psychiatry, 124:1542–1546, 1968.
21. Kantor, J.S., Zitrin, C.M. Zeldis, S.M.: Mitral valve prolapse syndrome in agoraphobic patients. Am J Psychiatry, 137:467–469, 1980.
22. Pariser, S.F., Pinta, E.R., Jones, B.A.: Mitral valve prolapse syndrome and anxiety neurosis/panic disorder. Am J Psychiatry, 135:246–247, 1978.
23. Weissman, M.M., Myers, J.K.: Affective disorders in an urban community. Arch Gen Psychiatry, 35:1304–1311, 1978.
24. Adler, L.E., Sadja, L., Wilets, G.: Cimetidine toxicity manifested as paranoia and hallucinations. Am J Psychiatry, 137:1112–1113, 1980.
25. Allen, R.M., Young, S.J.: Phencyclidine-induced psychosis. Am J Psychiatry, 135:1081–1084, 1978.
26. Arnold, E.S., Rudd, S.M., Kirshner, H.: Manic psychosis following rapid withdrawal from Baclofen. Am J Psychiatry, 137:1466–1467, 1980.
27. Biggs, J.T., Spiker, D.G., Petit, J.M., Ziegler, V.E.: Tricyclic antidepressant overdose: Incidence of symptoms. JAMA, 238:135–138, 1977.
28. Binder, R.I., Dickman, W.A.: Psychiatric manifestations of neurosyphilis in middle-aged patients. Am J Psychiatry, 137:741–742. 1980.
29. Block, S.H.: The grocery store high. Am J Psychiatry, 135:126–127, 1978.
30. Bond, T.C.: Recognition of acute delirious mania. Arch Gen Psychiatry, 37:553–554, 1980.
31. Bowers, M.B.: Psychoses precipitated by psychotomimetic drugs. A follow-up study. Arch Gen Psychiatry, 34:832–835, 1977.
32. Braden, W.: Response to lithium in a case of L-dopa-induced psychosis. Am J Psychiatry, 134:808–809, 1977.
33. Brenner, F.: Bromism: Alive and well. Am J Psychiatry. 135:857–858, 1978.
34. Brown, G.M., Stancer, H.C., Moldofsky, H., Harman, J., Murphy, J.T., Gupta, R.H.: Withdrawal from long-term, high-dose desipramine therapy. Arch Gen Psychiatry, 35:1261–1264, 1978.
35. Caine, E.D., Hunt, R.D., Weingarten, H., et al: Huntington's dementia: Clinical and neuropsychological features. Arch Gen Psychiatry, 35:377–384, 1978.
36. Chouinard, G., Jones, B.D., Neuroleptic-induced supersensitivity psychosis: clinical and pharmacologic characteristics. Am J Psychiatry, 137:16–21, 1980.
37. Crowder, M.K., Pate, J.K.: A case report of cimetidine-induced depressive syndrome. Am J Psychiatry, 137:1451, 1980.
38. DeBard, M.L.: Diazepam withdrawal syndrome: a case with psychosis, seizure and coma. Am J Psychiatry, 136:104–105, 1979.

39. Demers-Desrosiers, L.A.; Nestoros, J.N.; Vaillancourt, P.: Acute psychosis precipitated by withdrawal of anticonvulsant medication. Am J Psychiatry, 135:981–982, 1978.

40. Demuth, G.W., Rand, B.S.: Atypical major depression in a patient with severe primary degenerative dementia. Am J Psychiatry, 137:1609–1610, 1980.

41. Dysken, M.W., Chan, C.H.: Diazepam withdrawal psychosis: a case report. Am J Psychiatry, 134:573, 1977.

42. Epstein, R.S.: Withdrawal symptoms from chronic use of low-dose barbiturates. Am J Psychiatry, 137:107–108, 1980.

43. Faquet, R.A., Rowland, K.F.: "Spice cabinet" intoxication. Am J Psychiatry, 135:860–861, 1978.

44. Franks, R.D., Richter, A.J.: Schizophrenia-like psychosis associated with anticonvulsant toxicity. Am J Psychiatry, 136:973–974, 1979.

45. Gardos, G., Cole, J.O., Tarsy, D.: Withdrawal syndromes associated with antipsychotic drugs. Am J Psychiatry, 135:1321–1324, 1978.

46. Gawin, F.H., Markoff, R.A.: Panic anxiety after abrupt discontinuation of amitriptyline. Am J Psychiatry, 138:117–118, 1981.

47. Gelenberg, A.J., Mandel, M.R.: Catatonic reactions to high-potency neuroleptic drugs. Arch Gen Psychiatry, 34:947–950, 1977.

48. Gold, M.S., Bowers, M.B.: Neurobiological vulnerability to low-dose amphetamine psychosis. Am J Psychiatry, 135:1547–1548, 1978.

49. Greden, J.F.: Anxiety or caffeinism: a diagnostic dilemma. Am J Psychiatry, 131:1089, 1974.

50. Gualtieri, C.T., Staze, J.: Withdrawal symptoms after abrupt cessation of amitriptyline in an eight-year-old boy. Am J Psychiatry, 136:457–459, 1979.

51. Hall, R.C.W., Popkin, M.K., McHenry, L.E.: Angel's trumpet psychosis: a central nervous system anticholinergic syndrome. Am J Psychiatry, 134:312–314, 1977.

52. Hausner, R.S.: Amantadine-associated recurrence of psychosis. Am J Psychiatry, 137:240–242, 1980.

53. Heiser, J.F., Wilbert, D.E.: Reversal of delirium induced by tricyclic antidepressant drugs with physostigmine. Am J Psychiatry, 131:1275, 1974.

54. Heller, S.S., Kornfeld, D.S., Frank, K.A., Hoar, P.F.: Postcardiotomy delirium and cardiac output. Am J Psychiatry, 136:337–339, 1979.

55. Liebowitz, M.R., Wuetzel, E.J., Bowser, A.E., et al: Phenelzine and delusions of parasitosis: a case report. Am J Psychiatry, 135:1565–1566, 1978.

56. Luchins, D.J., Freed, W.J., Wyatt, R.J.: The role of cholinergic supersensitivity in the medical symptoms associated with withdrawal of antipsychotic drugs. Am J Psychiatry, 137:1395–1398, 1980.

57. MacKenzie, T.B., Popkin, M.K.: Psychological manifestations of nonbacterial thrombotic endocarditis. Am J Psychiatry, 137:972–973, 1980.

58. Mirin, S.M., Schatzberg, A.F., Creasy, D.E.: Hypomania and mania after withdrawal of tricyclic antidepressants. Am J Psychiatry, 138:87–89, 1981.

59. Mitchell, E., Matthews, L.L.: Gilles de la Tourette's disorder associated with Pemoline. Am J Psychiatry, 137:1618–1619, 1980.

60. Moskovitz, C., Moses, H., Klawans, H.L.: Levadopa-induced psychosis: a kindling phenomenon. Am J Psychiatry, 135:669–675, 1978.

61. Nelson, J.C., Bowers, M.B., Sweeney, D.R.: Exacerbation of psychosis by tricyclic antidepressants in delusional depression. Am J Psychiatry, 136:574–576, 1979.

62. Newton, R.W.: Physostigmine salicylate in the treatment of tricyclic antidepressant overdosage. JAMA, 231:941–944, 1975.

63. Pevnik, J.S., Jasinski, D.R., Haertzen, C.A.: Abrupt withdrawal from therapeutically administered diazepam. Report of a case. Arch Gen Psychiatry, 35:995–998, 1978.
64. Preskorn, S.H., Denner, L.J.: Benzodiazepines and withdrawal psychosis: report of three cases. JAMA, 237:36–38, 1977.
65. Rainey, J.M.: Disulfiram toxicity and carbon disulfide poisoning. Am J Psychiatry, 134:371–378, 1977.
66. Rampling, D.: Aggression: A paradoxical response to tricyclic antidepressants. Am J Psychiatry, 135:117–118, 1978.
67. Rappolt, R.T., Gay, G.R., Farris, R.D.: Emergency management of acute phencyclidine intoxication, JACEP, 8:68–76, 1979.
68. Rosen, A.: Case report: symptomatic mania and phencyclidine abuse. Am J Psychiatry, 136:118–119, 1979.
69. Rosenfeld, A.A.: Depression and psychotic regression following prolonged methylphenidate use and withdrawal: case report. Am J Psychiatry, 136:226–228, 1979.
70. Schaffer, C.B., Pauli, M.W.: Psychotic reaction caused by proprietary oral diet agents. Am J Psychiatry, 137:1256–1257, 1980.
71. Shear, M.K., Sacks, M.H.: Digitalis delirium: report of two cases. Am J Psychiatry, 135:109–110, 1978.
72. Sheehy, L.M., Maxmen, J.S.: Phenelzine-induced psychosis. Am J Psychiatry, 135:1422–1423, 1978.
73. Showalter, C.V., Thorton, W.E.: Clinical pharmacology of phencyclidine toxicity. Am J Psychiatry, 134:1134–1238, 1977.
74. Siegel, R.K.: Cocaine hallucinations. Am J Psychiatry. 135:309–314, 1978.
75. Sigell, L.T., Kapp, F.T., Fusaro, E.A., et al: Popping and snorting volatile nitrites: a current fact for getting high. Am J Psychiatry, 135:1216–1218, 1978.
76. Solomon, J.G., Solomon, S. Psychotic depression and bronchiogenic carcinoma. Am J Psychiatry, 135:859–860, 1978.
77. Stewart, R.B., Salem, R.B., Springer, P.K.: A case report of lorazepam withdrawal. Am J Psychiatry, 137:1113–1114, 1980.
78. Summers, W.K., Reich, T.C.: Delirium after cataract surgery: review and two cases. Am J Psychiatry, 136:386–391, 1979.
79. Van Scheyen, J.D., Van Kammen, D.P.: Clomipramine-induced mania in unipolar depression. Arch Gen Psychiatry, 36:560–565, 1979.
80. Weddington, W.W., Marks, R.C., Verghese, P.: Disulfiram encephalopathy as a cause of the catatonic syndrome. Am J Psychiatry, 137:1217–1219, 1980.
81. Winokur, A., Rickels, K., Guenblatt, D.J., et al: Withdrawal reaction from long-term low-dosage administration of diazepam. A double-blind, placebo-controlled case study. Arch Gen Psychiatry, 37:101–105, 1980.
82. Woods, S.W.: Catatonia in a patient with subdural hematomas. Am J Psychiatry, 137:983–984, 1980.
83. Woody, G.E., O'Brien, C.P., Greenstein, R.: Misuse and abuse of diazepam: an increasingly common medical problem. Int J Addictions, 10:843–845, 1975.

3

Staff Issues in Emergency Medical Settings

PAUL A. McCLELLAND

The most important stressor in many emergency medical settings is inadequate staff training in the issues most frequently confronted. Other stressors include unclear role definitions, poor leadership, and excessive exposure to the extremes of human suffering and cruelty. Although the same situation can be invigorating for one staff member and devastating for another, this paper will focus on the latter experience by discussing burnout, depression, alcoholism, and drug abuse. Prevention and treatment will be considered in the context of the psychiatric consultant's role. Other stressors are less subject to intervention and will not be discussed. Psychophysiological disturbances such as hypertension are beyond the scope of this paper and will not be dealt with here.

TRAINING

Occupational psychologists have identified inadequate training as a crucial factor in job dissatisfaction, frequent tardiness or absence, and accidents on the job, all major components of the burnout syndrome as defined by most authors[1,2]. The Maryland Institute for Emergency Medical Systems and Services serves as a training site each year for approximately 250 emergency physicians, surgeons, anesthesiologists, and other physicians from training programs located throughout the United States. Experience with this group suggests that physician training is very deficient in the area of behavioral emergencies. One explanation for this shortcoming stems from the major differences between diagnosis and management of behavioral emergencies and other medical emergencies. Ambiguity, reliance on subjective variables, and interventions that are somewhat less action-oriented make training in this area more difficult and less appealing for many. Nevertheless, the poorly trained staff member will experience repeated failures, create a greater burden for his colleagues, and expose himself to the risk of assaults by poorly managed patients. Parenthetically, the studies mentioned earlier have also shown that overtraining for a job is stressful. Much of what doctors and nurses actually do (starting IVs, obtaining EKGs, suturing lacerations, etc.) requires far less training than is provided by medical and nursing schools. However, unlike deficient training, this is one of the several potential stressors that cannot be removed. Similarly, although interesting and applicable in large part to emergency rooms, studies of intensive care unit staffs have identified few stressors that can be eliminated.

ROLE DEFINITIONS

Unclear role definitions are a major source of stress and division throughout medicine. This is a well-known fact thoroughly discussed in the literature, particularly in the area of doctor-nurse conflicts [4]. Understandably, it is the difficult patients such as those with behavioral emergencies that seem to exploit or call attention to organizational weaknesses such as this one. The mutual support and esprit de corps that bind staff members and that make emergency work attractive to many are the major casualties resulting from the failure of those in leadership to define and maintain the boundaries between disciplines.

Leadership

Competent leadership includes clarification of role or job descriptions as well as several other functions. Among the latter, two deserve special mention.

First, leaders cannot allow administrative decisions to be made inappropriately on the basis of race, sex, or any other arbitrary factor, because employees excluded from promotions and access to decision-making are far more likely to exhibit signs of stress [5]. Paramedics are an example of this; high turnover rates reflect their existence at the periphery of fire departments.

Second, leaders must not burden those beneath them with complaints and problems brought about by higher level leaders. For example, nurse supervisors who complain about the decisions of the head of nursing will undermine their own effectiveness and will lower morale because their personnel are not likely to be able to solve such problems. It is not surprising that poor leadership is a major problem in medicine because few nurses and fewer doctors have ever received adequate training as leaders.

TRAUMATIC EXPERIENCES

A fourth major stressor is the frequent exposure to massive injuries, mutilation, and death. Similarly, frequent contact with victims of rape, child abuse, and other assaults can be an overwhelming experience. Whereas virtually all personnel are stressed by poor training, role confusion, and poor leadership, some staff members seem to experience their contact with these conditions and such patients as a challenge and not as a burden. Nevertheless, the literature in post-traumatic stress disorders suggests that such experiences may provide fertile ground for pathological responses. Fenichel observed that events are more likely to be experienced as traumatic if the person is unable to be active (his example was the soldier unable to advance or retreat), if fatigue is present, and if the person has already encountered multiple traumatic events [6]. In varying degrees, all three of these factors characterize the work of emergency room staff. DSM-III requires of the traumatic event that it be one that is beyond the realm of anticipated life events [7]. Seeing and touching the grossly mutilated body of an accident victim is not an ordinary life event. The impact may be heightened if the victim is of the same sex or age as the observer.

The above discussion has highlighted certain features of emergency medical work that play substantial roles in the wide range of disorders seen in staff members referred for psychiatric consultation. The following four disorders are common, treatable, and disastrous to staff morale if left untreated.

Burnout

Burnout is a much abused label which can disguise a number of conditions ranging from mere job dissatisfaction to psychotic depression. Because of its popularity we are stuck with the term. To be a useful concept it must be more than job dissatisfaction, just as depression is more than unhappiness. If alcoholism or depression are present, they should be diagnosed and treated appropriately. However, there will still be a significant number of individuals who deserve attention. Such "burned out" workers will display what would otherwise be diagnosed as an adjustment reaction, often with anxiety and other symptoms suggestive of a post-traumatic stress disorder and depressive features such as anhedonia and diminished self-esteem. More completely, burnout is a life crisis highlighted by job dissatisfaction, questions about the integrity and effectiveness of one's self and one's colleagues, intrusive re-experiencing of work events, and mild depression. The keys to treatment are prevention and early diagnosis, discussed below. Untreated, the result can be a dramatic lowering of morale for those not yet burned out as well as personal losses such as marital breakups.

Depression

Depression in this population is diagnosed in the usual way. One well known suggestion that a nurse or doctor may themselves be depressed is the over or under-diagnosis of depression in their patients. Also of note is the tendency for such individuals to discount their own depression, often comparing themselves to their patients. Furthermore, friends, family members, and colleagues facilitate this process through their expectation that the nurse or doctor be a strong, self-sufficient caretaker. Since this expectation is part of most professionals' ego-ideal, acknowledging depression is a further threat to self-esteem. This dynamic may contribute to the increased risk for suicide in this group.

Alcoholism

Absenteeism, depression, impaired judgement on the job, and social withdrawal are only a few of the early signs of alcohol abuse. Untreated alcoholism is a devastating illness in this population for a variety of reasons. Colleagues are feared because of the medical profession's skepticism and intolerance towards alcoholics. Drinking on the job is extremely risky and yet, as the disease progresses, the person's confidence in his ability to make decisions rapidly and accurately can decline so drastically that the urge to drink while working becomes overwhelming.

Drug Addiction

As with many individuals in nonmedical settings, excessive drinking often grows out of attempts to self-medicate for insomnia, agitation, or pain. This theme is echoed in case reports of nurses who turn to narcotics instead of alcohol [8]. The ease with which emergency personnel can obtain and use narcotics without detection makes estimates of the incidence of such behavior very questionable. The risk to patients is clear, but less obvious is the catastrophic effect on staff morale. Staff members are both furious and frightened when such incidents occur. Anger with the leaders for allowing this to happen is matched by fear that colleagues and outsiders may suspect that they are also addicts. As a result, the unit undergoes a period characterized by unproductive challenges to the leader and loosening of bonds within the group. This makes it very difficult if not impossible for the addicted individual to continue as a member of the group even when he or she receives successful treatment.

ROLE OF THE PSYCHIATRIC CONSULTANT

The psychiatrist working part-time or full-time in an emergency medical setting can support the staff in a number of ways. Designing and implementing effective training in behavioral emergencies will diminish the demands imposed by these cases. Nurse chairmen and other leaders can be supported, particularly in their efforts to clarify role definitions. Nurses and doctors can be encouraged to use their vacation time and avoid unnecessary overtime. Similarly, rotating assignments within the unit may help to prevent individuals from being overwhelmed by continual exposure to the same stressors. This potential advantage must be weighed against the possibility of diminished individual effectiveness, since some individuals function well only in particular roles. Another possible drawback of mandatory rotations is decreased group cohesiveness.

Withdrawal and isolation from the rest of the staff pose threats both to the individual's wellbeing and to the strength of the group. This is particularly important at those times when the group may resolve a crisis by scapegoating one member. For example, when a staff member is assaulted by a patient, the group may fail to align itself with the victim against the patient (or, preferably, against the patient's behavior). Emergency rooms focus on controlling bleeding arrhythmias, etc., and when a patient's violence reveals the lack of control, the resulting crisis may be resolved by blaming the victim for provoking the assault or failing to protect himself. Later, the staff may split into several groups, one blaming the assaulted staff member, one supporting that person, one blaming the administration for inadequate security measures, and so forth. A group meeting involving all of the staff is one way to detect and resolve such crises in a more productive fashion. Held as soon as possible after the assault, the meeting allows all members to hear the victim's description of the event. The psychiatric consultant may need to lead the meeting to insure that the focus is on ventilation of feelings, support, and learning rather than on scapegoating. At other times when the staff is not in crisis it is more appropriate to encourage a withdrawn staff member to become more active in the group. Without discretion, such a move by the psychiatrist can be very intrusive and harmful to the individual involved. On the other hand, withdrawal is often the first sign of burnout or depression, and as such calls for an active role to insure that the chance for successful treatment is heightened and the risk to others is minimized.

Treatment for these disorders depends, as always, on accurate and early diagnosis. Specific treatment measures do not necessarily differ from those used with other patient populations. However, if psychotherapy is indicated and if one goal of treatment is to maintain the current job, then it will be very difficult for the psychiatric consultant to be the therapist. The issues that arise from shared work experiences may be overwhelming. For example, the role of therapist can conflict with the role of consultant when a valuable staff member decides in the context of psychotherapy that a change of jobs is indicated. On the other hand, the unit psychiatrist can be invaluable as a consultant to individuals on the staff. Awareness of working conditions can be useful in separating group and individual crises so that proper referrals can be made.

SUMMARY

Emergency medical settings can be extremely stressful for staff members. Inadequate training for behavioral emergencies, vague job definitions, and deficient leadership are correctible stressors. In addition to intervening in these areas, the psychiatric consultant can provide evaluations and referrals for members of the staff so that other personnel are not exposed to the cynical victims of burnout, the depressed or addicted individuals exhibiting self-destructive behaviors, and other untreated colleagues.

REFERENCES

1. Harrison, R.V.: Person — Environment Fit and Job Stress, In Stress at Work, Cooper, C.L. and Payne, R. (eds), John Wiley & Sons, pp. 175–205, 1978.
2. Marshall, R.E. and Kasman, C.: Burnout in the Neonatal Intensive Care Unit, Pediatrics, Vol. 65, No. 6, June, 1980.
3. Greenburg, A.G., Civetta, J.M. and Barnhill, G.: Neglected Components of Intensive Care, Journal of Surgical Research, 26, 494–498, 1979.
4. Firman, G.J. and Kaplan, M.P.: Staff "Splitting" on Medical-Surgical Wards, Psychiatry, Vol. 41, August 1978.
5. Cooper, C.L. and Marshall, J.: Sources of Managerial and White Collar Stress, In Stress at Work, Cooper, C.L. and Payne, R., John Wiley & Sons, pp. 81–105, 1978.
6. Fenichel, O.: The Psychoanalytic Theory of Neurosis, Norton & Co., 1945, New York.
7. DSM III (3rd Ed), American Psychiatric Association, Washington, D.C., 1980.
8. Levine, D.G., Preston, P.A. and Lipscomb, S.G.: A historical approach to understanding drug abuse among nurses, Am J Psychiatry, 131:9, September, 1974.

4

Violence in the Emergency Room

STEPHEN M. SOREFF

The emergency department (ED)—the attending physicians, the psychiatric consultant, the nurse, and the security personnel—has the responsibility and the mandate to control the violent patient, contain the violent situation, and bring both to resolution through swift, effective intervention. This mandate encompasses four aspects which constitute the thrust of this chapter: (1) an exploration of the ED as a focus for violence intervention, (2) the causes of violence, (3) the management of violence, and (4) staff difficulties in addressing the violent patient.

The ED has emerged as the focus of violence intervention for two reasons. First, the ED is the place in the medical and psychiatric system to which the violent patient comes or is brought. In essence, that is where the combative, disruptive, and dangerous person is. Second, and more important, that is where the violent patient should be. Specifically, the ED stands as that critical component of the community's response and treatment network which truly comprehensively intervenes with the violent patient. The ED swiftly and decisively addresses all the medical, psychiatric, and social aspects of violence. Violence represents the endpoint of a wide variety of factors ranging from drug ingestion to psychodynamic events, from trauma to social stresses, and from medical illnesses to intrapsychic eruptions. The ED evaluates, diagnoses, and manages all these factors.

The ED serves as a focus for violence intervention. This phenomenon reflects its very nature, its function in the community's medical network, and its responsibility for difficult cases. The ED's accessibility, consistent availability, unrestricted admissions, emphasis upon action, and instant response make it the natural place for the violent patient to come. Violence by definition is immediate. Emergency medicine is immediate.

The community recognizes the ED violence role. Civil authorities—police, sheriffs, fire officers—bring the out-of-control disruptive patient there. Courts refer patients there. EMTs transport their violent patients there. Families bring their unruly members there. Physicians send their erupting patients there. But, most importantly and significantly, patients come on their own to the ED seeking control for their violence [1]. And they will return there if their loss of control threatens to re-emerge.

The very type of patient the ED serves, and the very type of problems it addresses, combine to produce potentially explosive situations. The alcoholic patient, the suicidal patient, the paranoid patient, and the disoriented patient come to the ED. Each has a propensity toward violence. The "bad trip", the closed head injury, the diabetic crisis, and the drug ingestion all carry the possibility of disruption.

Since the ED provides the most accessible immediate assessment of the violent patient, what are the causes it must address? The causes of violence encompass ten categories. These include a psychodynamic explanation, a nonpsychiatric medication cause, a psychotropic medication cause, an alcohol explanation, an abused substance cause, a medical illness etiology, a surgical event, a physical trauma, a genetic contribution, and an environmental explanation.

DYNAMIC EXPLANATIONS

The life histories of violent patients contain many common factors including prior violence, exposure to violence, automobile accidents, parental loss, fire setting, cruelty to animals, enuresis, and truancy [2].

Violent patients often have been violent in the past. Their life stories are full of assaults, attacks, criminal activities, and striking out. They have shown murderous rage; they have engaged in numerous fights; they have been bullies. When faced with fight or flight, they choose to fight [3].

Violent people have been exposed to violence. As children and adolescents their parents inflicted physical pain upon them; they beat them. One study found that non-self-referred violent patients had a significant history of being beaten by their mothers [4]. They have been taught physical aggression as a solution to problems.

Their motor vehicle histories reflect their violence [2]. They have had automobile accidents, many of which have been serious. They have numerous moving violations.

The violent patient frequently has sustained a parental loss [2]. Among women prisoners, for example, there is a high correlation between early loss of one's mother and violent behavior [5]. Their histories reveal the loss, often early, of a parent and the subsequent absence of very significant persons in their lives.

Violence has been associated with a history of enuresis, fire setting, and cruelty to animals [6]. These childhood events frequently are found in the lives of violent patients [7].

Similarly, violence has been correlated with truancy, temper tantrums, and school problems [8]. These reflect the impulse control conflicts and disruptive behavior of these individuals.

A number of personality characteristics predispose individuals toward violent eruptions: impulsiveness, explosiveness, stubbornness, paranoia, self-centeredness, and immediacy. These qualities find expression in the historical correlations with assaults, automobile accidents, criminal activity, fire setting, truancy, and temper tantrums [4].

Impulsivity characterizes these patients. When confronted by dilemmas, faced with problems, or challenged by situations, they act. They do something, go somewhere, or respond somehow. They are not prone to reflection and contemplation. They act with explosiveness. They respond with swift, sudden, and dramatic behavior. They erupt.

Stubborness typifies violent individuals. They hold their ground, maintain their points of view, and vigorously resist any changes. They pride themselves upon their persistence. More importantly, they aggressively and physically respond to any challenge.

Many paranoid persons are aggressive [9]. They perceive themselves under attack, and in anticipation they attack. They remain constantly vigilant and on guard, ready to defend themselves at all times.

Violent patients are self-centered. They see themselves as the center of the universe, the center of attention, and the appropriate focus of everyone's attention. This characteristic accounts for their demandingness, impatience, intolerance, and arrogance.

Finally, there remains a sense of immediacy about violent patients. They convey the sense of urgency, presence, and action. They portray themselves as about to do something.

A variety of specific psychiatric symptoms lead to violence. These include auditory hallucinations and terrifying visual hallucinations. In the former, the patients experience "voices" telling them to act upon destructive impulses. These auditory hallucinations can be very powerful, irresistible, and highly dangerous. A 35-year-old man heard God "commanding him" to destroy his house after his wife left him alone. There must be "punishment", he was "told". Visually hallucinating patients become violent to escape terrifying visual images. They see extremely frightening, attacking and invading animals, people, and monsters; they respond with violence in order to get away from them or to defend against them.

Delusions of grandeur and persecution lead to violence. Grandiose people assert their right to insist upon and inflict their values, behavior, and standard of conduct upon all others. Such a view often dramatically brings them to violent conflict with others. The "persecuted" patients feel under assault from all sources at all times. They are prepared to defend themselves against the "enemy." Their defense frequently leads to violence.

Both affects of extreme anxiety and anger lead to violence. The highly anxious patients, in their attempts to control the panic, use aggressive solutions. The very angry patients strike out at their environment.

These hallucinations, delusions, and affect extremes are commonly encountered in the schizophrenic and the manic phase manic depressive patients [10].

The last key dynamic of violence revolves around three often interrelated factors: loss, depression, and suicide. Violent patients have experienced losses of spouse, of family, of a significant relationship, of a job, or of self-esteem. Loss causes depression; violent people very frequently are depressed. The aggression emerges as the chief manifestation of the desperation. Finally, depressed people become suicidal. Violent people have histories of self-destructive thoughts, threats, and behavior [4].

Medication — Nonpsychotropic

A variety of medications have been linked with violent, aggressive behavior. These include testosterone, phenacemide, an L-dyhydroxyphenylalanine (L-DOPA), and steroids. Testosterone long has been associated with aggressive behavior [11]. Many physicians have used injections of testosterone to treat impotence. Phenacemide, an anticonvulsant, has been reported to cause violent behavior [12]. It has been employed when the usually used antiseizure medications have proved unable to control convulsions. L-DOPA can produce violent behavior [13]. This antiparkinsonism drug has triggered eruptions of aggressive activity [11]. Steroid use has been linked with violent behavior in two ways [14]. First, violent behavior may occur when they are introduced [8]. Second, they may produce an aggressive picture when they are withdrawn.

Medication — Psychotropic

Two types of psychotropic medications have led to violence. The first are antidepressants, both the tricyclic and the monoamine oxidase inhibitors (MAO-inhibitors) [11]. The second class includes the minor tranquilizers.

The use of antidepressants has produced aggressive combative outbursts [15]. This more commonly is reported with the tricyclic type, possibly reflecting its more common use. In many instances, the patient with schizophrenia has been misdiagnosed as depressed and has been given a tricyclic preparation. The delusions deepen; the hallucinations increase; and violence erupts.

Minor tranquilizers also paradoxically produce violence [16]. These medications, prescribed to control anxiety, can actually trigger a violent episode through their disinhibiting action. Minor tranquilizers or sedatives may interfere with the hypervigilance of paranoid patients, thereby increasing anxiety and suspiciousness, leading to violence.

Alcohol

Alcohol produces violence in the various stages of its use: intoxication, idiosyncratic intoxication, hallucinosis, and withdrawal delirium [17]. Taken together they account for many of the psychiatric emergencies involving loss of control, aggression, and destructive behavior.

Alcohol intoxication represents the most commonly encountered alcohol violence syndrome. Here the acute use of alcohol uncovers repressed hostility, unleashes suppressed rage, and releases pent up anger. As a result the person drinking becomes aggressive, assaultive, and combative.

Alcohol idiosyncratic intoxication (pathological intoxication) involves an extreme degree of violent behavior following consumption of a small amount of alcohol. The ingestor often has no recall for these episodes.

Alcohol hallucinosis is a syndrome of hallucinations occurring in persons within 48 hours after they have stopped or decreased alcohol use. They have a clear sensorium. They manifest an aggressive response to frightening images.

Withdrawal delirium (delirium tremens) marks an extreme of alcohol withdrawal. This occurs usually 3 to 5 days following termination or diminished consumption, includes disorientation, hallucinations, temperature elevation, and frequently culminates in violent outbursts, panic, striking out, and seizures.

ABUSED SUBSTANCES

In a number of ways, a variety of abused substances produce violence in the users. The most common presentation occurs during and immediately following ingestion and intoxication. Some appear as a result of chronic involvement with the substance. Others develop during withdrawal. The most implicated substances include amphetamines, barbiturates, cocaine, hallucinogens, opiates, and phencyclidine [18].

People can behave violently during intoxication from a large variety of substances. Amphetamines acutely produce not only euphoria, but also marked experiences of paranoia. The users find and see enemies all around them; they fight "these intruders". Barbiturates paradoxically cause aggressive behavior [19]. Cocaine has triggered violent episodes [20]. Hallucinogens— lysergic acid diethylamide (LSD), mescaline, dimethyltryptamine (DMT), psilocybin, 2,5-dimethoxy-4-,ethyl-,amphetamine (STP)—can produce terrifying images, frightening experiences, "bad trips", hallucinations, and delusions which lead to violence. The users often act upon some strong unusual delusion or hallucination. Phencyclidine (PCP) not only causes a number of transient neurological symptoms but also triggers hallucinations and violence. PCP has been linked to murderous rage [21].

Chronic use of amphetamines leads to protracted projective thinking. This prolonged paranoid position makes the addict prone toward violence. One amphetamine user reports constantly carrying a weapon during and after periods of amphetamine use.

The withdrawal period from certain substances produces violence in two ways. First, the users experience physiological signs of withdrawal (e.g., sweating, tachycardia, fever, insomnia, and nausea with vomiting as in the case of opiate withdrawal, which result in restlessness, aggressiveness, irritability, and violence). Second, as a result of loss of supply and because of the intense craving, the users often turn to violence and crime to obtain their "fix," to regain their source, and to reverse the withdrawal signs.

MEDICAL ILLNESS

Many medical conditions, diseases, and syndromes either manifest themselves or are associated with violence. Anoxia from any cause can lead patients to display aggressive behavior. Central nervous system (CNS) lesions and infections cause violence. Various seizure states either produce or correlate with violence. Minimal brain dysfunction is also associated with aggressive behavior.

Extreme breathing difficulty causes people to become violent. Patients with chronic obstructive pulmonary disease (COPD), asthma, or cystic fibrosis during certain phases of their illness find themselves "fighting for breath." Dyspnea is a terrifying, overwhelming experience. Patients often aggressively respond to it. Generally this is associated with rather rapid onset of anoxia and produces behavior entirely out of the patient's control.

Similarly, life threatening illnesses such as a myocardial infarction in certain patients lead to a violent response.

CNS lesions and infections in certain patients present as violent behavior. These include temporal lobe neoplasms [1], limbic system tumors [11], hypothalamic area lesions [11], and tuberculoma [22]. Encephalitis—viral, bacterial, or fungal—often first reveals itself by violent disruptive behavior [8]. Certain seizures and EEG findings are linked to violence [5]. Temporal lobe epilepsy (psychomotor epilepsy) causes aggressive behavior. Seizures occur in the temporal lobe region or the limbic system. Four qualities characterize them: aura, autonomic nervous system activation, automatous movements, and amnesia [8]. The types of aura include deja vu, an epigastric sensation, or a hallucination. The automaton designates stereotyped behavior, including stamping, kicking, or scratching [23]. Nonspecific asymmetric EEG changes have been associated with violence [24]. Six and 14 per second spiking also has been linked to aggressive behavior [25]. Some patients become violent during the post-ictal phase [11].

Minimal brain dysfunction (MBD) in recent years has been thought to be related to aggressive activity [26]. Persons with this syndrome have EEG abnormalities, organicity on psychological testing, difficulty interpersonally, affective lability, histories of alcohol and drug abuse, and respond to either low dose imipramine or amphetamine without an addictive pattern.

SURGERY

Surgery accounts for violence in several ways. First, some patients aggressively respond to their need for surgery. Second, a combative assaultive picture erupts occasionally following cardiac surgery. Third, the immobility required after certain surgical procedures causes some patients to become violent.

Some patients respond aggressively to the prospect of anesthesia and surgery. "Going under," "submitting to the blade," "being cut upon," and "being on the table" evoke frightening and overwhelming images for many patients. Frequently they react violently by assault or with flight.

Violence can follow cardiac surgery [27]. After surgery the patients experience a "lucid interval" for several days and then they often develop disorientation, delusions, hallucinations and aggressive behavior. One post-cardiac surgery patient believed the hospital was trying to poison him and struck a nurse. He apologized after appropriate therapy.

Many procedures require the patient to be immobilized for a significant time period, post-operatively. These procedures include skin grafts, skin transfers on pedicles, traction, and casts. Often impulsive, action-oriented patients respond to this confinement with violence. One young motorcyclist in traction frequently obtained attention by throwing bed pans across the room.

TRAUMA

Trauma both correlates with and contributes to violence. Trauma has a number of historical correlates to violence. Trauma itself in a number of ways accounts for aggressive behavior.

The histories of many violent patients contain references to physical trauma, especially to the head [4]. Many have incurred severe injury to the head. A troublesome cycle emerges. Impulsiveness, alcohol abuse, a history of violence, and reckless driving all lead to vehicular accidents and head trauma. Head trauma leads to impulsiveness, alcohol use, and violence.

Trauma to the body causes aggressive behavior in at least two ways. First, some patients react to acute trauma with violence. They engage in combat with would-be helpers. In their fear, pain, apprehension, and confrontation with death they respond by striking out. Second, other patients become aggressive as they start to comprehend the devastation of the trauma— extensive burns, amputations, para- and quadriplegia, or disfigurement.

Head trauma produces both acute and protracted violent behavior. The patients in their disorientation, anxiety, and disorganization become acutely combative, assaultive, and destructive. Frequently, head injury patients react violently at the scene of the accident and in the ED. On a more chronic basis head trauma often produces long term and significant impairment of memory, loss of integration ability, and attention deficits. Patients with these deficits, when distressed by their limitations, can become violent [28]. Three months after a closed head injury a patient struck the examiner when asked the name of the President. The patient realized that she used to know the answer.

GENETIC CONTRIBUTION

Evidence along a number of lines suggests a genetic contribution to violence. Studies of families, adoptees, chromosomal patterns, and mental ability indicate that indeed genetics play a role in the manifestations of aggression.

Studies of genograms support the concept that "violence runs in the family"[26,29]. Clinically it is evident that patients with histories of violence also have family histories of violence. Evidence suggests that antisocial personality, alcoholism, drug dependence, and hysteria are over-represented in the criminal population and their families, both in their parents and in other first-degree relatives [26].

A more fascinating bit of support for the genetic contribution comes from adopted-away studies [11,26]. Offspring of antisocial parents who are adopted away and reared by others still demonstrate increased incidence of antisocial behavior [30].

Studies of chromosomes in the violent criminal populations indicated an over-representation of men with an XYY [26]. The extra Y is thought to be related to violence. However, the evidence is far from conclusive. The studies also indicate an excess of XYY men in psychiatric institutions, in facilities for the mentally retarded, in prisons, and in maximum-security confinement [31].

Similarly, studies in criminal and psychiatric institutions demonstrate an over-representation of mentally retarded individuals [11,27]. These patients' deficiencies, inability to negotiate complicated situations, and difficulty in aiding in their court defense may account for their violence and their numbers in those facilities.

ENVIRONMENT

Violence particularly erupts in certain settings. These environments can be described in several ways, involving emotions generated in the setting; the institution and its dynamics; and the impact of weapons.

The important contributory emotional features include intimacy of relationships, danger, intense affect, and dehumanization. Close relationships and high danger lead to intense affect and to defenses against it.

Settings that develop, promote, and sustain close intimate dependent relationships can also generate violence; this accounts for much of the eruption of violence within the family [32]. Lovers, spouses, and companions fill this role. Close working partners, combat groups, and athletic teams also share this relationship. In all these relationships intense feelings of love, hate, expectation, disappointment, hope, and fear develop. Plans, past experiences, and anticipated future are shared. When feelings are intense, disappointments can be severe and violence can result.

Danger produces violence. In combat, in a dark alley, and in the emergency department, people fear death. In situations in which individuals feel their lives threatened, many will strike back. The threat spurs them to constant vigilance. They respond to minor stimuli by attacking.

Certain intense emotions promote violence. These are anger, anxiety, and despair, each producing pressure for action, expression, and release; with each, violence may follow.

Finally, intimate dependent relationships, danger, and intense emotions result in dehumanization, the ultimate mental mechanism for attack [33]. The individuals see the people around them as not real, not important, and not human. They strike out at objects, not people.

Violence occurs in environments which accept it, promote it, and foster it. Many families, social organizations, athletic teams, prison populations, and military groups have developed direct physical aggression as their group norm. It is their way of settling issues, establishing relationships, maintaining group identity, and viewing themselves. They pride themselves upon their violent history and traditions. They accept and expect violence.

Finally, in any environment, the presence of weapons escalates and heightens the likelihood of violence. The availability of knives and guns changes an altercation to homicide, a fight to a murder, and a quarrel to death [3].

MANDATE IMPLEMENTATION

The ED must contain, control, and conclude the violent patient episode. This is the responsibility of the staff; this insures good, effective patient care. In order to achieve the control the ED staff must follow a number of practices requiring prompt, courteous, and firm intervention. The practices include the use of an office, the involvement of security personnel, the removal of weapons, the employment of restraints, the administration of medications, and constant supervision [34,35].

The ED intervention with the violent patient must be swift. Delays escalate aggressive behavior. As the violent patients wait, their anger, apprehension, and anxiety increase. The notions of "do nothing" or "hope they will go away" often result in patients becoming more assertive, demanding, and disruptive.

ED staff should identify themselves formally by their full names and professional title. They must address the patients by their full names also. This promotes a sense of professional competence and responsibility. This also serves to reverse the dehumanization. We are people helping people. This further checks any misidentification, misperceptions, or distortions that the patients hold toward people in their environment.

Courteousness has two facets: respect and appropriate distance. Staff must exercise and demonstrate respect for the patient. When patients perceive this respect, a major step has been achieved in the resolution of violence. Appropriate distance requires staff to appreciate and observe the body buffer zone [36]. Too close becomes too threatening; too far becomes too remote and dehumanizing. A near but not too close physical presence establishes a concerned, respectful noninvasive response.

A separate office with fixed pleasant furniture provides a safe place to control and contain the violent patient. It prevents elopement. It uses walls both to check the disruptive behavior and to limit the sensory over-stimulation from the rest of the ED. ED staff find it very difficult to control an aggressive person in the midst of a busy waiting room or among other patients in adjacent cubicles. The office provides the patient the opportunity to be interviewed privately, with dignity.

Security personnel are an important part of ED ecology. Their uniforms and their presence provide the message of control, order, and support.

In the actual deployment of security personnel certain guidelines have proven useful. First, security personnel must work ultimately only under the direction of the physician. The doctor uses them to establish the intervention under his orders. Second, display force before employing it. Frequently, having enough personnel present is enough to halt a disruption. Third, if security must physically gain control they must act in sufficient numbers, under the order of one person, the physician, and in a coordinated manner. Fourth, the security personnel may only cease their patient involvement after a physician's order. Fifth, the ED must develop a procedure protocol for the use of security personnel and the levels of their involvement.

Weapons must be removed. No effective patient care can be conducted while the patient remains armed. Staff must insist that implements of destruction, i.e., knives, guns, razors, bottles, and clubs, be turned over for the duration of the evaluation. Sharp instruments should be placed by the patient on a table, not handed directly to the interviewer. In the case of guns, the staff can obtain police involvement. Many ED's employ metal detectors. One other method has the patient change into a hospital gown for a physical examination. This permits staff to check the clothing for weapons.

Restraints provide another dimension of control and cover a number of intervention levels. The basic level focuses upon simply observing the patient. The next requires that the patient stay within the office. The ultimate is physical "four point" restraint. The patient should be on a stretcher with each extremity wrapped in strong, nonabrasive materials and with waist restraint. The patient's shoes should be removed. The wraps on each arm and leg must be checked frequently and circulation observed.

Medications control violence. In cases of drug ingestion of unknown type, diazepam (Valium) is most safe. However, the drug of choice remains haloperidol (Haldol) 2-5mg IM up to q½hour [37]. In situations of extreme violence, agitation, and loss of control, IV diazepam or, under an anesthesiologist's supervision, the use of muscle relaxants have proved effective. Equipment for external support of respiration is needed before either drug is used. Once staff have initiated the administration of medication vital signs must be checked frequently and clinical assessments conducted.

Finally, once the staff has commenced their intervention with the violent patient, they must have personnel accompany and supervise the patient at all times. This reassures the patient, provides a human contact, checks further disruptions, prevents elopement, and protects against complications of pharmacotherapy.

IMPEDIMENTS TO EFFECTIVE STAFF INTERVENTION WITH THE VIOLENT PATIENT

Various staff reactions to the violent patient impede effective intervention. The consequences of an ineffective response include elopement, escalation of disruption, injury to staff, to other ED patients or to the violent patient, and destruction of property. These impeding staff reactions include anger, underestimation, bias, fear, and affront [38].

Staff anger toward the violent patient has at least two causes. First, they are enraged that the patient is in their ED. The patient disrupts the routine, the order, and the system. Second, and more dynamically significant, the violent patient's demandingness, his self-centeredness, and his impulsivity challenge others to confrontation in kind, and professional staff are not exempt from these feelings. Essentially anger begets anger.

Often, staff underestimates the patient's violent potential. They deny the threats. They reduce the dangers to "just talk." They assume the patient will wait "just like everyone else."

Staff have clear bias against violent patients. They do not like them, their use of alcohol, their criminal activities, their histories of violence, and their disruptiveness. Staff have a disdain for dealing with the violent patients.

Staff fear the violent patient. They have good reason for such fear. The literature contains many references to assaults upon staff [39,40]. Their experiences have shown some patients do attack staff and staff are concerned with their own safety.

Finally, the violent patient is perceived by staff as an affront to their view of themselves. As one ED physician stated "I did not go into medicine to work with violent patients." ED staff see themselves as health professionals, helping people who want help. The violent patient challenges this highly prized value.

CONCLUSION — THE MANDATE

ED staff have the responsibility to contain, and to control the violent patient and to resolve the crisis. Not only has the ED emerged as the community's referral source for the violent patient, but also and more importantly, the ED stands as the place where these patients should come for evaluation and treatment. The ED can best acutely assess and intervene in the ten causes of violence: psychopathology, nonpsychotropic medications, psychotropic medications, alcohol, other abused substances, medical illness, reactions to surgery, trauma, genetic factors, and environmental stress.

Yet if the ED represents the most important access point, its staff members have their own reactions which impede the intervention. The solutions involve a four part program. First, acceptance by the ED staff of its mandate to intervene. Second, a realization that the violent patient not only desires help, but also benefits from the intervention. Violent patients frequently come on their own for assistance, for control, and for alternatives to aggression [1]. Many violent patients say "thank you." Third, a recognition and frank discussion of staff reactions to violent patients. Fourth, the implementation of the mandate by an intervention protocol utilizing a prompt, identified, courteous and firm response and employing a separate office, security personnel, removal of weapons, restraints, medication, and supervision. These provide the staff with the tools to contain and to control the violent patient.

REFERENCES

1. Lion, J.R., Bach-y-Rita G., Ervin, F.R.: Violent patients in the Emergency Room. Am J Psychiatry 125:1706–1711, 1969.
2. Mark, V.H. and Ervin, F.R.: Violence and the Brain. Harper and Row, New York, 1970.
3. Halleck, S.L.: Psychodynamic Aspects of Violence. Bulletin of American Academy of Psychiatry and the Law. 1979.
4. Climent, C.E. and Ervin, F.R.: Historical Data in the Evaluation of Violent Subjects. Arch Gen Psych 27:621–624. 1972.
5. Climent, C.E., Rollins, A., Ervin, F.R. and Plutchik, R.: Epidemiological Studies of Women Prisoners, I: Medical and Psychiatric Variables Related to Violent Behavior. Am J Psychiatry 130:985–990. 1973.
6. Hellman, D.S., Blackman, N.: Enuresis, Firesetting, and Cruelty to Animals: A triad predictive of adult crime. Am J Psychiatry 122:1431–1435. 1966.

7. Rubin, B.: Prediction of Dangerousness in Mentally Ill Criminals. Arch Gen Psych 27:397–407. 1972.
8. Soreff, S.M.: Management of the Psychiatric Emergency. John Wiley & Sons, New York, 1981.
9. Swanson, D.W., Bohnert, P.J., and Smith, J.A.: The Paranoid. Little, Brown and Co., Boston. 1970.
10. Skodol, A.E. and Karasu, T.B.: Emergency Psychiatry and the Assaultive Patient. Am J Psychiatry. 135:202–205. 1978.
11. Goldstein, M.: Brain research and violent behavior. Arch Neurol 30:1–35. 1974.
12. Hall, R.C.W. (ed.): Psychiatric Presentations of Medical Illness. SP Medical of Scientific Books. New York. 1980.
13. Goodwin, F.K.: Behavioral effects of L-dopa in man—in Shader, R.I. ed. Psychiatric Complications of Medical Drugs. Raven Press, New York, 1972. pp 149–174.
14. Glaser, G.H.: Psychotic reactions induced by corticotropin (ACTH) and cortisone. Psychosom Med 15:280–291. 1953.
15. Rampling, D.: Aggression: A paradoxical response to tricyclic antidepressant. Am J Psychiatry. 135:117–118. 1978.
16. Slaby, A.E., Lieb, J. and Trancredi, L.R.: Handbook of Psychiatric Emergencies. 2nd ed. Medical Examination Publishing Co., Flushing, New York. 1981.
17. Diagnostic and Statistical Manual of Mental Disorders, 3rd ed. American Psychiatric Association, Washington, D.C. 1980.
18. Rada, R.T.: The violent patient: Rapid assessment and management. Psychosomatics. 22:101–109. 1981.
19. Manschreck, T.C. and Petri, M.: The paranoid syndrome. Lancet 1:251–253. 1978.
20. Post, R.M.: Cocaine psychosis: A continuum model. Am J Psych 135:1079–1081. 1975.
21. Fauman, M.A. and Fauman, B.J. Violence associated with phencyclidine abuse. Am J Psych 136:1584–1586. 1979.
22. Simm, R.H. and Desilva, M.: Intracranial tuberculoma coexistent with unciate seizures and violent behavior. JAMA 245:1247–1248. 1981.
23. Benson, D.F. and Blumer, D.: Psychiatric Aspects of Neurological Disease. Grune, &. Stratton, New York. 1975.
24. Bach-y-Rita, G., Lion, J.R., Climent, C.E. and Ervin, F.R.: Episodic dyscontrol: A study of 130 violent patients. Am J Psychiatry 127:1473–1478. 1971.
25. Gibbs, E.L. and Gibbs, F.A.: Electroencephalographic evidence of thalamic and hypothalamic epilepsy. Neurology. 1:136–144. 1951.
26. Menuck, M. and Voineskos, G.: The Etiology of Violent Behavior. Gen Hosp Psych 3:37-47. 1981.
27. Kolb, L.C.: Modern Clinical Psychiatry, 8th ed. W.B. Saunders, Co. Philadelphia. 1973.
28. Goldstein, K.: After-effects of Brain Injuries in War, Grune & Stratton, New York, 1942.
29. Cloninger, C.R., Reich, T. and Guze, S.B.: The multifactorial model of disease transmission: II. Sex differences in the familial transmission of sociopathy (antisocial personality). Br J Psych 127:11–22. 1975.
30. Cadoret, R.J.: Psychopathology in adopted-away offspring of biologic parents with antisocial personality. Arch Gen Psych 35:176–184. 1978.
31. Hook, E.B.: Behavioral implications of the human XYY genotype. Science 179:139–150. 1973.
32. Barnhill, L.R.: Clinical assessment of intrafamilial violence. Hosp & Commun Psychiatry. 31:543–547. 1980.
33. Grant, D.A.: A model of violence. Aust NZ J Psych 12:123–126. 1978.

34. Fauman, B.J. and Fauman, M.A.: Emergency Psychiatry for the House Officer. Williams and Wilkins. Baltimore. 1981.
35. Perry, S.W. and Gilmore, M.M.: The disruptive patient or visitor. JAMA 245:755–757. 1981.
36. Hall, E.T.: The Hidden Dimension. Doubleday and Co., Garden City. 1966.
37. Donlon, P.T., Hopkin, J. and Tupin, J.P.: Overview: Efficiency and safety of the rapid neuroleptization method with injectable haldoperidol. Am J Psychiatry 136:273–278. 1979.
38. Lion, J.R. and Pasternak, S.A.: Countertransference Reactions to Violent Patients. Am J Psychiatry 130:207–210. 1973.
39. Whitman, R.M., Armao, B.B. and Dent, O.B.: Assault on the therapist. Am J Psychiatry, 133:426–429. 1976.
40. Lion, J.R., Snyder, W. and Merrill, G.L.: Underreporting of assaults on staff in a state hospital. Hosp & Comm Psychiatry. 32:497–498. 1981.

Victims of Violence

5

Abused Adults

BEVERLY J. FAUMAN

Every 30 seconds a violent crime is committed. The FBI reports for 1973 indicated that there were 828,150 homicides, rapes, robberies, or aggravated assaults [1]. It is estimated that there were 2,000,000 episodes of domestic violence annually [2]. In 1972, 31% of murders were of spouses or lovers [3]. The victims who survive these attacks, as well as the hundreds of thousands who do not report the crimes committed against them, constitute the population which may present to emergency departments with obvious or covert psychiatric problems. In addition to the direct victims of rape, assault, and domestic violence, there is another population who are also victims of violence. This includes the families of victims of rape, assault, and homicide, the children of domestic violence victims, and the perpetrators of these violent crimes.

REASONS FOR SEEKING HELP

There are many factors that motivate a victim to seek emergency help. Foremost, of course, may be the direct physical trauma that cannot be ignored. Fractures, lacerations, soft-tissue injuries, and organ damage are common sequellae to assault. Indirect effects are also present, however, and frequently constitute the only reason for seeking help. These include the psychological sequellae, especially depression, suicide attempts, and psycho-physiologic disorders. The patient may have decided that it was time to get out of a repetitive violent situation. An abusive parent or spouse may recognize the lethal potential of his or her behavior, and be frightened enough by the threat of loss of the victim that he or she presents seeking help. A perpetrator may also be coerced into asking for help by the threatened or actual loss of the victim through separation or formal court action. Families of homicide victims, and boyfriends or spouses of rape victims may present to an emergency department some time after the violent event. It is important to remember that they are frequently unaware of the relationship between their symptoms and the violence, or are embarrassed by or defensive about the assaultive situation. Further, victims of violence come to an emergency department or other agency when efforts at self-treatment fail, not necessarily when the injury occurs.

MEDICAL PRESENTATIONS SUGGESTIVE OF VICTIM STATUS

The staff in an emergency department is in a particularly good position to identify victims of violence, although it is estimated that only 10% of domestic violence victims seek medical attention [4]. Many of these victims are treated without the true cause of the injuries being identified. For the victim of domestic violence, there are certain predictable characteristics of injuries that should raise the index of suspicion (See Table 1). Multiple traumatic injuries, unexplainable injuries, and specific kinds of trauma, in males or females, are the most common clues. Specific injuries to look for include maxillo-facial bruises or fractures, eye injuries, hematomas or ecchymoses on the trunk (especially breasts). Sprains, strains, and fractures of the arms, and ecchymoses on the shins should be particularly alerting [4].

Some physical injuries sustained during domestic assaults may cause pain without visible trauma, while other injuries are confined to areas of the body normally concealed by clothing. Therefore, a complete examination of the disrobed patient must be performed. Even if the cause of the injury seems plausible, the medical history should be reviewed to determine if the patient is sustaining an inordinate number of "accidents."

Symptoms and signs of chronic stress reactions are common medical presentations for both victims and perpetrators of rape and domestic violence [5]. Insomnia, nightmares, headaches, anorexia, or vague psychosomatic complaints impel the physician to inquire further; requests for sleeping pills, minor tranquilizers, or pain medication are also signals that the patient is asking for help with a stressful situation. Symptoms referable to the gastrointestinal tract, "bleeding disorders," and generally poor nutritional status may

Table 1. Components of the Battered Spouse Syndrome

1. Repeated emergency center visits for minor injuries
2. History of being "accident prone"
3. Soft tissue injuries
4. Injuries on areas of the body normally covered by clothing
5. Implausible explanations for injuries
6. Simplistic or vague explanations for injuries
7. Psychosomatic complaints
8. Depression
9. Pain — especially chronic
10. Substance abuse in patient or spouse
11. Suicidal gestures or attempts
12. Psychiatric history in patient or spouse
13. Previous marriage counseling
14. History of prior physical abuse
15. History of observing someone else being abused
16. History of sexual abuse

From: Goldberg W, and Carey A: Domestic violence in the emergency setting. Topics in Emergency Medicine: Human Violence, Warner CG and Braen GR (eds) 3(4):65-83, January, 1982.

also suggest a past or present violence syndrome. Any unusual difficulties during pregnancy should be thoroughly explored to determine if the patient is being beaten.

Psychiatric symptoms are very common in this population. Depression, anxiety, suicidal or homicidal feelings, hostility, painfully low self-esteem, and phobias are frequent, in victims and perpetrators. The development of phobias is particularly suggestive of rape or child abuse.

Sometimes patients present to physicians with a description of symptoms in others that can serve as an alert to a violence syndrome. Behavioral symptoms in a child may suggest that the child is a direct victim of abuse, incest, or rape, but may also be a signal that the child is observing domestic violence or severe marital strife. Symptoms in children include bedwetting, truancy, running away, learning disorders, suicidal behavior, or depression [5]. When a parent brings a child in because of one of these symptoms, the parent should be questioned in a nonthreatening, nonjudgmental way to determine whether any of the violence syndromes are present.

The health care practitioner should bear in mind that many perpetrators of violence syndromes present in covert ways, hoping to be discovered or stopped.

IDENTIFICATION

Once there is a commitment to treat the violence syndrome, there must be a systematic way to identify the treatment population. In some cases, the victim's presentation is overt — he or she reports being battered, assaulted, or raped, and requests some form of assistance. More often the presentation is covert, which requires that the health care professional take an active role in identifying these victims [6, 7]. One approach to identification of domestic violence victims is to question patients directly. It is helpful to remember that nonjudgmental, direct, supportive questioning has been demonstrated to be both informative to the health care professional, and a relief to the patient [7]. The gender of the interviewer doesn't matter; what does is a neutral attitude. A large population of domestic violence victims could be identified simply by asking patients if they have had certain experiences. Many of these patients have not consciously acknowledged that they are battered. Many times, asking these questions first awakens the patient to the pathological nature of her experiences.

The domestic violence victim is a person under chronic stress. Therefore, victims commonly present with psychosomatic or functional complaints secondary to the stress of their violent relationship. It may be more "acceptable" to seek treatment for headaches, loss of sleep, or depression than to acknowledge domestic violence. The development of pain, suicidal gestures, and problems of substance abuse have been seen also in both partners. The husband or father who is violent was commonly abused as a child. There is conflicting evidence regarding whether the battered wife observed any more violence in her family of origin than other women.

The acute phase of the rape-trauma syndrome includes the following physical symptoms [8]: soreness, disturbances in sleeping and eating habits, and symptoms directly related to the specific assault. Emotional reactions may include continuing fear of injury, mutilation, or death; guilt, shame, or self-blame; anger and a desire for revenge; and "undoing"—obsessive thoughts related to the details of the assault and the attacker, related to a wish that it would not have happened if the victim behaved differently. Over the next weeks or months, there are a number of behaviors which are associated with being a victim of rape, and which may be used to identify emergency department patients who have experienced rape in the past. The victim may make certain changes in her life-style. She may restrict her social activities, move, and frequently suffers a disruption in a dating or marital relationship. Dreams and nightmares are common, as will be experiences of reliving the assault, or mastering it by changing the outcome or undoing the beginning. Phobias as mentioned above are common. They are frequently experienced as fear of crowds, fear of being alone, or to specific characteristics of the assailant or the assault. Sometimes the patient experiences anxiety over the fact that it is taking so long to recover from the assault. It is useful to remember and to advise her that it can take weeks to months to get over the experience and that this is normal.

Abusive parents are commonly isolated, mistrustful, lonely, sensitive to criticism, and unable to ask for help [9]. A small number have clinically significant psychiatric disorders. They typically demand high performance from themselves as well as their children, although they are unable to express mild or moderate anger. They are unable to acknowledge or to be empathic to the child's needs, wanting instead for the child to fulfill parental needs. They are at higher risk to abuse or neglect their children when either partner is ill, the family suffers financial setbacks, or a stress occurs that lowers a parent's self-esteem. Thus, many "ordinary" emergency situations may prompt an increase in child abuse. The psychological profile of a sex offender includes some of the same characteristics. There is a high correlation with a history of abuse or neglect in childhood, a problem expressing anger, difficulty asking for help, and a feeling that he is not "OK" [10].

Although family members who are indirect victims of homicide or rape have not been studied extensively, there are some characteristics which can be found regularly [1]. Initially, family members undergo an acute grief reaction, which is complicated both by the untimely, unexpected death or injury and the horror of the manner of the assault. If the victim died, there is concern about how much suffering was experienced, and an urgency about wanting to know the details. This urgency is often coupled with the reality of having to help the police reconstruct the victim's movements and contacts. For the families of rape victims, feelings of guilt and irrational anger at the victim commonly surface. Family members experience sleep disturbances, somatic complaints, "numbness" (or just not remembering), and anxiety which may be related to a desire for revenge. The victim-perpetrator dichotomy is oversimplified; often an adult is both sequentially and in parallel. In many families, multiple violence syndromes are present. Furthermore, all parties within a violent or incestuous family are in collusion, willingly or not [5].

BARRIERS TO IDENTIFICATION

Professionals who encounter victims of abuse have a variety of attitudes that can interfere with diagnosis and treatment. Ignorance is the most superficial reason for missing the diagnosis. Someone who has grown up in a nonabusive environment may not believe that human beings are capable of inflicting such violence on each other. In that sense the whole experience of working in an emergency department creates culture shock. Beneath the naiveté, there are many professional responses that interfere with adequate assessment and treatment. The patient reinforces many of these responses, for several reasons. The patient may try to deny that the situation is as bad as it is, or may feel she doesn't deserve anything better anyway. She often perceives the professional's helplessness and consequent anger, and tries to relieve those feelings by minimizing her need for help. The professional may react to the feeling of helplessness by denial or by identifying with the aggressor. This is expressed as believing the woman wanted to be raped, the child is whiney, or the wife is a masochist. Aggressiveness can also be expressed by giving help only on a conditional basis, e.g., only treating a woman if she agrees to leave her husband [4].

The professional may try to avoid feelings of outrage and helplessness by tending to the medical needs, or the social needs of reporting the rape or abuse, or finding a temporary shelter. It may only be possible to respond to those obvious needs; however, the therapist should be aware that the psychological issues exist.

The therapist may also feel that there is no point in interfering with a domestic violence situation, because if the woman wanted to be out of it, she'd get out. This condescending attitude overlooks the terror and helplessness experienced by the victim. If the patient or parent disguises the origins of the injuries in a case of abuse, the professional fears challenging the story.

A lack of education and training regarding current useful approaches for violence victims, the general underdeveloped "state of the art," and a lack of community resources contribute to the health care professional's feelings of inadequacy. Feelings of helplessness may be particularly aroused when treating a victim who has been in a violent situation for years, and has already made several unsuccessful attempts to get help. While this victim might appear to have a poorer outlook than someone seeking help for the first time, those who eventually get out of abusive relationships are often older, have been involved in abusive relationships longer, and have sought help before [4].

Human violence situations can produce strong responses from the well-meaning but naive care giver. Over-reaction by the helping person may result in frightening the victim into silence, or even into defending the assailant. This prevents the victim from assessing her own feelings and needs. The victim's task is to recognize, express, and channel her anger constructively. Therefore, treatment must remain focused on the victim, not on the outraged professional.

Sometimes, observation of the assailant's solicitous concern and apologetic behavior toward the victim may result in the health care professional's encouraging the couple to continue the relationship despite evidence of a long history of abuse. Recommending counseling while the couple continues living together is risky. Certainly, the assailant requires professional help, but this requirement does not diminish the victim's need to extricate herself from this potentially life-threatening situation [4].

Finally, professionals must avoid becoming callous. Because the physician or nurse has seen worse injuries, more horrible rapes, or younger victims of child abuse, the present patient may not be recognized as experiencing overwhelming distress. For the patient, the worst abuse she knows is the one she experienced herself. The therapeutic role is to be empathic to that, not to put it into the perspective of others' problems for the patient. The therapist sometimes may not believe the patient, but here again the role of the medical professional is to treat, not judge the case [11, 12].

SOCIETAL ATTITUDES ABOUT VIOLENCE VICTIMS

Both the therapist and the patient who is a victim are subject to the attitudes of the society to which they belong. The common attitudes that interfere with therapy of the child abuse or domestic violence victim are concerns about family sanctity, parental rights, and marital privacy. Police departments, neighbors, and physicians may feel they don't have the right to interfere [3,13,14], and the patient feels embarrassed at revealing family secrets. In addition, there are prevailing societal myths about masculinity and femininity that can impede treatment. For a woman, the common stereotypes are of the masochist, who likes to be beaten or raped [15,16], the vamp, who teases a man until he has no other choice but to be violent; the martyr, who needs to be victimized to feel worthwhile; and the tramp, who deserves to be treated badly. The stereotypes of men that serve to rationalize abusive behavior include the idea "men are like that," that men have the right to control their women and children, and that men are simply stronger, so it is natural that the woman gets hurt [13,16].

It is a common belief that people control their own destinies. It is rather unsettling to believe that events beyond our control affect our lives in severely destructive ways. For that reason, women often accept the blame for provoking violence by "letting dinner get cold," rather than feeling helpless at the irrational behavior of an abusive spouse. Domestic violence may include the components of high coercion/high control inherent in brainwashing and kidnapping, and can cause people with normal psychological profiles to behave in a bizarre or irrational manner [17,18,19], to stay in a dangerous or pathological situation when it seems obvious that one should leave.

Even if a woman chooses a series of abusive mates, she should not be "blamed" for this. Each abusive encounter reinforces the woman's own sense of worthlessness and the worthlessness of women in general. Masochistic behavior should not be reinforced by health care providers who subtly infer that it is the victim's fault for choosing such partners, and provoking such violence.

Individuals who are chronically exposed to extreme forms of violence, either at home or in their jobs, tend to become impervious to lesser forms of violence. A slashed arm seems minor compared to a gunshot wound and a kick may be perceived as trivial compared to the slashed arm. A person who has been repeatedly shaken and pinched by a spouse may not be thought of as a victim of violence at all. This diminished state of perception hinders prevention, early identification, and treatment of domestic violence. A similar phenomenon is a victim's tendency to use nonspecific descriptors and minimizing language to deny the seriousness of the situation to themselves and others. Phrases such as "he pushed me" and "we were just squabbling," may not activate suspicion that the patient may be a victim of severe on-going violence. Although there are many psychosocial reasons for the victim's denial, what is most important is that imprecise language is used, and that health care professionals must anticipate it, recognize it, interpret it, and validate it with the victim. Persistent questioning, which requires the victim to specify the details of her experience, will clarify the violent nature of the relationship, and may break through the victim's conscious denial [4].

Domestic violence victims often impede helping agencies from mobilizing on their behalf. While requesting assistance, they simultaneously exhibit overwhelming dependency, passivity, and resistance to change. The thought of leaving a known but oppressive environment engenders ambivalence within the victim, which may be perceived as disinterest or laziness. The female victim may believe she is incapable of surviving emotionally or economically outside of the relationship, she dreads retribution by the assailant, the thought of single parenthood is intolerable, and, perceiving her partner's fragility, she fears his self-destruction if she leaves. Simultaneously, the victim can no longer cope with the chronic unpredictable stress, she values her children's well-being, and she dreads continuing a potentially lethal relationship. Domestic violence victims are often psychologically and physiologically debilitated by the time they seek professional help. They lack the energy to look at their situation objectively, and cannot imagine a better future. Only through persistence of the helping professional can domestic violence victims sufficiently restore their resources to choose healthy alternatives to their current situation [4].

PSYCHOLOGICAL ISSUES OF VICTIMS OF VIOLENCE

The reality of being a victim prompts certain predictable responses [20]. The first time anyone is victimized, there is a sudden realization of one's mortality. Trust in others is broken (in the instance of infant and child abuse, trust may never develop). The recognition that one human can inflict such harm on another is an isolating experience, which makes it difficult for the patient to trust in a therapist. The more frequent, early, and harsh the abuse, the greater is this isolation and distrust. The terror of the assault and the anticipation of further violence are more of an issue than the violence itself [21]. The sequence of brutality, then kindness, and then a fear of further beatings or rapes if the child or woman does not comply creates somewhat of a hostage mentality, in which the victim begins to identify with the captor, and may experience guilt for "making" him beat her.

For all victims of violence there is concern with being believed [5,13]. Many adults who were victimized in one way or another as children relate that they told no one because they didn't think they would be believed, or did try to tell someone who could not believe the child's stories. Rape and incest victims who felt they were somewhat responsible for an attack may not report it also because they fear not being believed or being blamed. Victims of child or spouse abuse may never report the abuse because they keep hoping for a change in the situation, or may actually see intermittent change [22,23]. They may try to ignore the fact that the abuse is occurring or continuing.

The reality of each specific abuse situation may also contain elements that are unanticipated, severe, or bizarre, such as recognizing that the assailant was actually psychotic, there was significant physical injury including mutilation, or there were multiple or prolonged abuses.

In addition, there are reactions that are more specific for specific types of violence. A rape victim is often reacting to the life threat: If she resisted she might have been killed but if she submitted she could have been killed anyway, or may find it hard to live with herself afterwards. The rape victim has internalized a lifetime of societal attitudes that "nice" girls don't get raped, that women secretly are supposed to enjoy it, and that a woman can't be raped if she doesn't want to be. After an assault, she will feel guilty, dirty, embarrassed, and frightened. If the assault occurs under any circumstances that reinforce the common cultural myths, the patient is even more likely to feel isolated and guilty for having allowed the rape to occur. For instance, if the assailant was known to the victim, or even attractive to her, she may believe that she invited it. Feelings of helplessness and fear for her life can become overwhelming in subsequent life situations that do not warrant such reactions [8,16,17,21].

For a child abuse victim, there is genuine helplessness, powerlessness, and dependency on the parent or guardian who is beating the child [5,9]. The child may perceive that the parent is sick and immature, and needs an inordinate amount of understanding and caretaking. This is often how the child survives. Internally, however, the child has learned not to trust adults (more accurately, probably never learned to trust), often feels responsible for evoking the beating, and in addition is in a complicated predicament; namely, if he tells anyone about his beatings, he may be removed from his home, siblings, and parents. Because these beatings may be the major mode of communication between the child and his abusive parent, he may provoke the same sort of behavior in foster parents and physicians. Most important, he grows up to become an adult victim of one of the violence syndromes; child abuser, victim or perpetrator of spouse abuse, or other violent offender [2,5,24–27].

The perpetrator of spouse abuse commonly grew up in a family in which abuse and violence were common [2,5,27]. The issues of trust, guilt, self-esteem, and role-reversal mentioned above are also active in domestic violence, and may be reenacted in the therapy situation. For the victim of domestic violence, the abusive husband may resent her receiving therapy, and may sabotage or directly interfere with her therapy. His methods include beating her, threatening her, or threatening to kill himself. She commonly recognizes that he is so fragile that he will kill himself or her if she attempts to leave. He may limit her mobility and finances so that she can neither get to treatment nor pay for it. In seeking treatment, she experiences fear of a subsequent attack, retaliation, and the fact that the marriage will most likely end [11,22,27–29].

MOTIVATION FOR TREATMENT

For the victim of domestic violence, the most common motivation for entering psychotherapy is the wish to maintain the marital relationship. The fantasy that the relationship can improve usually persists for a prolonged period, even with no reinforcement [11,14,27]. The decision to leave an abusive situation, or seek treatment, usually represents a change in the wife's behavior, not the husband's. It is useful to ask why the patient has chosen this particular time to seek treatment [15].

The perpetrator is sometimes motivated to enter treatment because he is unhappy about his lack of control, or recognizes the threat to the relationship. He may have made a decision to change, and needs therapy to support that change. He may also enter individual or marital therapy somewhat unwill-

ingly, but as a demonstration that he wants to maintain the marital relationship [11].

The rape victim may enter therapy to deal with the acute traumatic event
or to feel supported while pressing charges and going through court proceedings. While rape crisis counseling and family involvement can provide some of
the emotional support in a general way, the particular reason the rape was
traumatic to a specific victim is more appropriately explored in therapy. Brief
therapy may also enable her to deal with issues that come up with her spouse
or boyfriend, parents, friends, or employer as they react to the fact that she has
been raped and deal with their fantasy about how she has been damaged [11].

The child victim of abuse often enters treatment when he or she has been
removed from the family and is either recognized to have psychiatric problems
or has difficulty within a foster or adoptive family. More commonly, the
person who has been abused or involved in an incestuous relationship as a
child does not enter therapy until adulthood, for problems that may or may
not appear to be related to the earlier relationship [5,24].

When the predominant behavior is action-oriented, the patient is angry,
outraged, plans to file charges, wants to leave an abusive relationship, etc., the
patient's prognosis is fairly good. If, however, there is guilt, self-effacement,
delay in recovery, the development of physical symptoms or use of drugs or
alcohol to control feelings, treatment may be more complicated. The combination of the internal psychological set (not necessarily psychological health)
plus the reality of the assault creates the disequilibrium [15,30].

SPECIFIC INTERVENTIONS

The key to making an effective intervention begins with identifying the
problem as one of the violence syndromes [31]. A high index of suspicion, a
therapeutic attitude, and knowledge of specific interventions and available
resources are essential. It is also imperative to plan for one-time-only interventions. Many violence victims do not return for follow-up. Fear, embarrassment, and lack of predictability in lifestyle impede the victim's ability to
comply with scheduled appointments. In one emergency room study, only
35% of the women requesting help for problems related to domestic violence
actually returned for follow-up appointments [30]. Therefore, treatment
which cannot be completed during the initial contact is not likely to be
rendered at all. Efforts must be made to develop intervention strategies which
can be successfully completed during a single emergency center visit, and
simultaneously apply to the changing needs of the patient during subsequent
visits. Second, crisis theory has shown that timely intervention during the

acute phase of a crisis can prevent serious morbidity and can promote resolution of the crisis to the premorbid level of functioning or above [32], while poorly timed intervention can result in either a lack of therapeutic gain, or in serious aberrations and even mortality [30-32].

Delaying treatment for the victim of repeated violence may, in fact, result in loss of life or limb even though her psychological "vital signs" are within normal limits. If potential threats to the victim are inadequately explored, the victim's next presentation may be to the morgue.

FOCUS OF SHORT-TERM INTERVENTION

The therapy of any victim of violence should focus initially on the acute trauma. In this sense, the patient may be viewed as a post-traumatic stress disorder, and the initial treatment is similar, whether the abuse occurred years ago or the same day. The object of the initial intervention is to enable the patient to share the horror, and feelings of helplessness [8,12,17]. The therapist must ask in detail about the event or multiple episodes of abuse, going over the details in a nonjudgmental way. Begin by asking directly what occurred. Ask the patient to relate things in sequence. It is particularly important to ask the patient what the most distressing part was, and whether the patient can identify why it was so distressing. Never assume what was upsetting, as you cannot know what the patient's prior experiences were. Do not minimize or reassure, because this has the effect of closing off emotionally charged memories without resolving anything. Allow and encourage the patient to retell the story; details that were suppressed in the first telling (because they were too upsetting) gradually enter the memory as the patient feels more capable of handling them. Ask what symptoms the patient is experiencing, but do not prescribe medication for them. This is to determine a baseline, and in order to understand the meaning of the abuse episode; medication interferes with the therapeutic process when it relieves symptoms before the patient has explored their origins [12].

If the patient still has medical or legal sequellae, the therapist can provide emotional support. The responsibility here is to listen empathically, and to offer occasional interpretations, not to advise, recommend, or join in the outrage. For example, when a patient complains about some frustrating legal interrogation, the therapist might suggest that the patient's distress is related to feeling like she is being raped again, rather than to offer to call the lawyer, find her another, or advise her to drop the charges. Although a single session with the patient's family may be useful, the patient must handle subsequent family issues that are stirred up by the patient's assault. The role of the therapist is to enable the patient to identify those aspects of her family's response that are realistic, those that are not, and those that stir up deeper psychological issues for her, and to help her to understand why.

The most important task of short-term intervention for any victim of violence is to convert inappropriate and paralyzing feelings into feelings that are useful and appropriate, and that can motivate the patient into corrective actions [22]. The common inappropriate feelings experienced are guilt, shame, and self-deprecation [8,16]. These feelings will be repeated in the therapeutic relationship, in which the patient may feel ashamed to be talking about these things, guilty for taking up the therapist's time, unworthy of concern, particularly when the patient has not made any apparent move to improve the situation, and excessively responsible when the therapist expresses any frustration or annoyance. It is important to identify these feelings whenever they come up within the therapeutic relationship, or when the therapist perceives his or her own irritation with the patient or with the lack of progress of therapy. The therapist's goal is to awaken in the patient the recognition that no one has the right to abuse another human, and that the patient should be angry, even outraged, at the violator's behavior. Once the patient stops accepting the guilt and the blame for another's abuse, the patient can begin corrective maneuvers to protect himself or herself. Before terminating brief therapy, advise the patient that it can take weeks to months to get over the experience, and that that is normal [12].

There are some common rationalizations that need to be confronted to mobilize a patient to seek treatment—the patient deserved the beating because she provoked it, didn't perform some tasks, or isn't as good a person as the assailant; it's not that bad; there was no weapon, it only lasted a few minutes, the gun wasn't even loaded, or the bruises healed quickly; "But I love him." This response to any attempt at questioning the patient's acceptance of abuse must be addressed directly by such inquiries as "What do you love about him?" "What does he love about you?," or "What are your rewards in this relationship?" "If only I hadn't . . . ," Again, the patient invests energy in assuming the responsibility for the assault or abuse. The therapist must recognize that this is a defense against the helplessness the patient would otherwise recognize.

All of these rationalizations are common [5,15,29]. The role of the therapist is to question these kinds of statements, so that the patient may begin to question them too.

The stereotypes mentioned earlier, that men have the right, that marriage permits the behavior, and that women are obliged to accept it, also are amenable to confrontation.

The victim of a violence syndrome sometimes feels or recognizes that he or she was in collusion with the perpetrator; that is, the victim achieves some goal by being a victim [5,28]. The wife may recognize that in the aftermath of a family battle she is likely to be treated very well, or that he will feel profoundly guilty for several days, which she can use to her advantage. The child who is a victim of incest often recognizes that she is in a special place within the family [5]. The rape victim may appreciate that she has wounded her boyfriend or spouse by being raped by a stranger [16]. In each of these instances, the therapist must be alert to the underlying concern of the patient that she wanted to be hurt. This is not masochism. The therapist may interpret to the patient that this is an adaptive method of dealing with a bad situation, but it does not mean the patient created or wanted the situation. When a therapist prematurely "takes the patient's side," the therapist precludes the patient from acknowledging this sense of complicity.

Pain and suffering may be the focus for some people's lives. Without such immediate discomforts, they are faced with the more significant decisions of what to do with their lives. For a woman who is fearful of her own aggressiveness or competence, it is defensive to be involved with a man who is intermittently violent and impotent. She can feel sorry for him, and has less to lose than if he were competent. For some couples, battering, violence, and subsequent making up and tenderness are their only experience of intimacy. Their lives are often structured around violence, recovery, and repeated separations [22,28].

TREATMENT OF AN OFFENDER

A perpetrator of a violence syndrome is often as much a captive of his actions as his victim [5,26,28]. He may enter therapy because he really wants to change, fears the consequences of his uncontrolled actions, or fears the loss of a relationship. The battering or assaulting person usually feels powerless and often has low self-esteem. Having power over another human serves to relieve these feelings temporarily, and may be seen as antipsychotic, antidepressant, and anxiolytic. The spouse-victim frequently recognizes the perpetrator's need to beat in order to maintain some psychological equilibrium, and in that sense is an accomplice. The wife of a "powerful," "aggressive," "masculine" wife-beater may feel more feminine, powerful, or capable, because she is married to such a person [5,28]. Furthermore, she really feels that she controls him, since she can get him to beat her. The offender may find it difficult to acknowledge these issues, but can experience considerable relief when he begins to see the mutual reinforcers of the beatings. It is useful to identify those situations in which violence is more likely to erupt, or which have led to the present unsatisfactory state. Common stressors include a history of violence in the family of origin [5], unemployment or economic deprivation, unwanted or illegitimate pregnancy, mixed marriage, social isolation, and children.

SUMMARY

The medical professional who works in an emergency department has the opportunity to direct victims of violence to treatment that may improve not only their own lives, but the lives of their spouses and children. Early and effective intervention may demonstrate its usefulness on subsequent generations who may be spared the injuries and psychiatric sequellae of human violence. The emergency department personnel must avoid being judgmental, setting up expectations that are doomed to failure, or contributing to the destructive process by ignoring, denying, or criticizing the patient's situation. Motivation for treatment can be enhanced by repeated emotional support over time, by questioning the patient's acceptance of violence, and by knowing the resources that are available. Inprovement can occur in therapy by the use of focused, short-term treatment techniques.

REFERENCES

1. Burgess, A.W.: Family reaction to homicide, Am J Orthopsychiatry, 45:391-398, 1975.
2. Rosenbaum, A. and O'Leary K.D.: Children: The unintended victims of marital violence, Amer J Orthopsychiatry 51(4):692-699, 1981.
3. Field, M. and Field H.: Marital violence and the criminal process: neither justice nor peace, Soc Serv Rev 47:221-240, 1973.
4. Goldberg, W. and Carey, A.: Domestic violence victims in the emergency setting, in Warner, C.G., Braen, G.R. (eds), Topics in Emergency Medicine: Human Violence 3(4):65–83, January, 1982.
5. Weissberg, M.: Victims and perpetrators of violence, In Fauman, B.J., Fauman, M.A.: Emergency Psychiatry for the House Officer, Baltimore, Williams & Wilkins, 1981.
6. Stark, E. Flitcraft, A. Frazier, W.: Medicine and patriarchal violence: the social construction of a "private" event. International Journal of Health Services, 9(3):461-492, 1979.
7. Parker, B.: Communicating with battered women. Topics in Clinical Nursing 1(3):49-53, 1979.
8. Burgess, A.W. and Holmstrem L.L.: Rape trauma syndrome, Am J Psychiatry 131:981-986, 1974.
9. Helfer, R. and Kempe, C.(eds): The Battered Child, Chicago University Press, 1968.
10. The psychological profile of the apprehended sex offender. Sexual Assault Council, Denver Colorado, 1977.
11. Fauman B.J.: Psychiatric intervention with victims of violence. In Warner, C.G., Braen, G.R.(eds): Topics in Emergency Medicine: Human Violence 3(4):85-93, January, 1982.
12. Fauman, B.J., and Fauman, M.A.: Emergency Psychiatry for the House Officer, Baltimore, Williams & Wilkins, 1981.

13. Domestic Assault: A report on family violence in Michigan. Lansing, Michigan, Women's Commission, 1977.
14. Martin, D.: Battered Wives, San Francisco, Glide, 1976.
15. Gelles, R.J.: Abused wives: Why do they stay? J Marriage and the Family, 38:659-668, 1976.
16. Brownmiller, S.: Against Our Will: Men, Women, and Rape. New York, Simon and Schuster, 1975.
17. Symonds, M.: Victims of violence: psychological effects and after-effects, Am J Psychoanal 35:19-26, 1975.
18. Steinmetz, S.K.: The Cycle of Violence: Assertive, Aggressive, and Abusive Family Interaction. New York, Praeger Publishing Company, 1977.
19. Singer, M.T.: Coming out of the cults, Psychology Today 12(8):72-82, 1979.
20. Symonds, M.: The rape victim: Psychological patterns of response, Am J Psychoanal 36:27-34, 1976.
21. Hilberman, E.: The impact of rape, In Notman, M.T., Nadelson, C.C. (eds): The Woman Patient, Vol I, New York, Plenum Press, 1978.
22. Appleton W. The battered woman syndrome. Ann Emerg Med 9:84-91, 1980.
23. Ball, P.G., Wyman, E.: Battered wives and powerlessness: What can counselors do? Victimology: An International Journal 2(314):545–552, 1977–1978.
24. Feinfeld, L.: The nature of child abuse and its treatment, in Pyrooz-Sholevar G (ed): Emotional Disorders in Children and Adolescents, New York, Spectrum, 1980.
25. Sadoff, R.: Clinical observations on parricide. Psychiat Quart 45:65-59, 1971.
26. Lystad, M.G.: Violence at home, Am J Orthopsychiat 45:328-345, 1975.
27. Hilberman E.: Overview: the "wife-beater's wife" reconsidered, Am J Psychiatry 137:1336-1347, 1980.
28. Hanks, S.E. and, Rosenbaum, C.P.: Battered women: A study of women who live with violent alcohol abusing men, Am J Orthopsychiat, 47:291-306, 1977.
29. Snell, J.E., Rosenwald R.J., Robey A.: The wifebeater's wife: A study of family interaction. Arch Gen Psychiatry 11:107-112, 1964.
30. Rounsaville, B.J., Weissman, M.M.: Battered women: A medical problem requiring detection. Int J Psychiatry in Medicine, 8(2):191-202, 1977-1978.
31. Rounsaville B.J.: Battered wives: Barriers to identification and treatment, Am J Orthopsychiat 48(3):487-494, 1978.
32. Aquilera, D.C., Messick J.M.: Crisis Intervention: Theory and Methodology, 3rd Ed, St. Louis, CV Mosby Company, 1978.

6

Suicide — Emergency Issues

BETSY S. COMSTOCK

ILLUSTRATIVE CASE

A 27-year-old white male, John T., was brought to the emergency center by friends who said he had had a seizure. He promptly had another seizure in the emergency room and in a period of observation the EEG continued to show seizure activity; his level of consciousness varied; periodically he had additional peripheral discharges.

When he recovered, the patient at first denied any epileptogenic activity but eventually admitted that he and his friends had injected large doses of Preludin during a three-day party. This patient admitted having twice attempted suicide by barbiturate overdose, one such attempt having eventuated in medical then psychiatric hospitalization. When asked if he meant to kill himself with Preludin he responded, "I didn't care. It was something to do." He reported that he worked erratically in a labor pool, being unable to support himself as an artist. His ideas about the future were that he would be recognized as a brilliant artist and live on easy street. He denied any close friendships but often spent time with the group who brought him to the hospital. Several women in the group had shown interest in him but he complained they didn't really understand him and he found them undeserving. He was cut off by his family because they disapproved of his "Bohemian" life style.

THE EMERGENCY PROBLEMS ARE:

A. Is there a suicide risk?
B. How great is the risk?
C. How can suicidal risk be understood in terms of psychopathology and life stress?
D. How can a therapeutic alliance be built?
E. What interventions are needed?
F. What referral and follow-up are indicated?
G. What will be the outcome?

SUICIDE IN GENERAL

Suicide is not a disease, not a diagnosis. As a means of death it ranks high and consequential, however. In most years it is the 10th leading cause of death. Among college-aged people it is the second most common cause of death, led only by accidents; and on some college campuses it is the leading cause of death. The number of suicides occurring annually is estimated at 30,000 to 50,000 in the U.S., or at least 12 per 100,000 citizens [1, 2].

Demographic information is of low relevance in emergency situations, and so will be summarized only briefly. It is derived from the annual reports of the Center for Disease Control and is gathered from coroners' reports; thus it is believed substantially to underrepresent true incidence [3]. The statistics fluctuate from year to year and only can be understood from the perspective of relatively long-term trends. Suicide is more common in males than in females, at a ratio of about 3 to 1. Suicide is more common among whites than blacks, although over the past 15 years that difference has declined steadily. Black women are least likely to die by suicide; but they have followed the trend of increased incidence shown by black men [2, 4]. Although suicide rates increase with age and begin to plateau around 45 or 50, early in the last decade there was noted a rapid acceleration in suicide deaths in the 15-25-year-old age group. The increase now may have stabilized, such that almost as many young people as older people now kill themselves each year [5]. Murphy and Wetzel have reexamined the death statistics for cohorts defined by year of birth and they suggest that there is an on-going increase in likelihood of suicide as new year-of-birth cohorts are added [6].

Suicide does not vary significantly with socioeconomic status although it does vary with interpersonal status. The dramatic exception to this is that suicide rates are especially high among professionals. Not only doctors but lawyers, engineers, teachers in institutions of higher learning, all have risk rates 3 or 4 times that of the population as a whole [7]. The graduates of one U.S. medical school are needed annually merely to replace the physicians who kill themselves.

Suicide also varies with locations. Very high rates in Seattle, Washington and in San Francisco never have been adequately explained in comparison with low rates in other major cities including Houston, Texas. Possibly the differences relate to reporting practices but more likely they are multiply determined by complex factors of quality of life.

Finally, suicide risk varies with many aspects of individual life, and these will be considered in detail when we return to the subject of risk-assessment.

SUICIDE AS AN EMERGENCY PROBLEM

Thus far we have considered suicide in general, mainly with reference to death by suicide. Emergency center personnel do deal with death by suicide when dead(-on-arrival) or dead(-with-emergency-procedures-in-process) cases are considered. The major psychological aspects of these cases have to do with the survivors after suicide, and these will be discussed later.

Most emergency situations involve patients who have made suicide attempts and lived or who present because they are alarmed by their own suicidal thoughts.

A third category of suicidal patients are those who harbor self-destructive impulses. These may be conscious or unconscious impulses, but are not offered directly by the patient. The emergency-center staff has the task of identifying these individuals. The patient, John T., described at the beginning of this chapter, illustrates such a case.

A final category of suicide-related emergency center problems includes patients who are actively behaviorally suicidal in the emergency center. These patients place exceptional demands on the staff for immediate death-prevention efforts, and these also will be discussed later in this chapter.

In summary, then, the emergency categories relevant to suicide include: (1) survivors after the suicide of a close friend or relative, (2) patients who have made suicide attempts, (3) patients who fear they may commit suicide, (4) patients at risk for suicide when their risk-status has not been identified, and (5) patients actively trying to kill themselves in the emergency center.

One category omitted from this tabulation involves nonpatients at large in the community or patients in other treatment settings who generate emergency circumstances as they try to kill themselves. Much of what will be discussed with specific reference to emergency centers can be applied to these individuals.

The population of patients defined by suicide-related emergencies can be described. Various hospitals with active emergency centers, especially public hospitals, have reported that suicide-related emergencies account for from 5 to 10% of all registrants [8]. Emergency centers thus concentrate suicide-related problems in a way unmatched by any other setting or type of program. In the author's experience suicide-related emergencies account for about 40% of emergency referrals to psychiatry in a general public teaching hospital. Estimates of the number of such cases identified nationally each year stood at about 350,000 a decade ago [9], but more recent experience with hospital registrants suggests a far higher figure. Although not all suicide attempts reach the emergency center, and estimates involve considerable uncertainty because of lack of uniform reporting, still it is clear that emergency center cases are a major cause for concern. Follow-up studies after suicide attempts have indicated a high incidence of completed suicide in the year after suicide attempt, and a decreasing incidence thereafter. The death-by-suicide rate for the entire group within 5 years is reported between 5 and 15% [10]. Using the most conservative figures available, it appears that at least 20% of the reported suicides each year have been seen in some emergency center in a suicide-related emergency in the previous year. Emergency personnel thus have tremendous potential for suicide-prevention.

IDENTIFICATION OF SUICIDE RISK

Is John T., whose case was reviewed at the outset, at risk for suicide? When asked if he meant to kill himself, he said it wouldn't matter. The important thing here is that it occurred to someone to ask the question. The description doesn't tell us in what spirit the question was asked. "You idiot. Are you trying to kill yourself?" Or perhaps, "Don't you know that mainlining that stuff is sure death?" Or conversely, "Look, if you expect to die you'd better go back to trying barbiturates." Or, "Drugs are mellow but guns are surer."

I used to think that such quotations had shock value. Now, I suspect that the reader has heard these or could add equally unsettling reports of hostility and devaluation directed toward taxing emergency center patients, including suicidal "failures," drug and alcohol abusers, sex offenders, and the rank and file of socially unstable citizens. This is not written either to condemn or to condone such retorts. It is written as a consciousness raising effort. We cannot expect ourselves to identify with the life values of patients, but our work often will be biased against our patients if we are not sensitive to conflicts in values between them and us. The help-giving professions are pro-life, perhaps not as that word currently is used, meaning antiabortion, but in the sense that life and health are valued and preserving them is our work. When a patient's values are so divergent as to support suicide, that person is out of register with us. Self-awareness is all that stands between us and direct or indirect, blatant or hidden mistreatment of that person. Mistreatment, undertreatment, or neglect are common. If this is less than obvious to any reader, then better self-awareness probably is needed.

In situations where self-destructive impulses are important but not volunteered, the emergency task is to identify them. Certain hints may lead the way. Others important to the patient may voice the fear that an emergency presentation results from self-destructive impulses. The circumstances may be suggestive, such as in unusually careless auto-pedestrian injuries. "She walked in front of a car but it stopped," suggests the need for more than treatment of abrasions. Single-occupant single automobile wrecks, serious recreational drug overdoses, injuries from falls from considerable heights, injuries associated with inordinate risk-taking, victim-precipitated fights all suggest the intent of self-destruction.

The basis of suicide case investigation is inquiry. Ask the patient if there was suicidal intent. Ask the family if there has been recent behavior change. Ask the observers if they think there was suicidal intent. Ask the patient if he or she considers that unconscious suicidal impulses could have been involved. Ask the emergency staff to pay attention to each patient's attitude toward his or her injuries.

Recently, a man with bilateral deep lacerations of the neck was sutured and was being discharged. These were razor cuts which just missed the major vessels. The surgery staff was so intrigued by his anomalous survival and the patient was so noncommittal that psychiatric evaluation was overlooked. If appropriate questions aren't asked, answers will not be heard.

RISK ASSESSMENT

The starting place for intervention is evaluation. For suicidal patients evaluation requires both understanding the individual to the greatest degree consonant with the rapid work in emergency settings and estimation of the degree of risk involved. We will consider the second aspect first because it is the more urgent task in the emergency center and because risk evaluation supplies some of the answers that will be needed for general understanding of the individual.

Many teachers, including the present author, say something like, "There is no substitute for experienced clinical judgement." Personal conviction about suicide risk, based on global judgement, outweighs any scoring device derived from population studies and factor analysis. Certain reservations are necessary, however. No refinement of measuring instruments has yet provided more than relatively weak correlations with suicide risk. Our ability to predict future acts is severely limited. Clinical judgement is a highly complex thing, derived from past experience, scientific information, empathic resonance with the psychological state of the patient, personal values and biases, and guess work. Assertions of confidence in clinical judgement also is based on what one has been taught. Clinicians emulate their teachers and repeat the mistakes of their teachers.

With all these disclaimers, we can return to the question of what is known about risk for suicide.

Early correlational studies established now well-known factors which can help predict who may die from suicide [11]. Risk is higher for the elderly but, as already stated, age is far less predictive today than it was 15 years ago because of the sharp rise in suicide among young people. Black-white and male-female differences also have decreased. The existence of an example of suicide in the patient's past history is relevant, and can be supplied either by a former suicide attempt by the patient or by attempted or completed suicide by a friend or relative. The suicide of a parent weighs especially heavily.

Any recent major loss increases the likelihood of suicide. This may be loss of a loved one, loss of work, financial reverses, or loss of social status.

Situations of social isolation are ominous in suicidal individuals. The lack of supportive others in the household, and inability to attract close friends deprive the patient of personal encouragement, and of dependency gratifications.

Other significant factors include poor physical or mental health, and alcohol or drug abuse.

Since the early correlational studies which identified the factors listed above, additional studies have focused on issues of patient-attitude [12]. Expressions of hopelessness and of helplessness are found to be especially important. These are best explored through questions about the patient's future. Are there fantasies about future life on earth? Are they realistic? John T., the patient with whom we began, had fantasies of living happily ever after, but no realistic plans for connecting his present discouraging and future blissful existences. Patients who see life as very problematic and who lack any sense of personal resources for meeting their problems, have increased risk for suicide.

In an opposite direction, patients who have difficulty accepting help from others also are at increased risk. Such individuals often deny the seriousness of very real problems, do not want to be patients, and even reject befriending overtures made by others.

In recent years, increased attention has been given to the life course of suicidal individuals. Focus on demographic factors and on current attitudes is not sufficient. A case can be made for what Maris has called suicidal careers [13]. To evaluate a patient from this perspective, it is necessary to know his or her life story. Individuals whose family of origin had multiple problems show increased risk. Those who lost a parent in childhood have increased risk. Those whose life story is marked by social instability, who tend to be impulse ridden as shown by frequent change of job, residence, and lovers and by educational disruption and multiple legal problems, are more at risk. Studies which measure the number of life change events in the recent past [14, 15] show some correlation with suicide, but this may relate more to identification of impulse-ridden individuals than it does to the suicidogenic aspects of making changes.

Two other types of inquiry may be useful in estimating suicide risk. We have considered demographic factors, the patient's current attitude toward life and especially to future life, and the significance of a long-term, troubled life story. The remaining factors are specific psychopathology and the patient's declaration of suicidal intent.

Approximately two-thirds of those who die by suicide are considered to have been depressed in the interval preceding the death [16]. The incidence of depressive illness is so great that it alone cannot be taken as a strong predictor; but the same can be said for all of the factors considered thus far. Within the types of affective disorders, manic-depressive illness deserves special mention. The death rate from suicide is higher, probably about 15%, among manic-depressive patients than among those in any other diagnostic category [17 18]. A subgroup of all psychotic patients warrants second mention, namely that group having specific delusions relating to death. "I can hear my dead mother calling me to come across the grave" obviously warrants very careful suicide precautions.

Informed readers have by now suspected the importance of another type of psychopathology. The risk factors already discussed point strongly to the borderline personality disorder. Indeed, this is the most common diagnosis given to patients identified in emergency programs because of suicide risk. These patients see the world and themselves in black/white polarities resulting from ego-splitting. They have strong yearning for attachments to others but are impulsive and typically generate disorderly or chaotic lives for themselves. They tolerate losses poorly, hence are especially prone to suicide as a solution when losses are experienced.

Another personality designation, that of narcissistic personality also deserves mention. Psychiatric nosology currently seems unsettled with respect to the proper use of this term. Many or most individuals, even some who function very well indeed, have narcissistic features. There is considerable overlap, in addition, between borderline and narcissistic states. Nevertheless, narcissistic injury figures greatly in the dynamics of suicide. John T., our illustrative case, offers several hints of narcissistic pathology. He believes his artistic gifts have been ignored and his sense of entitlement and expected recognition has interfered with his ability to work productively. He complains that women who like him nevertheless don't understand him well enough and aren't deserving of his reciprocal affection. One senses that life is pretty boring for him and that this boredom and disaffection are poor defenses against his ongoing disappointment that he does not receive recognition and approval from others. When these defenses fail, he experiences considerable dysphoria. Drug abuse may mask this but is a manifestation of his poor adaptation in general and of poorly regulated self-destructive trends as well.

The final factor in risk assessment returns us to the starting admonition, "You have to ask the patient." With respect to suicide-intent you have to ask the patient very specifically not just, "Is suicide an issue?", but "Exactly how likely do you think it is that you might kill yourself?" When a patient responds, "I am going to do it," that must be taken seriously. A direct declaration of suicidal intent constitutes an on-going emergency for as long as it lasts. If the patient is determined, the risk is high indeed. Some deaths, in fact, can't be prevented despite heroic efforts by others.

Disbelief in a patient's expressed determination to kill himself or herself is a treacherous choice. Experienced emergency center personnel probably can recall not one but many patients who made such declarations not once but on many return trips to the hospital. Most recognize that the dangers in such cases escalate as time passes. After numerous suicide attempts, and out of exhaustion or miscalculation, an attempt will succeed. Every center seems to have a star case, the patient everyone knows, everyone is exasperated with, and whose eventual death seems inevitable. The patient seems to delight in sabotaging every logical or desperate intervention, and succeeds in transferring his own or her own psychic discomfort onto those trying to help.

Despite the problems posed by such patients, to whom we will return when we discuss intervention, the general principle should be followed that a patient's direct declaration of suicidal intent must be taken seriously. In the author's estimation, techniques which rely on paradoxical intention and lead therapists to direct patients to be sick and to kill themselves if necessary are unwarranted. The risks simply are too great, even though good results sometimes can be cited.

UNDERSTANDING SUICIDE RISK

In discussing risk-assessment we have touched on several issues of psycho-dynamics.

This overview paper cannot provide exhaustive treatment of the subject. The usual disclaimers can be invoked: the subject is too complicated; it goes far beyond what is relevant to emergency psychiatry; it has been treated in depth elsewhere. All these are true, but the supervening reason is that there is no unified explanation for suicide which is coherent and generally accepted. Faced with this dilemma, we will mention briefly the Freudian view, systems approaches to understanding suicide, behavioral theory, and the already mentioned role of narcissistic injury.

Freud's belief in the existence of a death-instinct underwent some reformation as he evolved his own understanding. It is largely discarded by modern theorists with the possible exception of Karl Menninger. However, Freud's elucidation of the defensive transformations of aggressive impulses is validated repeatedly in clinical experience. Two thirds of the people who commit suicide are depressed at the time just preceding death, and a significant number of those have the symptoms of guilt, self-blame, and sense of worthlessness which are associated with introjected hostility. When the psyche turns on itself, when patients become their own worst enemies, outward aggression is turned inward and both great psychic pain and self-destruction can result. In emergency practice, the key point in this is the recognition of self-blame and guilt as defining a specific sub-type of depressive illness, not by phenomenologic criteria, but by psychodynamic criteria which have specific implications for treatment. These depressions may be very difficult but by and large are more treatable than other affective disturbance in which the focus is more on bad world than on bad self.

Systems theorists point out strongly that patients do not fall ill in a vacuum. Manifest symptoms are meaningful not only to patients but to others having influence on the patient. That influence may extend across generations and may relate to efforts to solve very old problems. Patients are those who bear symptoms for the system of interlocking lives and who have come to the attention of care-givers. Treatment, on the other hand, may involve the patient only as the point of entry into the system. Interventions may be made more effectively with a spouse, a parent or grandparent, or with the large system treated in family therapy. This orientation also has implications for emergency practice since around the suicide crisis the extended sytem often is mobilized, is accessible, and can be engaged for ongoing therapy. Unfortunately, the relevant people may sit unidentified in a waiting room. Anyone accompanying or waiting for a suicidal patient should be interviewed as part of the evaluation, to protect the possibility of an on-site system intervention. Indeed, such evaluations inevitably initiate such interventions, and the staff only at some point of review will decide either to continue or to shift from this approach.

Emergency interventions with suicidal patients have relied historically on crisis-intervention techniques derived basically from behavioral theory. This approach emphasizes adverse learning experiences in the patient's life and relies on the possibility that the patient can learn to make self-protective choices in problem solving. This refutes the idea that symptoms are troublesome compromises made in response to unconscious conflicts and relies on identifying faulty decision-making habits and helping the patient learn to make decisions in more rewarding ways. The therapist becomes leader and teacher. The strength and indeed the demonstrated success of these techniques in treatment of affective disorders makes them important for emergency practice.

The final issue of psychodynamics which will be mentioned here is that of emergency approaches informed by the theory of narcissistic injury. I am strongly impressed by the prevalence of suicidal presentations in which there is substantial psychological disorganization resulting from some experience involving immediate and severe disappointment. Part of every evaluation must ask, "Why is this happening now? Why not last week or last year?" The answers regularly reveal what can be termed a narcissistic injury, a severe frustration or disappointment which disrupts the patient's ability to maintain enough self-approval to make life seem worthwhile. Individuals who are vulnerable for narcissistic injury are vulnerable for suicide. These are patients whose self-esteem mechanisms are faulty. They react to injury by an inordinately severe deterioration of functioning. However, their usual level of functioning tends to be restored by specific kinds of interactions with others. The self-psychology theorists have found that patients with pathologic narcissism tend to relate to others as either mirroring or as idealized objects. "Self-objects" is a more accurate term. This has been observed mainly in extended psychoanalytic therapy and requires the willingness of the therapist to be so perceived by the patient. In our experience, similar tendencies for establishing self-objects can be observed in emergency presentations, and acceptance of the perceived role can allow the therapist the chance to help the injured personality stabilize in a more adaptive way. The mirroring transference refers to the situation in which the patient perceives the therapist as much admiring and in effect allows the therapist to reflect back to the patient his or her positive perception of himself or herself. The patient's experience is something like "I must be pretty good after all. It is clear that the doctor thinks I am." The idealizing transference refers to the situation where the patient perceives the therapist as good, powerful, benevolent, and prestigious. The patient's experience is something like, "I'm in solid since I have such an exceptional doctor. Things are really going well for me." These transference roles have been studied primarily in the setting of long-term psychoanalytic work. Their potential for immediately stabilizing patients in crisis barely has been noted. Nevertheless, they work well if therapists can learn to let themselves be perceived in whichever of these roles the patient chooses. Success in crisis management depends on the therapist's remaining receptive long enough to understand which transference manifestation is emerging and then to promote it.

A patient's suicidal crisis also can be better understood if attention is paid to the developmental tasks with which the patient is involved. Numerous elaborations of life stages are available, and thorough discussion of these is beyond the scope of this chapter. They are amplified elsewhere in this volume with respect to adolescents and children. Separation and individuation, oedipal resolution, adolescent identity crisis, parenting, mid-life crisis, retirement, and aging are familiar terms which suggest special life-stage stresses. Attention to any of these which may be operative in a suicidal patient will direct both evaluation and interventions in relevant channels.

CRISIS ALLIANCE

The preceding discussion has identified several different approaches to suicide crisis intervention, informed by several very different theoretical orientations. All have in common the need for an alliance with the patient. Experienced readers will be aware that in discussing evaluation and its implications for intervention, a major step indeed has been omitted, i.e., that of establishing rapport. In practice, suicidal patients don't slip easily into the role of therapy-recipients. They don't expect to be helped if they feel helpless. They may want to perpetuate the role of distressed person if that role seems to be mobilizing the concern of important others. They often still want to die and they see intervention as an interference. And often they already feel they have been badly treated in the emergency setting. "Bad treatment" may refer to gastric lavage after overdose, hardly a pleasant introduction to receiving help. It usually includes vena puncture and often other tubes-in-various-orifices experiences. Probably it includes having been kept waiting, usually in an environment of frightening exposure to the suffering of other emergency patients. Sometimes it includes the experiences described earlier when staff biases against suicidal patients generate adversive treatment. When a benevolent doctor at last sits down to talk about self-destruction, sadness, helplessness, and hope for better coping, the reaction is just what could be expected. "Get lost. Go to hell. I don't need you. Just get me out of here." The model therapist is supposed to convert that into an opportunity for useful intervention. How? With gentle persistence of course. With reassurance to the patient, with real attention to the real discomforts of emergency patienthood, with empathetic listening, and with humanness, by which I mean efforts to rise above the inevitable and often unnecessary emergency-orientation to anonymous patient X, a case of this or that. A case of ruptured gastric ulcer can be a patient X and the OR readied and the surgical emergency appropriately resolved. Patients presenting with a psychiatric emergency cannot be treated anonymously if the purpose is to understand them psychologically and to intervene in their very private lives.

Rapport is facilitated by playing hero to the extent of relieving body discomfort, such as by getting the tubes removed as soon as possible, if possible getting the patient reunited with his or her own clothes, and by providing a calm, private place for the interview, and a calm and receptive listener, yourself. When all else fails, time usually is on the doctor's side. If a patient is unapproachable, try again later. Psychological states alter rapidly in the course of a suicide crisis. What fails now often will succeed in the next hour. In the meantime it may be possible to interview important others. A word of caution, however; always inform the patient about any anticipated interviews and be bound by his or her refusal or consent to have you talk to others.

When rapport cannot be established it is extremely difficult to make the necessary judgements about safety for discharge or indications for involuntary treatment. As a last resort this dilemma can be explained to the patient. This won't produce rapport but usually it will allow for enough cooperation to accomplish history-taking and the further opportunity to establish yourself on the basis of real concern for the patient's needs.

INTERVENTIONS

Emergency interventions in suicide crisis, once evaluation has been accomplished, are of three types: (1) those directed toward reduction of suicide intention, (2) those directed to an immediate danger of self-destructive behavior, and (3) those which initiate longer term treatment.

In the earlier discussion of dynamics of suicide, several types of intervention were identified. Crisis goals include reduction in the level of distress experienced by the patient, control of external events in the patient's life which are causing distress, modifications within the interpersonal system to relieve the necessity for self-destructive symptoms, and support for adaptive defenses or ego strengths which will help the patient deal with the crisis.

In suicide intervention it often is important to decide what individual or individuals will work with a suicidal patient. The patient's demonstrated affiliation with a specific staff member should be noted. If the patient expresses a preference, that staff member probably should be assigned. Decisions about style of intervention will depend on the theoretical orientation of the therapist as well as on specific aspects of the crisis. The easiest interventions are those which invoke medical authority as a means of reducing external stresses in the patient's life. It is relatively easy to get a work assignment changed or midterm exams delayed. The difficulty in such environmental change interventions is in deciding whether the relief from stress warrants the interference on behalf of the patient. Such interventions may reinforce self-destructive behavior as a means to problem solving. They certainly reinforce the patient's sense of personal failure and lack of internal resources. Interpersonal interventions based on systems approaches have fewer complications related to future suicidal crisis and should be attempted whenever possible. When patient cooperation is good, the patient can be engaged in one to one efforts to reduce discomfort through ventilation of problems, and to seek better solutions through rational approaches to problem solving.

Patient safety may be an immediate concern to emergency center personnel. Guns, knives, and other weapons commonly are brought into the emergency center and must be removed. Other potential weapons are part of hospital supplies and equipment and these warrant separate attention. These include pajama belts for hanging, scalpels off suture trays, and supplies of emergency medication. It generally is easier in the emergency setting to provide continuous observation of the patient than it is to make the area free of objects which can be misused in a self-destructive act. Even under continuous observation, patients may make a sudden suicide attempt. In recent years several suicidologists have attempted to define what a hospital can be expected to do to reduce the risk of on-site suicide. There is not general agreement about what constitutes satisfactory protection of the patient from himself or herself and it is conceded that no fully reliable set of practices has been found.

Several years ago we had a patient in bed beside the nurses's station under continuous observation. Because the patient was an injured felon, he was guarded for three shifts daily by police officers at the bedside. Despite these precautions, a gun was deposited under his pillow by a visitor and he shot himself. Such a death, in my judgment, was unpreventable.

In general, however, one on one nursing attention seems the best safeguard. Another precaution applicable to emergency centers and to any hospital setting involves asking suicidal patients what means of suicide they have considered while in the hospital. The imagination and inventiveness of the patients provide a useful guide to increasing safety precautions.

The third task in emergency interventions is that of referral for ongoing treatment. Most patients involved in a suicide crisis will need referral. The optimal situation is the one where the crisis worker can also provide ongoing care. Unfortunately, most hospital staffing situations can not make this possible. Research has shown that successful referrals are made from public hospital emergency centers only about 20% of the time as measured by kept appointments for follow-up [19]. When programs focus on this problem it has been possible to raise the kept appointment rate to 85 or 90%. It is sobering to realize that close to 80% of emergency work with suicidal patients may be, in effect, aborted by inadequate attention to referral strategies. Studies have shown that the level of psychopathology is as great among those who fail to follow-up as among those who accept continued treatment [20].

Successful strategies include all of the following: (1) Explain to the patient why the referral is made, identifying expected goals of continued therapy. (2) Involve important others in supporting the referral if possible. (3) Tell the patient as concretely as possible what to expect. (4) Anticipate what patient-resistances to the referral are likely and deal with them. Will transportation be a problem? Can the patient afford therapy? Is a letter to job or school needed to secure the time away? Will the patient decide that he or she was silly, over-reacting in the crisis, or not as seriously disturbed as seemed the case? (5) Request a signed release of information authorization so that medical records can be transferred promptly to the treatment facility. (6) Follow-up by telephone calls to the patient and to the treating facility to correct any mishap that might interfere with the success of the referral.

These activities place significant demands upon program staff, but should be a carefully structured component of programs which regularly see suicidal patients. Staff accept this added responsibility when they become aware of how their emergency work is often wasted without effective referrals.

The discussion of referrals has not included the possibility of hospitalization for ongoing treatment. Psychiatrists differ in their judgements about indications for hospitalization. A useful test is to question whether the hospital offers needed services which cannot be obtained in any out-patient setting. Against the advantages of hospital care must be weighed the problems of identifying the patient as being too ill to cope, and of postponing the patient's efforts to deal with environmental stresses. Since separation anxiety is a prevalent problem among suicidal patients, the dependency fostering aspects of the hospital can lead to painful discharge conflicts with recrudescence of the suicidal crisis. In my judgement, absolute indications for hospitalization include major affective disorders with suicidal intention, any acute psychosis manifesting delusions involving death, suicidal thinking in manic-depressive patients, and any other case when the direct expression of suicide intent cannot be altered by crisis-intervention efforts. Hospitalization merely to provide a safer environment for a patient may be contraindicated. It must be remembered that suicidal intention is not static. Typically it peaks in a crisis and falls rapidly afterward. Effective emergency interventions are much more powerful than protective custody.

The discussion of interventions cannot be completed without returning to the difficulties of the "star-case," the individual who is chronically suicidal and who becomes an unwanted emergency center fixture. Everyone has horror stories to tell about such patients. Usually they are diagnosed as borderline personalities. Commonly they are young, as young as 12 or 13. They are helped most by the establishment of long-term therapy with a very constant therapist who doesn't want to go to the emergency center. However, part of the problem is that the patient may be as help-rejecting as he or she is help-seeking. Until a therapeutic alliance can be built, the problems of repeated self-destructive acts can stress the staff beyond its capacity for compassion and decent behavior. Staff conferences are helpful in establishing treatment plans which can be followed uniformly. This will stop the patient's exasperating habit of peering through the door to see what doctor is working before deciding whether to overdose. The case conference also can redirect attention to the patient's pathology and can relieve the problems of staff members blaming one another for everyone's failure to be effective with the patient. A recent innovation in one emergency setting was the staging of a mock funeral in which staff members could identify their own sense of helplessness and resentment. The patient did not directly benefit but staff tension related to the patient was greatly reduced.

OUTCOME

The scarcity of outcome data is a major problem in psychiatric emergency care. This is as true for suicidal patients as for others. Deaths occur without coming to the attention of the personnel who offered emergency treatment. In closely followed samples, the five-year death rate from suicide ranges from 5 to 15%. Patients in long-term treatment seem to have a lower death rate, but many cases are lost to follow-up. The impulsive behavior and social instability of most suicidal patients makes it very difficult to find them even when they have agreed to participate in follow-up studies. Those who drop out may be more at risk than those who maintain contact.

The situation sometimes seems analogous to the familiar medical dilemma of treating patients with red throats. There are lots of them and most of them will be all right even without treatment; the incidence of rheumatic fever, death and disability only can be reduced by extensive evaluation, vigorous treatment, and follow-up. Is it worth it? Surely. Is it easy? No. Do we have the satisfaction of knowing when we succeed? No!

SURVIVORS

There are other victims of suicide, those close to the suicide victim who remain as survivors. This includes therapy staff and the friends and relatives of the dead person. These tend to be symptomatic groups with special needs for help in the mourning process. Children are affected profoundly by the suicide of a parent. Suicidal individuals generally understand that their death can have major emotional impact on loved ones. Their fantasies range from, "They'll be better off without me," to, "Maybe they'll be sorry after I'm gone." The latter reaction reflects well the degree of hostility in many suicidal acts. Survivors have to deal with the related questions of "How could he or she do this to us?" or even, "It's a relief finally to have it all over." Emotional support is needed for survivors who are themselves conflicted because of the unattractive and hateful aspects of such responses. Emergency centers are optimal settings for beginning the task of reassuring survivors that such conflictual feelings are natural and predictable.

CONCLUSION

Emergency centers are the best available facilities for suicide-prevention efforts. These programs annually see a very large number of suicidal individuals. Approximately 2% of these will account for about 20% of any community's deaths from suicide in the subsequent year. The level of risk can be identified only in approximate ways. Dismissing any case as only manipulative or as merely a gesture is unwise since there is so little correlation between the apparent seriousness of an attempt and the likelihood of eventual lethality. Interventions must be planned in an individualized way, depending on assessments of individual psychopathology. Interventions include medical attention free from judgemental bias against the patient, on-site crisis intervention techniques, and careful and disciplined attention to referral for on-going therapy, with decisions about indications for hospitalization. Special attention is required to assure the safety of those patients who remain suicidal in the hospital setting. Additional specific attention is needed in the event of a completed suicide for assisting identified survivors in beginning the troublesome psychological work of mourning for a loved one who has inflicted great hardship by choosing to take his or her own life. Staff members themselves have to be willing to accept the disappointment that occurs when some patients are reported dead despite heroic efforts. As one wise mentor said, "Those who think we won't lose patients don't understand the nature of the work we do."

REFERENCES

1. Monk, M.: Epidemiology in A Handbook for the Study of Suicide. Edited by Perlin, S. Oxford University Press, Inc., 1975.
2. Kramer, M., Pollack, C.A., Redick, R.W., Locke, B.Z.: Suicide in Mental Disorders/Suicide. Howard University Press, 1972.
3. Nelson, F.L., Farberow, N.L., and MacKinnon, R.R.: The certification of suicide in eleven western states: An inquiry into the validity of reported suicide rates. Suicide and Life-Threatening Behavior 8 (2) 75-88, 1978.
4. Davis, Robert: Black suicides in the seventies: Current trends. Suicide and Life-Threatening Behavior 9 (3) 131-140, 1979.
5. Hillon, C.P., Salomon, M.I.: Suicide and age in Alberta, Canada, 1951 to 1977. Arch Gen Psychiatry 37 (5) 505-510.
6. Murphy, G.E., Wetzel, R.D.: Suicide risk by birth cohort in the United States, 1949 - 1974. Arch Gen Psychiatry 37 (5) 519-523.
7. Holinger, P.C.: Violent deaths among the young: Recent trends in suicide, homocide, and accidents. Am J Psychiatry, 136 (9): 1144-1147, 1979.
8. Nigro, S.A.: A psychiatrist's experiences in general practice in a hospital emergency room. JAMA 214 (9): 1657-1660, 1970.
9. Weissman, M., et al: Suicide attempts in an urban community, 1955 and 1970. Soc Psychiatry 8: 82-91, 1973.
10. Ritterstöl, N.: The future fate of suicide attempts. Life-Threatening Behavior 4:4, 1974.
11. Turkman, J., Youngman, W.F.: A Scale for assessing suicide risks of attempted suicides. J Clin Psychol 24, 17-19, 1968.
12. Kiev, A.: The Suicidal Patient. Nelson - Hall. 1971.
13. Maris, R.W.: Pathways to Suicide: A Survey of Self-Destructive Behaviors. Johns Hopkins University Press, 1981.
14. Holmes, T.H., Rake, R.H.: The social readjustment rating scale, J Psychosom Res 11: 213-218, 1967.
15. Paykel, E.S., Prusoff, B.A., Myers, J.K.: Suicide attempts and recent life events: A controlled comparison. Arch Gen Psychiatry 32:327-333, 1975.
16. Sainsbury, P.: Community Psychiatry in a Handbook for the Study of Suicide. Edited by Perlin, S. Oxford University Press, Inc. 1975.

17. Guye, S.B., Robins, E.: Suicide and primary affective disorder. Br J Psychiatry, 117:437-38, 1970.
18. Pokorny, A.D.: Suicide rates in various psychiatric disorders. J Nerv Ment Dis, 139:499-506, 1964.
19. Kirstein, J., Weissman, M.M., Prusoff, B.: Utilization Review and Suicide Attempts. J Nerv Ment Dis, 160(1) 49-56, 1975.
20. Comstock, B.: Final Report—NIMH Grant—MH-19709-01. Suicide Attempt and Emergency Referral, 1971.

7

Physical Abuse of Children

LARRY B. SILVER

Psychiatric emergencies with children and adolescents may be the result of a direct crisis with the youth, such as physical trauma, or the consequence of a broader crisis, such as injury or death of a close family member, or may reflect the impact of being the victim of a complex act of violence. Physical abuse and sexual abuse of children and adolescents are sad examples of this latter type. This chapter focuses on physical abuse and neglect of children and the psychiatric consequences.

These fundamental betrayals of childhood trust by adults who take advantage of the helplessness and powerlessness of the young are difficult for helping professionals to accept or understand. Often psychological avoidance or "blindness" to the possibility of physical cruelty to children by adults is among the primary problems in establishing the correct diagnosis, intervening effectively in the crisis, and developing a long-range plan of treatment.

The feelings experienced by physicians and other helping professionals when confronted with such situations are often such that they react in ways that might add to the physical and emotional trauma experienced by the youth and family. The best way to prevent avoidance, denial, or less-than-helpful reactions is to be knowledgeable about these clinical problems.

Violence against children has been known since recorded history. Over the centuries children have been killed, maimed, starved, abandoned, and neglected. Children were the sole property of their parents. The justifications for the behavior of abusive adults have been based on religious beliefs, to maintain discipline, to transmit educational ideas, to please certain gods, or to expel evil spirits. Some children were maimed to help them be more appealing as beggars or to qualify as eunuchs for harems. During the early years of the industrial revolution, children as young as 5 worked up to 16 hours a day. They often were starved and beaten.

In 1961 a symposium on the Battered Child Syndrome was held by the American Academy of Pediatrics [1]. This symposium brought into focus the increasing professional recognition of the problem. In 1962, Kempe et al presented evidence of the prevalence of the syndrome and alerted physicians to consider this diagnosis and to be aware of their duty and responsibility to the child [2]. Since 1962 numerous articles have been published on the incidence, clinical manifestations, social and psychological characteristics of both the battered child and the battering parent, and the physician's responsibilities [3].

DEFINITION

Child abuse represents a spectrum of clinical conditions. At one end of this spectrum would be child neglect, manifested by malnourishment, starving, and some forms of failure to thrive. At the other end of the spectrum would be the child who has been severely traumatized physically. It is not clear if psychological abuse should be included.

Delsordo [4], in his study of abused children in Pennsylvania, and Connell [5] in his review of willful injuries to children, each defined child abuse in terms of violent person-to-child physical assault. Kempe et al [2] defined the "battered child syndrome" as a "clinical condition in young children who have received serious physical abuse."

Some authors have attempted to distinguish between child abuse and neglect. Elizabeth Elmer defined abused children as those physically assaulted by adults; neglect as the chronic failure of adults to protect children from obvious physical danger [6]. A joint committee of the British Medical Association and the Magistrates' Association on Cruelty and Neglect to Children attempted to define these terms and concluded, "Cruelty and neglect are not easily definable separately [7]." In general, they constitute treatment as the result of which a child's potential development is retarded or completely suppressed by mental, emotional and/or physical suffering produced as the outcome of a deprivation of minimum requirements.

INCIDENCE

Accurate statistics are difficult to obtain. The major difficulty is in recognizing and reporting a case. There are differing definitions. Cases may not come to the attention of professionals. Cases may be brought to medical attention but not be suspected or diagnosed. There are cases, also, that are suspected but not reported [8].

Kempe's study in 1962 [2] reviewed incidence in 71 hospitals. He learned of 302 cases of "battered child syndrome." Thirty-three of the children died; 85 received permanent injury. Kempe and his group emphasized the prevalence of the problem and felt that their statistics were not a total reflection of the problem in the United States. In the same year Jacobziner of the New York City Department of Health noted that about 4,000 cases of child neglect came to the attention of the city's courts [9]. Kempe's survey alerted hospitals to possible cases of child abuse; one hospital in his survey reported no known cases of battered child syndrome; yet a year later the same hospital reported over 50 cases of child abuse.

Chesser, in reporting on the work of England's National Society for the Prevention of Cruelty to Children, concluded that between six and seven percent of all children are, at some time during their life, "so neglected or ill-treated or become so maladjusted as to require the help of the National Society for the Prevention of Cruelty to Children" [10]. A 1964 study in California suggested a minimum of approximately 20,000 children in need of protective services in their state alone [11]. A more recent survey suggests that the number of cases in the United States is between 200,000 and 250,000 children each year [12]. Unfortunately, all such data are probably underestimates.

THE EVALUATION: EMERGENCY ROOM AND HOSPITAL WARD

Perhaps a major problem in recognizing clues suggestive of child abuse which could lead to further questioning, studies, or reporting is the physician's difficulty in thinking of child abuse. Kempe et al noted

"Physicians have great difficulty both in believing that parents could have attacked their children and in undertaking the essential questioning of parents on this subject. Many physicians find it hard to believe that such an attack could have occurred and they attempt to obliterate such suspicion from their minds, even in the face of obvious circumstantial evidence" [2].

The author, in surveying the physicians in one metropolitan area, noted that one in five physicians surveyed reported that they rarely or never considered child abuse in seeing an injured child [8]. In addition, the survey revealed that one in six physicians mistakenly had not considered child abuse in cases that they had seen in the past; one in two physicians did not know the correct procedure to follow in their community; one in three physicians did not know what follow-up procedures were used; and one in four physicians stated that they would not report a case of suspected Child Abuse Syndrome even with legal protection. These physicians were concerned that their evidence would not stand up in court, that the legal time lost in court proceedings was too lengthy, or that there were implications to their practice by reporting a suspected case. In general, this survey suggested that some physicians have difficulty admitting that such an entity could exist and hesitated to follow through on a suspicion of child abuse. The study also suggested that many physicians do not report a suspected case of child abuse because of past experiences or frustrations encountered when dealing with community or legal agencies.

Another concern is the fear of establishing an incorrect diagnosis. The major emphasis has been in being alert to the possibility of willful injury; but the problem of missing a case of child abuse is equally matched by the danger of incorrectly labeling a case of child abuse. A child, after an ordinary slap or push by a parent, intended only to be normal punishment, may be propelled against the sharp edge of a table or bed and this unintentional secondary injury may induce fatal laceration of the liver, spleen, or brain, or tear the communicating veins to produce fatal subdural bleeding. The use of reasonable and usually safe force in the punishment of a child by parents may produce unintentional secondary injuries which are serious and sometimes fatal; and the innocent parents may suddenly find themselves in confrontation with the law charged with child abuse or even murder when they actually set out to correct the child by moderate or mild punishment.

It is important for the physician to remember that his or her only responsibility is to report suspected cases of child abuse. The physician does not have to prove or legally establish that abuse did occur. This task is a legal one.

CHARACTERISTICS OF THE ABUSING PARENT

Morris et al compared the typical reactions and attitudes of protective parents to their children's injuries with the typical reactions and attitudes of neglecting, battering parents [13]. In so doing they offered useful general guides one might use in evaluating parents of suspected child abuse cases. The typical reactions and attitudes of protective parents to their children's injuries were noted to be (1) voluble and spontaneous reports of details of a child's illness or injury, (2) concern about the degree of the damage, (3) concern about treatment, (4) concern about the possibility of residual damage, (5) exhibiting a sense of guilt; this guilt and remorse is frequently found even when the parent has had no part in the child's injury, (6) inquiring about the prognosis of the child's condition, (7) difficulty in detaching from the child on admission, (8) attempting restitution through frequent visits, toys, gifts, and apologies to the child, (9) interest in discharge date, (10) concern about follow-up care, (11) identification with the child's feelings, both physical and emotional, (12) positive relations to the child. Typical attitudes and reactions of neglecting, battering parents were noted to be (1) failure to volunteer information about the child's illness or injury, (2) evasiveness or self-contradiction regarding the circumstances under which the child's condition occurred, (3) irritation at being asked about the development of the child's symptoms, (4) criticism of the child and anger with him or her for being injured, (5) absence of apparent guilt or remorse regarding the child's condition, (6) no apparent concern about the injury, (7) no apparent concern about the treatment, (8) no apparent concern about the prognosis, (9) frequent disappearance from the hospital during examination or shortly after admission, (10) failure to visit the child in the hospital, (11) refusal to touch the child or look at the child, (12) failure to involve themselves in the child's care in the hospital, (13) failure to inquire about the discharge date (14) failure to ask about follow-up care, (15) an attitude that the child's injuries are an assault on them, (16) failure to respond to the child or inappropriate responses, (17) absence of apparent perception of how a child could feel physically or emotionally, and (18) consistent criticism of the child.

CHARACTERISTICS OF THE ABUSED CHILD

Morris et al also compared some typical forms of behavior of well-nurtured children in a hospital with some typical forms of behavior of neglected and battered children in the hospital [13]. As with the comparison of parents, the differences are general guides one might use in evaluating suspected child abuse cases. Well-nurtured children in the hospital were typically noted to (1) cling to parents when they are brought in, (2) turn to their parents for assurance, (3) turn to their parents for comfort during and after examination and treatment, (4) consistently show by words and action that they want their parents and want to go home, (5) be reassured by their parents' visits. Neglected and battered children in the hospital were typically noted to (1) cry hopelessly under treatment and examination, (2) cry very little in general, (3) not look to parents for assurance, (4) show no real expectation of being comforted, (5) be wary of physical contact initiated by parents or anyone else, (6) be apprehensive when other children cry and watch them with curiosity, (7) become apprehensive when adults approach some other crying child, (8) seem to seek safety in sizing up the situation, rather than in their parents, (9) be consistently on the alert for danger, (10) consistently ask in words and actions what will happen next, (11) ask "When am I going home?" or announce "I'm not going home," rather than crying "I want to go home," and (12) assume a flat "poker face" when discharged home or when discharge is mentioned.

Differential Diagnosis:

When the history of the injury is clear, the signs of trauma are immediately attributed by the doctor to injury. However, these same clinical signs, in the absence of history of injury, become deep diagnostic puzzles for they raise the question of all of the nontraumatic diseases which produce physical signs. Fever is common after internal bleeding and may falsely suggest infection. Convulsions which follow known injury are immediately attributed to subdural hematoma or cerebral lacerations but the same convulsions, in the absence of history of injury, suggest first brain tumor or, in the case of associated fever, some kind of meningoencephalitis.

Scurvy also produces large calcifying subperiosteal hemorrhages due to trauma; however, scurvy is a systemic disease in which all of the bones show the generalized osteoporosis associated with the disease. Vitamin C content of the blood is normal with abused children.

Syphilis in the first months of life can result in metaphyseal and periosteal lesions similar to those resulting from multiple and repeated trauma; however, the bone lesions of syphilis tend to be symmetrical and are usually accompanied by other stigmata of the disease. Multiple lytic areas are often seen. The Serology Test for Syphilis is useful in establishing this diagnosis.

Osteogenesis imperfecta also has bony changes which may be confused with those due to trauma; but it, too, is a generalized disease and evidence of the disorder should be present in the bones other than those traumatized. Even in skull fractures, the mosaic ossification pattern of the cranial vault, characteristic of osteogenesis imperfecta, is not seen in abused children. Fractures of osteogenesis imperfecta are commonly of the shafts; in the abused child it is in the metaphyseal regions. Blue sclerae, skeletal deformities, and family history will assist in establishing the diagnosis.

Infantile cortical hyperostosis produces diaphyseal lesions; however, the metaphyseal lesions of unrecognized trauma serve to differentiate the two conditions. The characteristic mandibular involvement of infantile cortical hyperostosis does not occur following trauma, although an obvious mandibular fracture may be produced.

Pyogenic osteomyelitis usually produces frank bone destruction with involucrum and sequestrum formation; these are not seen in trauma.

Tuberculosis of bone is also destructive. The tuberculin test helps to distinguish this disease from traumatic sources of bone damage.

Leukemia and metastatic neoplasms bear no resemblance to unsuspected trauma. Primary bone neoplasms are almost unheard of in infants.

Other disease processes which produce bone changes may be considered: blood dyscrasia, rickets, congenital hip disease, poliomyelitis. Laboratory studies assist in differentiating these entities from trauma.

The radiologic manifestations of trauma are specific. The metaphyseal lesions, in particular, occur in no other known disease.

In obtaining a clinical history from the family, one frequently, if not consistently, finds a contrast between the history given and the clinical findings observed. For example, a mother might state that a child rolled over in its crib and in so doing broke its arm or fractured its skull. One usually elicits a negative history of trauma. Failure to obtain a satisfactory explanation of fractures, subdural hematoma, failure to thrive, soft tissue swellings, bruising or sudden death, should alert the examining physician to seriously consider the possibility of child abuse. A history of injury to smaller children may frequently be withheld by their parents and others deliberately in some cases and inadvertently in others. This history may be negative for trauma because the informant is unaware that the child has been injured, e.g., if the child was injured by someone else, or out of the parents' presence. Older children who have been injured may not mention or may deny the trauma in the interest of avoiding punishment.

Gaffey commented that, "The pediatrician supposes that he will be given the full and honest history about all aspects of the child, including trauma, and he passes it by unless it is presented to him voluntarily" [14]. He feels that "This erroneous supposition by the physician is one of the important deterrents to early, accurate diagnosis of infantile and juvenile injuries and abuse."

THE CAUSE OF CHILD ABUSE

The actions of parents or other caretakers which result in abuse do not fall into any standard diagnostic category of psychiatric disorders, nor should they be considered a separate specific psychiatric disorder themselves. Yet, to consider child abuse as a derailed pattern of child rearing rather than as a psychotic disorder does not mean that abusing or neglecting parents are free of emotional problems or mental illness. They may have many psychiatric disorders, much the same as the general population. They have the normal incidence and distribution of neuroses, psychoses, and character disorders. Such psychiatric conditions may warrant appropriate treatment in their own right regardless of the co-existence of patterns of abuse.

Less than 10 percent of studied cases of abusive parents involve a serious psychotic disorder. When present they might be schizophrenia, serious post-partum or other types of depression. Also in this group are those parents who suffer from severe alcoholism, drug abuse, or significant sexual pathology.

Steele's research on abusive parents has helped to clarify the natural history of child abuse [15]. Almost without exception, abusive parents studied in his program were neglected and abused to some degree in their earliest lives by their own parents. In essence they are rearing their own children in the same fashion in which they themselves were brought up. Thus, abusive behavior is related to a life-long pattern deeply embedded in the character structure. The neglect he refers to was of two types, material neglect, a lack of adequate food, clothing, shelter, etc., and emotional neglect, a lack of the warm sensitive interactions that are necessary for the child's optimal healthy growth and development.

Most abusive parents whom Steele studied believe babies should not be "given in to" or allowed to "get away with anything." They should not be picked up and comforted when they cry nor should they be permitted to become too dependent; they must periodically be shown "who is boss" and to respect authority.

The effects on the abusing parent of this inadequate empathic care or lack of positive mothering during the early years of life are profound and enduring. A deep lack of basic trust and confidence, and a low sense of self-esteem are most evident.

The ability to be the empathic caretaker of an infant is directly related to the degree of empathic care received by the parent in his or her own first months of life. Steele feels that inadequate care during the infantile experience will result in inadequacy of adult ability unless remedial interventions occur.

In addition to having been raised with inadequate attention to their needs, abusive parents experienced in some way a higher than average degree of demand and expectation for performance to satisfy their caretakers. Much too much was expected of them too soon in their lives. Inevitably they could not meet all the high standards of behavior set for them and they were scolded, criticized, belittled, pictured as ineffective, and frequently physically punished for their failures. Such physical punishment inflicted on the child because of perceived misbehavior or otherwise unsanctioned behavior is the cause of the bruises, lacerations, fractures, burns, and other injuries which characterize the picture of child abuse.

Earlier studies suggested that the punitive parental attack was a haphazard, uncontrolled, impulsive discharge of aggression by the parent upon the child. Steele found it to be a specifically organized unit of behavior designed to punish or correct specific bad conduct or inadequacy on the part of the child.

The problem lies in the parents' unrealistic estimates of what the infant is able to understand and to do, and in misperceptions of what the infant is like and what his or her intentions are. The baby is seen by the parent as more mature than he really is and as able to satisfy the caretakers' wishes. Failure to do so implies stubbornness or actual purposeful meanness by the baby, behavior which the parent has the moral right and duty to correct.

Much of what the parent finds wrong in his or her child are the same things for which they were criticized and punished as a child. Thus, the punishment of the child carries the approval of traditional family authority and an aura of righteousness. This concept of the aggression released by the parent as a rather specifically structured action is supported by the usual observation that only one child in a family may be abused while others go free, and that children are only punished for certain misbehaviors and not for others.

Steele concluded that it is the triad of insufficient empathic love and care, extremely high premature demand for performance, and excessive criticism and physical punishment for failure that constitutes the essence of child abuse.

INTERVENTIONS

The major goals of intervention are to protect the child and to assist the family in making use of whatever community facilities it may need to insure that a chronic malignant process is interrupted. After evaluating the parent or parents, appropriate action can be initiated. Some parents may need social or psychiatric help, some parents may need hospitalization, other parents may need criminal court action. Penalizing the parent or placing the parent in jail does not help the problem; in fact, in many cases it may complicate the problem by depriving the family of the wage earner or by removing the mother, thus creating even greater disruptions of family life and creating the need for a variety of community services, such as public assistance, foster home placement, homemaker service, or other supportive measures.

The essential task is to protect the child. Following this, the major emphasis should be in helping to minimize the family or individual stress which created the battering need. With help and not prosecution, the parents may be more able to look at their family and personal difficulties and to accept community and individual assistance in coping with the difficulties.

The physician and other professionals must consider the possibility of abuse when presented an injured child. Unless recognized and reported, the child may not be protected from future abuse and the family may not get the necessary help. Equally critical, since violence breeds violence, without intervention today's child may become tomorrow's abuser [16].

REFERENCES

1. Bain. K: The physically abused child. Pediatrics. 31:895-897, 1963.
2. Kempe, C.H., Silverman, F.N., Steele, B.F., et al.: The battered-child syndrome. JAMA 181:17-24, 1962.
3. Bibliography on the Battered Child. Clearinghouse for Research in Child Life, Children's Bureau, Department of Health, Education, and Welfare, May, 1966.
4. Delsordo, J.D.: Protective casework for abused children. Children 213-218, Nov-Dec, 1963.
5. Connell, J.R.: The devil's battered children. J Kansas Med Soc 64:385-391, 1963.
6. Elmer, E: Identification of abused children. Children 180-184, Sept-Oct 1963.
7. Odlum, D.M.: Neglected children. Roy Soc Health J 79:737-743, 1959.
8. Silver, L.B., Barton W., Dublin C.C.: Child abuse laws—Are they enough? JAMA 199:65-68, 1967.
9. Shaw, A.: How to help the battered child. Resident Intern Senior Student 6:71-104, 1963.
10. Chesser, E.: Cruelty to Children. New York, Philosophical Library, 1952.
11. Planning for the Protection and Care of Neglected Children in California. Sacramento California, National Study Service, 1964.
12. Zalba, S.R.: The abused child: I. A survey of the problem. Soc Wk 11:3-16, 1966.
13. Morris, M.F., Gould R.W., Matthews, P.J.: Toward prevention of child abuse. Children 11:55-60, 1964.
14. Caffey, J.: Significance of the history in the diagnosis of traumatic injury to children. J Pediatrics 67:1009-1014, 1965. Cited in Sullivan E Symposium: Battered child syndrome. Clin Proceedings of Childrens Hospital (Washington D.C.) 20:229-239, 1964.
15. Steele, B.F.: Working with Abusive Parents from a Psychiatric Point of View. DHEW Publ No (OHD) 75-70, Washington D.C., U. S. Department of Health, Education, and Welfare, 1979.
16. Silver, L.B., Dublin, C.C., Lourie, R.S.: Does violence breed violence? Contributions from a study of the child abuse syndrome. Am J Psychiatry 126:404-407, 1969.

8

Sexual Abuse of Children

LARRY B. SILVER

INTRODUCTION

Almost all societies have cultural taboos against incest and other forms of sexual contact with children, and the problem of child sexual abuse has apparently always existed. The universal revulsion felt toward acts of child sexual abuse and the strong emotional reaction of most people toward the adult who sexually abuses a child are rarely coupled with an understanding of the problem, its causes, or its effect. This poverty of knowledge is common to professionals as well as lay people.

Many of the common beliefs regarding sexual abuse are based on misinformation and hearsay. In order to understand and prevent child sexual abuse, such myths must be dispelled. Warnings such as, "Don't take candy from a stranger!" or, "Don't accept rides from people you don't know!" are given to children in hopes of protecting them from sexual abuse. Yet, most children are sexually abused by people they know and trust. Children who are sexually abused are not special children with special characteristics; they are not of one age, one sex, one race, or one social class. They are not victims of any particular offense. Their role in the offense, their disclosure of the incident, and their reaction to the abuse all differ.

DEFINITION

Child sexual abuse can be defined as contact or interactions between a child and an adult when the child is being used as an object of gratification for adult sexual needs or desires [1].

The National Center on Child Abuse and Neglect expanded that above definition to better clarify legal issues:

Contacts or interactions between a child and an adult when the child is being used for the sexual stimulation of that adult or another person. Sexual abuse may also be committed by a person under the age of 18 when that person is either significantly older than the victim or when the abuser is in a position of power or control over another child [2].

Types of Sexual Abuse

Child sexual abuse encompasses a wide range of behavior from fondling and exhibitions to forcible rape and commercial exploitation for purposes of prostitution or the production of pornographic materials. The child victim can be a girl or a boy. Sexually abused children can range in age from infancy to young adulthood; the average age is 11 [3,4]. Girls are more likely to be the victim as preadolescents, while abused boys are usually somewhat older. Female victims outnumber male victims among reported cases ten to one [3,4,5,6,7].

Types of offenses against girls include exhibitionism, fondling, genital contact, vaginal, oral, or anal intercourse. Nearly all male experiences with sexual abuse involved a male offender and included fondling, mutual masturbation, anal intercourse, and fellatio [3,4,6,7].

Because of the child's trusting relationship with the offender, the use of physical force is rarely necessary to engage a child in sexual activity. Thus, the proportion of children who suffer serious physical injury is low. Adolescent victims are more likely to encounter physical force or violence than are younger children.

Incidence

It is difficult to determine the actual number of sexually abused children in the United States. Children may keep an assault secret from their families for many reasons. They may fear rejection, blame, punishment, or abandonment. They may feel their parents will not believe them. Children in general are more likely to report a single assault by a stranger. The closer the relationship of the offender to the child or family, the less likely it is that the child will report the incident [8].

Even when the abuse is disclosed, parents may be reluctant to report the incident to the police or social service agencies [8]. This reluctance may relate to cultural taboos, fears of social censure, blame or punishment; or to a lack of physical injury to the child; or to apprehension about involving the child in legal proceedings. The identity of the offender may also affect the parents' decision to report. They may fear retaliation by the offender, or they may feel a need to protect an offender who is a family member or friend, especially if reporting the offense could precipitate the loss of economic or emotional support.

THE ABUSER

The familiar images of "perverts," "molesters," and "dirty old men" are not accurate portraits of the majority of persons responsible for sexual abuse of children [9]. Studies of sexually abused children show that a large proportion of such cases involve parents or other familiar figures to the child. At least half, and possibly as many as 80 percent of all child victims are sexually abused by people well known to them [3,6,10,11,12,13,14]. Parents, parent substitutes, or relatives are responsible for from 30 percent to 50 percent of all cases [3,11–14].

The dynamics of the abuser differ depending on whether he or she is a stranger or someone with whom the child is closely acquainted. The behavior of the abuser is more likely to be an expression of a sexual preference for children in cases of assault by a stranger than is found in incest cases, where an individual's normal sexual preference for adults may have become thwarted, disoriented, or inappropriately directed toward a child.

While there are cases of sexual abuse by adult women, the overwhelming majority of abusers are men. This may reflect the incidence of reporting by a child and then by a parent. Retrospective studies with adults suggest that exhibitionism or fondling may not be uncommon with female babysitters and male children or male babysitters and female children. Studies suggest that most male abusers are heterosexual in their adult orientation even when they abuse male children [15].

Pedophiles are most often males and may have heterosexual or no sexual interest in their adult orientation. Penetration is not usually attempted. Body contact, fondling, and oral contacts are more typical. Gender roles are less binding; a man may be attracted to boys as well as girls. Most pedophiles are gentle and seek tenderness. They might back off from fear and resistance.

Studies of abusers have been conducted only on those who have been apprehended; thus, these studies have focused on sex offenders in general. The findings suggest that the adult who is convicted of sexually abusing a child usually does not fit the stereotype of a mentally defective or the clinical category of pedophilia. Most are males; their average age is about 30 [3,4,6]. In one study, 80 percent had at least attended high school, and 60 percent had an adequate job history [6]. Approximately two thirds were described as having some personality disorder, though few were psychotic. Some studies show that as many as 24 percent of the offenders have a history of an excessive use of alcohol [6,16,17,18].

Although sex offenders cannot be stereotyped, and the role of the child in the offense varies, it is not difficult to assign responsibility. This responsibility clearly rests with the adult.

Effects on the Child

Both the initial and the long-term effects of a sexual assault on a child are related to the child's age and relative maturity, the child's relationship to the offender, and the degree of force or violence associated with the offense. Of equal importance is the family's and society's reaction to the assault, the prior existence of any family pathology, and the legal process [8]. In general, it appears that the closer the offender-child relationship, the more invasive or violent the assault, the more disrupted the home, and the longer the court process, the more likely it is that the initial emotional impact of the abuse will be stressful and that psychological damage will result.

As will be discussed later, the role and activities of the medical professionals in the hospital or emergency room also plays a significant role in the effect of the abuse on the child.

Sexually assaulted infants become frightened. This fear is not necessarily related to the sexual experience itself but rather to the general behavior of the assailant. Infants cannot understand the nature of the abuse and appear to perceive only that they are in the hands of someone who is not meeting their needs in an expected manner. Forceful sexual assault may be perceived only as something painful and terrifying. Infants who have undergone such an experience may display anxiety through excessive crying and generally fretful behavior. They may react with physical ailments such as feeding or bowel disturbances, vomiting, or failure to thrive.

Very young children, like infants, do not have the intellectual or emotional coping abilities to fully comprehend the significance of the abuse. In cases involving a stranger, the toddler may understand only that he or she was faced with someone new and frightening and that pain was experienced. If the parent or caregiver did not respond to cries for help, the child might sense abandonment with an intensifying of the fears and confusion.

By age three, a child's perceptions become more sophisticated. They may experience feelings of shame or guilt if these emotions are communicated to them by parents or other adults. Frequently they misinterpret the source of the parents' displeasure. For example, a parent might react with anger toward the assailant; the child might perceive the anger as directed toward him or her. Sometimes children find the sexual stimulation pleasurable; guilt feelings may be experienced.

Young children experience nonreality-based magical thinking. Their difficulty in separating fact from fantasy may influence their reactions to the sexual assault. The child may be more influenced by what they imagine occurred than by what actually occurred. When questioned, the child may report the event or his fantasies or both combined and believe all to be true. For example, a child might imagine that the offending adult wanted to urinate on him. The incident may be remembered as unpleasant but with no sexual connotations.

Young children are confronted with a difficult dilemma when the offender is someone well known to them. They may be confused when a known and trusted adult demands that they participate in activities which make them uncomfortable or seem wrong.

If confusion, anxiety, guilt, or shame result from the abuse, toddlers and preschoolers often manifest these feelings by regressing to earlier forms of behavior. They may revert to thumb-sucking, baby talk, or bed-wetting. They might show fears, such as of the dark, or of being alone. They may become more fretful, whining, or clinging.

Six- to ten-year old children are generally better able to separate fantasy from reality. They can provide an accurate account of the incident. They can channel their anxiety through talking and through play; thus, they may be better able to cope. School-age children who have been sexually abused may also show more regression in behavior. They may have fears or have nightmares or other sleep disturbances or may experience school difficulties. Physical symptoms, such as abdominal pain or urinary difficulty may occur.

Adolescents are particularly vulnerable to sexual assault as they are in the process of striving for independence and assuming their adultlike sexual identity. Forcible rape, a frightening and shocking experience for anyone, may be especially devastating to a teenager. The passivity and humiliation can damage their emerging sense of autonomy and self-sufficiency. Adolescents' reactions to rape often parallel those of adults. They may feel grief over the loss of virginity, fear of a recurrence of the attack, anger over being forced into a situation beyond their control, and degradation and depression over such an invasion of their persons. A violent rape may cause the victim to fear further sexual encounters of any kind. In cases of homosexual assault, the adolescent's normal sex-related fears and conflicts may be intensified.

Adolescents who become involved in long-term sexual relationships with close adults may have severe difficulty when the relationship is discovered.

They may have little self-esteem and feel rejected or betrayed. If their anger is directed inward, it may lead to serious long-term problems including suicidal thoughts or gestures or drug or alcohol abuse. They may run away, become involved in an early marriage, or become promiscuous.

Less is known about the long-term effects of sexual abuse since much of the research is clinical, based on small numbers of cases, and retrospective. Such retrospective cases have shown, as noted earlier, a relationship between a history of sexual abuse, especially incest, and promiscuity or prostitution. However, the fact that many women reveal such a history while involved in therapy for other problems suggests that the damage from sexual abuse may be related to other problems for which they are seeking help [9]. Depression and confusion about their own identities are common reactions of many victims. Some jump into early marriages as a means of escaping their family situation and dealing with their feelings. Some report feeling "marked" or stigmatized for life and may have suicidal tendencies [9]. Some victims of incest come to the attention of the courts for antisocial behavior and may go through the active justice system without even revealing their underlying problems [16]. There is no doubt, therefore, that in some cases child sexual abuse influences the personality and behavior of the victim for the rest of his or her life. Possible long-term effects may include the repetition of self-destructive behavior patterns, such as drug or alcohol abuse, self-mutilation, and the development of symptoms of sexual dysfunction, such as frigidity.

THE FAMILY, ITS REACTIONS AND ROLE

The parents' reaction is probably the greatest prognostic indicator of the emotional effects of an incident of sexual abuse on a child.

It is not difficult to understand why some incidents of sexual abuse by a stranger may be far less traumatic to a family than those committed by someone close to the child. In most instances, the parents will rally to the aid of the child, and, while they may overreact to the situation, their anger and feelings of retribution are generally directed toward the perpetrator. It is less likely that provocation on the part of the child will be suspected, and the child will generally receive expressions of concern, protection, and support from family and friends.

Sexual abuse by members of the family, including that initiated by persons whom the child or other family members hold in high esteem, usually has a far more complicated impact on the family. The public disclosure of incest may cause feelings of guilt associated with denial and depression. If the mother has been aware of the situation, she may deny any knowledge of the matter, accusing her daughter of lying. The father's guilt, shame, and fear of retribution also may overwhelm any concern for his daughter's feelings. Thus, the child may be rejected by both parents, perceived as guilty, and seen as a betrayer of her family.

De Francis, in a 1969 study of sexually abused children in New York City, described initial parental reactions as being in one of three general categories: child-oriented, self-oriented, and offender-oriented [3].

When the parents' response is primarily child-oriented, the child usually has a better chance of recovering from the assault within a minimal period of time. Such responses are most common in families where the child was forcibly assaulted by a stranger or by someone known to the family but not part of the primary family system. Parents express strong concern for their child. They usually are shocked that anyone would approach their child sexually and often are frustrated or angry when findings from the physical examination are not sufficient to prove or disprove sexual abuse. Usually, these parents are receptive to police investigation. Involving the authorities may help relieve their feelings of helplessness while providing an appropriate way to channel their anger against the offender.

Self-oriented responses may be natural for all parents. When their child is threatened or injured, most parents feel some guilt or inadequacy for having failed to provide sufficient protection. If the parent was subjected to a sexual assault as a child, the new incident of abuse may awaken painful memories, making it difficult for the mother or father to focus on the needs of the child. There is particular reason for concern in such cases when the parents' unresolved conflicts are projected onto the child.

DeFrancis divided offender-oriented responses into two categories: aggressive or protective. Frequently, parents who have real concern for the safety of their child will want the offender identified immediately and apprehended by the authorities. If the offender is known to the family, an angry parent may want to conduct his or her own search with the aim of getting revenge. In the second type of offender-oriented response, the parent wants to protect the offender from the authorities. Usually, the offender in these cases is someone close to the family, a family member, a step-parent, or a boyfriend. Particular concern is warranted in such cases when, in the face of convincing evidence to the contrary, a parent persistently denies the possibility of abuse and focuses his or her anger on the child. The parent may be reluctant to accept the child's explanation for fear of losing a spouse or boyfriend. The threat of such personal emotional and/or economic loss may be intolerable and may override concern for the child. If the child is perceived as a willing participant in the incident, the parent may reject the child's story out of anger or jealousy.

INCEST

Incest is a special form of child sexual abuse in which the abuser and the child victim are members of the same family. It is a highly emotionally charged and socially intolerable form of sexual abuse. For most people, incest is the most threatening and difficult form of sexual abuse to understand and accept. It is also the most difficult form of sexual abuse to detect because incest, by its very nature, tends to remain a family secret. Generalization about its etiology, effects, and treatment are necessarily tentative because most published research on the subject is based on small numbers of cases.

Incest is considered to be a universal taboo, a taboo that has been explained as deriving from an innate biological mandate against inbreeding [19,20], and as a social measure to maintain the integrity of the family unit [10,21,22], avoid role strain and role confusion among family members [21,23,24], and eliminate disruptive and competitive family rivalries [25,26,27]. Since ancient times, incest has been prohibited in most societies. The taboo was originally enforced by the tribe and later by the church. Today it is enforced through the courts as well.

In law, incest is defined as sexual intercourse between persons who are too closely related to legally marry [26]. While laws vary from jurisdiction to jurisdiction, marriage usually is prohibited between blood relatives closer than first cousins.

The actual incidence of incest is not known. In an incidence study done by Weinberg in 1955, the yearly average rate of reported incest in the United States was computed to be 1.9 cases per million population [10]. In contrast, the Children's Division of the American Humane Association estimates in 1969 that at least 5,000 cases of incest occur nationally each year, a comparative rate of 40 cases per one million population [27].

Since father/daughter incest is the type most commonly reported to authorities, it is the type most commonly studied and about which most is known. It is usually a symptom of general dysfunction within the family.

Weinberg [28] divided fathers who commit incest into three personality categories: one type shows psychopathology with indiscriminate promiscuity [10]. A second type of father is socially immature and psychosexually retarded with a pedophilic orientation toward his own and other children. The third and probably most common type is the father who is introverted with an extreme intra-familial orientation.

Reported characteristics of fathers who commit incest include an emotionally deprived childhood and chaotic family life [29,30,31,32], an extreme emotional dependency on their wives [33], and a nonaggressive and ineffectual personality with poor impulse control [31,34]. In addition, they often have an immature sexual orientation and poor sexual adjustment [29,35]. Some are poor providers with a history of frequent separations from the family [31]. Others are socially well adjusted and appear to be good fathers and husbands [25]. Many have been found to have a history of alcoholism [17,31]. Most are in their thirties and early forties when the incestuous relationship begins [27,35].

It is often the mother who provides the key to the father/daughter incest relationship. Reports of case studies indicate that such incest sometimes involves at least unconscious participation and/or sanction by the mother [31,32,36]. The mother in such a family usually has experienced physical or psychological desertion during childhood; as a result, she often has strong residual dependency needs. Her poor concept of mothering and her own need to be mothered may cause her to cast her daughter in the maternal role. In addition, the mother usually fears any close relationship and is frequently sexually rejecting of her husband. Eventually, this role reversal of mother and daughter may place the daughter in a position where she is called upon to meet the sexual needs of the father. Although it is believed that in many cases the mother knows consciously or unconsciously of the sexual relationship, few of the reports of incest are made by the mother [10,31,37,38].

The child victim is usually the oldest daughter [10,32,37]. However, case studies indicate that the relative sexual maturity of the daughter does not contribute significantly to the occurrence of incest. One study noted the average age of the daughter to be ten years when her father begins his sexual advances [25]. Although often sexually immature, the daughters usually exhibit pseudo-maturity and are often caretakers of the home and younger children [32]. They often assume this role at an early age because of the state of the family unit. The child may fear her mother and receive little affection from her.

Prior to the actual incestuous relationship, the child may exhibit coy or flirtatious behavior toward the father. This behavior is not intended to obtain sexual gratification, but instead, is an attempt to secure the affection she is denied by her mother [32,33,39,40]. The daughter's affection-seeking behavior, combined with her fear of family disruption and her sense of maternal responsibility, allows the child eventually to become involved in a physically close, giving and receiving relationship with her father. This relationship may evolve gradually, with the daughter assuming a passive role and offering no physical resistance to her father's increasingly aggressive sexual advances [10,29,36]. Sexual intercourse between the two may be the pathological result of this increasingly intimate contact.

The incestuous relationship may continue for years [29,31,32,36]. In some cases it may be inherited by the next youngest daughter when her older sister leaves home [10]. In some cases, the child, after achieving some degree of social and sexual awareness, leaves home, seeks help for herself, or requests protection for her younger sisters [41,42]. At times the relationship comes to the attention of authorities when the girl becomes pregnant. Occasionally, a history of incest is obtained from a runaway who refuses to return home or from a child who has made a suicidal gesture.

When an accusation of incest is made against a family, the feelings experienced by each member may include anxiety and guilt, depression and disgrace [41].

The effects of incest on the daughter vary and depend on her age, her level of functioning prior to the relationship, and her experiences in the social and legal systems after disclosure. Preadolescent girls may be less affected by an incestuous relationship than older girls, possibly because younger children do not have such firm concepts of right and wrong and lack awareness of the possible social repercussions [29,43]. Some case studies indicate that adolescents may be relatively unaffected if they were well adjusted prior to the experience and if both parents display little guilt or anxiety when the incestuous relationship is discovered [44].

Some studies report that the daughter's feelings of guilt, depression, and anxiety appear to be more closely related to the break-up of the home following disclosure than to the incest experience itself [31].

In the treatment of incest, it is important to focus on the family dynamics and to consider the incestuous relationship as a symptom of sexual dysfunction [25,36,41]. The immediate emotional impact can be lessened by effective crisis intervention techniques. Identification and treatment of incestuous families also can serve as a preventive measure; there is some evidence that incest may be passed from generation to generation [34,45]. Further, other daughters can be protected from possible future sexual abuse. Other children in the family may need professional attention. Siblings may have intense conflicts over the incestuous relationships between their sister and their father which can result in long-term emotional problems [46].

INTERVENTION: THE EMERGENCY ROOM

It is possible to prevent or lessen much of the damage caused by childhood sexual abuse, even after the actual assault has occurred. Such prevention can begin as soon as the child and family arrive in the hospital emergency room.

To a child, who may have had little understanding of the significance of the incident at the time it occurred, intense emotional reactions on the part of adults can be frightening and confusing. When a sexually abused child is confronted with strong negative reactions, the abusive experience may take on new significance; its immediate impact may be intensified, and the possibility of long-term negative effects increased.

When parents and children in this state of crisis arrive in the emergency room, it is important that they be received with special care and consideration. All personnel who come in contact with the family should be knowledgeable about child sexual abuse. Each has an opportunity to help stabilize the situation. If curiosity and speculation are minimized, if parents are helped to regain composure and perspective, and if the child is treated with respect and sensitivity throughout the initial interview and physical examination, many of the effects of the crisis can be alleviated, and many of the family needs can be met.

A complaint of sexual abuse always should be taken seriously. In general, the possibility of sexual abuse should be considered when there is someone who claims to be an eyewitness, when the child confides in someone about the incident or hints about involvement in sexual activity, when the child's play with peers or dolls persistently indicates inappropriate sexual behavior, when suspicious stains or blood are found on the child's underwear, when the child complains of pain in the anal and/or genital area, or when the child is found to have venereal disease. Often, however, there is no eyewitness and little or no physical evidence to support the allegation of abuse. This does not negate the complaint. Any allegation of sexual abuse, whether true or false, is a cry for help.

The initial emergency room interviews with the child and family are extremely important and can set the tone for all that follows. The purpose of these interviews is not to find out exactly who did what to whom nor to prove or disprove the story presented. The primary objectives are to determine the nature of the child's problems and how to prevent further problems, to understand the functioning of the family, and how best to help in bringing about a satisfactory resolution to the crisis. A sensitive and patient interviewer, one who can communicate sincere concern and understanding of the family's conflicts and distress, usually can gain the confidence of both child and parents and obtain the needed information.

Often, the child and parents may come to the emergency room presenting other complaints. The emergency room professional may suspect child sexual abuse from the history, examination, or laboratory results. The first step in such a recognition is the willingness to entertain the possibility that such a situation could exist. Social and cultural taboos and values as well as personal anxiety and ignorance may contribute to a failure to recognize such cases. It may be difficult to acknowledge that child sexual abuse could occur in middle-class and upper-class families.

Before the child and parents leave the emergency room, certain anticipatory guidance can be provided. Ensure that the child is adequately protected from further encounters. Reassure the family that their feelings and concerns are appropriate; suggest ways of coping with them. Offer reassurance, if appropriate, for the way the parents are handling the situation and suggest additional ideas. Reassure the parents that the psychological effects of a one-time incident need not be long lasting. Alert the parents to possible short-term reactions by the child such as fears, a need to talk, thumbsucking, bedwetting, or sleep problems and let them know where they could get further help if needed.

Confidentiality vs. sharing information obtained from a parent or parents or from the child must be handled in a sensitive way. The wishes of the parent or child should be respected, yet police may need to know certain facts. At times, information shared by the child may have to be told to a parent to protect the child from future incidents of abuse. The professionals' responsibilities to the child, to the parents, and to the police may not be compatible. Decisions must be made with the best interest of the child in mind.

Sharing information about the identity of the offender should be approached with special care, as this may evoke strong emotional reactions with parents. This is especially true when the offender is identified as a parent, other family member, friend, or babysitter. In such cases, ensuring the safety of the child and assessing the family's need for follow-up services are of critical concern.

The physical examination usually follows immediately after the interview with the child. This exam and its results are considered an integral part of the diagnosis of sexual abuse. The examination can take on a false importance. Many parents depend on physical findings to confirm or disprove their child's story of assault. Police officers and prosecutors rely on positive findings for legal evidence. When the results of the examination are inconclusive, as is often the case, everyone involved may feel dissatisfied. Regardless of the physical findings, the needs of the child must be met.

In this examination, there should be three primary concerns: medical, psychological, and legal. First, a medical examination is needed to assess physical injury, to provide treatment, and to obtain samples for laboratory studies for venereal disease. Second, the examination may provide information useful in reassuring the child and family that no permanent damage has occurred and that future childbearing potential has not been affected. Third, the exam may yield physical findings that can be used as legal evidence to corroborate the child's story.

In summary, crisis intervention techniques used throughout the initial contact with the child victim and his or her family are of critical importance. It is during this time that many of the fears and anxieties of the parents can be addressed; guilt can be alleviated; and concern for the child can be emphasized. Trained and sensitive professionals can provide the basic supports needed by parents and child to help them return to a normal life by integrating the sexual assault into their life experiences with as little permanent damage as possible. Prevention of further sexual abuse and follow-up mental health services can be initiated.

CONCLUSION

I have reviewed the clinical issues of child sexual abuse, including approaches to emergency interventions. The goals of this overview have been to help the physician and other professionals be more aware of the possibility of such acts against children and adolescents and to help prepare such professionals to intervene in a sensitive and positive way.

These are not pleasant or easy clinical problems. Although the damage cannot be undone, the short-term and long-term consequences can be influenced by the correct interventions. The crises faced by the victim and family can be lessened and the possibility of future negative behavior or the development of psychopathology by the victim might be minimized or prevented.

REFERENCES

1. Sexual Abuse of Children: Selected Readings. DHHS Publ No (OHDS) 78-30161, Washington, D.C., US Dept Health and Human Services, 1980, p 1.
2. Child Sexual Abuse: Incest, Assault, and Sexual Exploitation. DHHS Publ No (OHDS) 81-30166, Washington D.C., Dept Health and Human Services, 1981, p 1.
3. DeFrancis, V.: Protecting the Child Victim of Sex Crimes Committed by Adults. Denver, Children's Division, American Humane Association, 1969.
4. Jaffe, A.C., Dynneson, L., ten Bensel, R.W.: Sexual abuse of children: An epidemiologic study. J Dis Children 129:689–692, 1975.
5. Landis, J.T.: Experiences of 500 children with adult sexual deviation. Psychiatric Quarterly Supplement 30:91–109, 1956.
6. Swanson, D.W.: Adult sexual abuse of children (the man and the circumstances). Dis Nerv Syst 29:677–683, 1968.
7. Voight, J.: Sexual offenses in Copenhagen: A medico-legal study. Forensic Science 1:67–76, 1972.
8. Schultz, L.G.: Psychotherapeutic and legal approaches to the sexually victimized child. International J Child Psychotherapy 1:115–128, 1972.
9. MacFarlane, K.: Sexual abuse of children. in The Victimization of Women. Edited by J Chapman and M Gates. Hollywood, Calif, Sage Publications, 1978, pp 81–109.

10. Peters, J.J., Meyer, L.C., Carroll, N.E.: The Philadelphia Assault Victim Study. Final Report: National Institute of Mental Health, Center for Studies in Crime and Delinquency (Grant NO RO1MH21304). Philadelphia Center for Rape Control, Philadelphia General Hospital, 1976.

11. Burgess, A.W., Holmstrom, L.L.: Sexual trauma of children and adolescents: Sex, pressure, and secrecy. Nursing Clinics of North America 10:551-563, 1975.

12. McGeorge, J.: Sexual assaults on children. Medicine, Science, and Law 4:245-253, 1955.

13. Sgroi, S.M.: Sexual molestation of children: The last frontier in child abuse. Children Today 4:19-44, 1975.

14. Weiss, J., Rogers, E., Darwin, M.R., et al.: A study of girl sex victims. Psychiatric Quarterly 29:1-27, 1955.

15. Sarafino, E.P.: An estimate of nationwide incidence of sexual offenses against children. Child Welfare 58:127-134, 1979.

16. Hayman, C.R., Lanza, C.: Sexual assault on women and girls. Am J Obs and Gynec 109:480-486, 1971.

17. Sidley, N.T., Stolarz, J.D.: A proposed dangerous sex offender law. Am J Psychiatry 130:765-768, 1973.

18. Virkkunen, M.: Victim-precipitated pedophilia offenses. Brit J Criminology 15:175-180, 1975.

19. Lindzey, G.: Some remarks concerning incest, the incest taboo, and psychoanalytic theory. Am Psychologist 22:1051-1059, 1967.

20. Seemanova, E.: A study of children of incestuous matings. Human Heredity 21:108-128, 1971.

21. Lester, D.: Incest. The J of Sex Research 8:268-285, 1972.

22. Seligman, B.Z.: The incest barrier. Br J Psychology 22:250-276, 1932.

23. Coult, A.D.: Causality and cross-sex prohibitions. Am Anthropologist 65:266-277, 1963.

24. Wahl, C.W.: The psychodynamics of consummated maternal incest. Arch Gen Psychiatry 3:96-101, 1960.

25. Giaretto, H.: The treatment of father-daughter incest: A psycho-social approach. Children Today 5:2-35, 1976.

26. Parsons, T.: The incest taboo in relation to social structure and the socialization of children. Br J Sociol 5:101-117, 1954.

27. Tormes, Y.M.: Child Victims of Incest. Denver, Children's Division, American Humane Association, (undated).

28. Weinberg, S.K.: Incest Behavior. New York, Citadel Press, 1955.

29. Weiner, I.B.: On incest: A survey. Excerpta Criminologica 4:137-155, 1964.

30. Cavallin, H.: Incestuous fathers: A clinical report. Am J Psychiatry 122:1132-1138, 1966.

31. Kaufman, I., Peck, A.L., Tagiuri, C.K.: The family constellation and overt incestuous relations between father and daughter. Am J Orthopsychiatry 24:266-279, 1954.

32. Lustig, N., Dresser, J.W., Spellman, S.W., et al: Incest: A family group survival pattern. Arch Gen Psychiatry 14:31-40, 1966.

33. Magal, V., Winnik, H.Z.: Role of incest in family structure. Israel Annals of Psychiatry and Related Disciplines 6:173-189, 1968.

34. Raphling, D.L., Carpenter, B.L., Davis, A.: Incest: A genealogical study. Arch Gen Psychiatry 16:501-511, 1967.

35. Sarles, R.M.: Incest. Pediatric Clinics of North America 22:633-642, 1975.

36. Machotka, P., Pittman, F.S., Flomenhaft, K.: Incest as a family affair. Family Process 6:98-116, 1967.

37. Henderson, D.J.: Incest: A synthesis of data. Canadian Psychiatric Assn J 17:299-313, 1972.

38. Vikkunen, M.: Incest offenses and alcoholism. Medicine, Science, and the Law 14:124–128, 1974.

39. Bender, L., Blau, A.: The reaction of children to sexual relations with adults. Am J Orthopsychiatry 7:500–518, 1937.

40. Gordon, L.: Incest as revenge against the pre-oedipal mother. Psychoanalytic Review 42:284–292, 1955.

41. Cormier, B.M., Kennedy, M., Sangowicz, J.M.: Psychodynamics of father-daughter incest. Canadian Psychiatric Assn J 7:203–217, 1962.

42. Molner, G., Cameron, P.: Incest syndromes: Observations in a general hospital psychiatric unit. Canadian Psychiatric Assn J 20:373–377, 1975.

43. Sloane, P., Karpinski, E.: Effects of incest on the participants. Am J Orthopsychiatry 12:666–673, 1942.

44. Barry, B.J., Johnson, A.M.: The incest barrier. Psychoanalytic Quarterly 27:485–500, 1958.

45. Berry, G.W.: Incest: Some clinical variations on a classical theme. J Am Acad Psychoanalysis 3:151–161, 1975.

46. Eist, H.I., Mandel, A.U.: Family treatment of ongoing incest behavior. Family Process 7:216–232, 1968.

9

Civil Disaster Planning: A Psychiatric Perspective

PERRY OTTENBERG

Psychiatry is the scientific study and treatment of irrational behavior. At times of disaster, when people regress to unusual forms of behavior, they may turn to psychiatry for assistance. This disorganization can occur as a result of overwhelming external or internal stress. Psychiatry as a medical specialty is eminently qualified to cope with massive grief, personal loss and sudden death that accompany civil disasters.

The ability of people to accept tragedy truly is amazing. The resilience and fortitude of most individuals and families are a tribute to the human condition. It is only the few who break down in crises. Factors that contribute to chaos are organizational ineptness, media abuses, failed leadership, public apathy and dehumanization. Psychiatrists have learned a good deal about how people react to civil disaster, about grief work and about the long-range impact of chronic traumatic experiences.

Psychiatry is also the field of human behavior that focuses on adaptive and maladaptive defense mechanisms. We are trained to recognize distortions, excesses, denials and displacements in people's thinking and behavior. It is important in psychotherapy to ascertain the difference between real immediate danger, past danger, suspicions of danger, projected danger, latent danger, and misperceived danger. There is also danger that has been institutionalized into the thinking of certain political, religious and cult leaders. My mother had a systematic sense of danger that I as a child succumbed to—a mysterious entity she called "viruses" that lurked in any pleasurable activity. All traffic became dangerous when I learned to ride a bike, swimming was dangerous in the polio season, and numerous other potential calamities were associated with new foods, ideas or girl friends. Generalized suspiciousness, exaggeration of the likelihood of attack, and xenophobic reactions to new and different values undermine our ability to cope with threats and to plan for civil disaster.

Psychiatric therapy centers on a sensitive involvement with individuals and families that makes us aware of the ways in which groups and individuals deny, destroy, and avoid coping with realistic dangers. The various avoidance stratagems that people employ need to be brought into the open. Dehumanization in leaders, groups and individuals can furnish a cloak of apathy to the civil disaster planning so sorely needed.

Psychiatrists have partially emerged from their sanctuary by being involved in crisis resolution around terrorist activity, hostage-taking and other community conflict situations. Our training and sensitivity to the extremes of human behavior, mental breakdown, psychosis, and what is secretly threatening to frightened or disturbed people make possible our role in civil disaster planning. We have an important contribution to make in exposing conflict, ethnocentric distortions, narcissistic leadership positions, and polarized thinking.

Psychiatrists also are prepared to face their responsibility as part of a team, participating in civil disaster planning and assisting in the recognition of transcultural and class attitudes that affect reciprocal understanding and cooperation.

DEFINITION OF CIVIL DISASTER: GENERAL FACTORS

A civil disaster can be defined as a sudden massive unfavorable change in the patterns of activities of a social system resulting from internal or external forces [1]. The system affected can be a small group or the entire society, the event anticipated or out of the blue, impacting on part or all of the system. The civil disaster may be a physical event such as flood, fire, earthquake, hurricane, tidal wave, or volcano. It may be economic collapse or a change in power relations. The emergency phase of the disaster can persist for hours or indefinitely, depending on the time it takes to return to the pre-existing relations. A new stabilized system of common expectations may follow the old.

During a civil disaster there are several foci: the individual, a small group, or a formal organization. The scope of the impact determines the focus. If civil disaster strikes only a fragment of the society, the existing organizations will persist and can concentrate on individual and family problems. If the civil disaster is extensive, beyond the capacity of local organizations, then the individual and small group become less central. Response to assist the injured, trapped, or isolated is the basis for all activity. Effectiveness will depend on the prior degree of preparedness by formal and informal social units to handle the catastrophe.

Civil disaster that threatens the community's capacity for normal services requires the creation of a temporary social structure to provide rescue, transportation, medical care, food, shelter, information, psychiatric support, and the restoration of community facilities. Care of children, the injured and the aged, and public order and utilities are the first priorities.

Local citizens invariably come to the rescue. Most essential services arise from public response rather than from professionals. Assistance usually arrives immediately from volunteers and survivors within the disaster area and only later from outside. Massive assistance generally springs from spontaneous collective action but often lacks people with specialized skills such as surgeons or movers of heavy equipment. The rate of maladaptive behavior in civil disaster is generally low, even in situations such as Hiroshima after the nuclear bombing. Primary group affiliation provides survival strength and support. Borrowed skills and careful following of orders help nonprofessional people to perform tasks outside their usual competence. Even with wide cultural differences, language barriers, and racial and religious tensions of long standing, there appears to be a strongly motivated urge worldwide to help others in catastrophes where the victims are blameless. Massive sharing of necessities for the bereaved community is a typical response in the Western World.

Simple solutions to alleviate suffering appear. If the victims are injured, treat them; if hungry, feed them; if homeless, shelter them; if anxious and in pain, comfort them; if trapped, free them. Disaster assistance, however, is temporary and outside the frame of permanent reciprocal social interaction.

DEHUMANIZATION AND CIVIL DISASTER PLANNING

Most individuals bypass involvement in the social dimensions of disaster. Entire societies can be oblivious as they routinely dehumanize others in small, inevitable bureaucratic steps. Dehumanization allows for technological efficiency without the guilt or shame that would otherwise paralyze such action. We tend to ignore the disasters of the past and slowly permit the disasters of the future to accumulate, even as we sit.

Our perception of social reality often is based more on a misperception from the past than on current realities. The time to cope with this helplessness is now, and the first step is consciousness-raising about the issues of civil disaster planning. The second step is organizations—group support for each other to bind the emergent anxiety. The third step is a program of action that brings enormous pressure upon the political leadership that has sidestepped painful decisions on civil disaster planning for decades.

To challenge attitudes set within a rhetoric of outmoded belief systems is a necessity for survival. To use nuclear weapons in a massive war, to exhaust the ozone layer, to poison the environment with chemicals, to allow natural disasters to remain not understood, and to disregard social conflict make disasters inevitable. It is a double bind to follow leaders who are lost. Most leaders are really followers, trying to avoid innovation, change or unpopularity.

A crucial moment occurs in every emergent movement when individuals band together into a likeminded group. Lethargy and helplessness are shaken off. A Rosa Parks precedes a Martin Luther King. Youths and idealists confront the police, military and government as a new movement takes shape, and 350,000 people congregate in a city to express their fear of nuclear war. Some scientists, lawyers, teachers, physicians, politicians and citizens risk their careers for their beliefs—sometimes in the wrong cause. Environmental protection organizations and the antinuclear movement share some beliefs about technological advances, population shifts and deeply held values about the meaning of life.

Civil disaster planning must challenge the acceptance of irrational belief systems that avoid the troublesome process of consciousness-raising in nuclear, environmental and social disasters.

Mass civil disasters are not inevitable or inherent in human nature. War, nuclear pollution, toxic waste, racial conflict, maldistribution of food, health care, and political power are all modifiable. Although the human species is partly genetically influenced, our main problems with mass catastrophe are institutional.

Democratic tolerance and scientific objectivity do not require abstention from a political stand for civil disaster planning or discussion of controversial social issues. Disturbing issues in civil disaster planning are often avoided out of a feeling of impotence, although in actuality human concerns are passionately felt. Some people fear that discussion of civil disaster planning will disrupt the delicate balance of cooperation that cities, political parties, and society require to function. Exposure of the real risks may be temporarily disruptive but ultimately leads to the kind of democratic process that strengthens the society. Some disasters may actually bring the community closer together through their social impact.

DENIAL AND OTHER EXCESSIVE
APPROACHES TO DANGER

Research on crisis populations suggests that people are capable of living with chronic danger for years. Rationalizations, excuses and fantasies that distort reality may cloak their sense of danger. People live on earthquake faults. Farmers work river valleys just below dams. Jews and others stayed in Nazi Germany long after they were marked for extinction. The capacity to deny danger under varying circumstances can block effective planning for civil disaster.

In a small pilot study of 130 children in the lower grades, I found, interestingly enough, that they wanted more training in urban evacuation. Perhaps as we age we use more denial against our vulnerability and approaching death. Children can sense realistic dangers when adults have modified their perceptions of danger. Harry Truman, who lived in a cabin on the side of Mount St. Helens, chose to stay there in a fully conscious decision that led to his death. Many people, however, who live on earthquake faults seem to lack awareness of the inevitable danger that the slippage of tectonic plates represents. One of the first steps in civil disaster planning is alerting people to real dangers.

An approach to civil disaster planning that is hysterical, phobic or millennial, or that exaggerates the real dangers, can easily end up being counterproductive. Scaring people does not usually lead to effective action—in fact, it may lead to more denial, apathy, hedonism or other forms of escape. Some civil disaster planners blame the victims for their plight. It does not matter so much why people look into the abyss. What is important is offering them a hand when they're ready to back away. I expressed concern to an old federal ranger at Mount Washington in New Hampshire about the scantily dressed young children going up the mountain in late afternoon into some of the worst weather in America, worrying that they would inevitably be trapped on the mountain overnight. He replied, "Son, you can't tell anybody anything. I get up there in the morning and I see kids running around in diapers and bare feet in the snow." All over the trail are signs pointing out the dangers and the necessity to be prepared with proper clothing, food, and shelter, but so many people pay no attention.

Civic institutions cannot bear the entire burden of control. Police, firefighters, elected leaders, national guard, park rangers, and physicians provide only the expectation of control. It takes cooperation, compliance and volunteering on the part of all of us to make civil disaster planning work. Internalized custom and habit provide law and order, not the police. Predictable behavior in civil disaster planning depends not on threats but on organized cooperation and awareness of human needs.

The time between recognition of the danger and moving away may be years. The fault lines of earth are real. The increasing toxic gas emissions are real. Yet people who live on faults cannot grasp the inescapable consequences. Modifying one's own and collective belief systems may involve great suffering and shock before one gives up self-deluding thinking. Even after leaving an area of civil disaster, some people return to the scene of the catastrophe out of unresolved ties to their place of security and origin.

Everyday activities mask reality testing or adaptive escape. The reality of disaster is avoided through unconscious mechanisms of defense including repression, rationalization, fantasy formation, isolation and identification with leaders.

THE LIBERTY CITY AND
BRIXTON RIOTS

A tour of Liberty City (Dade County, Florida) revealed it to be no northern urban ghetto like the South Bronx. Much of the area is uncrowded, with low, detached homes and other buildings. Driving through the peripheral streets at the time of the riots in May 1980, one found gutted and charred ruins, often on widely separated blocks. One hundred and fifty-seven businesses were totally or partially destroyed, perhaps selectively. About 3,000 jobs were lost. The gruesome aftermath included 19 deaths, more than 400 injuries, 1,300 persons arrested, 149 buildings burned or looted, and incalculable permanent scars in the community. The wide dispersal of the damage impressed me with the difficulty of simultaneously fighting fires and looting. For reasonable social control in a community, local acquiescence to law and order is needed. This respect was notably lacking for several days. Some "outsiders" traversing the streets on ordinary business were killed.

Before this violent upheaval, knowledgeable community relations experts had been worried about mounting tension. The highest-paid black public official in Florida, John Jones, had been expeditiously tried by a white judge and convicted by a white jury for misapplication of $8,000 in school board funds. The black community leadership rallied to his support. In the black community, televised segments of the trial were viewed every night. Their reaction to this trial was resentment, and opinion within the black community coalesced in response to what was seen as a dual standard of justice. Three other black/white police incidents, all highly publicized, contributed to the community tension engendered by routine police practices and a self-exonerating system for review of public complaints.

Soon thereafter, the McDuffie trial took place. Several police officers had participated in a nighttime chase ending in the violent beating and death of McDuffie, a middle-class black father, an insurance salesman. This trial gripped the community for months. An all-white jury, trying five white policemen who had been seen beating McDuffie to death with a heavy steel object, threw out 17 counts of criminality. The other police officers involved in this incident turned state's evidence. A change in venue from Dade County to Tampa was no more than a change in geography. After the exoneration of the police officers there were many mass meetings. Spokesmen did not always represent the local residents, and some observers saw demagogic political opportunism in the speeches.

When these antisocial episodes occurred in Liberty City and simultaneously in numerous other Florida suburbs, they proved to be unmanageable because of the intense psychosocial conflict. The agencies of society, the police and firefighters, could not respond appropriately to the arson and looting in Liberty City because they were seen as the cause of the antisocial outburst in the first place. The police could not enter the area where they were most needed because they would certainly have been attacked.

The Dade County Chamber of Commerce held a community meeting immediately after the riots, during which a one-cent "riot tax" on all sales was suggested but was defeated. The speeches at the Chamber of Commerce meeting echoed the liberal ideology of the 50s and 60s, with residents appealing for more money for housing, education, public services, and insurance coverage—speeches filled with self-serving platitudes. One black resident was reported to have said in effect, "Gentlemen, I have a good house, I have a good job, insurance and social services. Mr. McDuffie, the one who died, had a good job and a good house. What we need is protection from our protectors. In the black community we live in fear of the police, for ourselves and our children."

In other instances of urban rioting, for example, New York City after the electrical blackout in July 1977, police cordoned off the affected area but were unable to stop the looting, arson and other violent behavior. The reluctance of the police to stop the unlawfulness was lauded as appropriate restraint by some commentators and public officials. Many people believe that if the violence had spread into middle-class Manhattan or Miami, there would have been much less restraint and patience. It must also be recorded that a large number of New York City police did not report for duty during the rioting, apparently for private reasons that reflected certain attitudes toward professional responsibility for public safety in that black and Hispanic area. This role conflict between one's job and one's private life is rarely discussed openly. It could just as easily occur in a hospital among psychiatrists, in legislatures, schools or nursing homes.

Lessons from the Riots

The local community mental health center at the University of Miami recommended seven steps [2] in civil disaster planning after the three days of racial urban violence in Liberty City in May 1980: (1) Task force organization, (2) Assessment of riot impact on patients and center operations, (3) Outreach and formation of street miniclinics, (4) Outreach to schools, (5) Home visits to victims, (6) Agency liaison, (7) Generation and funding of primary prevention projects.

The findings give reasons why people burn down their own community stores, homes and property and surrender to an outpouring of uncontrolled hatred.

The *Miami Herald* interviewed 444 local residents and found that more than 25% admitted to participating in this antisocial episode. Those who rioted (or rebelled, as some described the behavior) could not be distinguished from those who did not by their attitudes toward the police, the courts and local government. This implies a general community rejection of these establishments. At the time of the Liberty City riots, several other Dade County communities started to respond with crowds, fires, and antisocial looting, but local leaders, pastors, and businessmen were able to quell the mounting violence, control the gangs and keep order without the police presence.

Immediately after the civil disaster in Liberty City, the community mental health center organized a task force for outreach to all victims. Case-finding, using hospital emergency room records, helped to identify the injured and the families of those who had died. Street activity led to many others who were not listed in the medical records. The community mental health teams were organized to reflect the ethnic composition of the local population. Being aware of their catchment area, they were ready to serve almost day and night during the crisis, use referral knowledge, maintain resource centers, and provide services directly to the needy. Home visits, school visits, and gang control activity were part of the community approach.

The unique role of youth gangs and other young people in the days of disaster needs special attention. High-risk groups of young people who have dropped out of school, are unskilled for industrial work and have a history of police involvement may spark social conflagration. The period of time before lawlessness takes over can be but a few minutes. A massive self-image of being excluded by "the system" from power and the opportunity to "make it" contributes to the outpouring of rage. Many community programs are perceived by residents as serving the interests of the administrators rather than those of the local population.

In New York City on July 13, 1977, after the lights went out, the looting commenced. Armed with chains and crowbars and driving trucks as if they were tanks, the looters tore steel shutters and grills off storefronts the way soda cans are opened, often scooping out the desired contents of the store before torching the remnants. There was a sequence to the type of store looted—first liquor, large appliances, sports goods, and jewelry. Only later were food and clothing stolen. Trucks were loaded for resale. It was a gruesome carnival. Looters hit black, Hispanic, and white owners alike, not selectively the white ones, as in the 1960s. Local black or Hispanic ownership did not protect them. Eight of 16 Fedco Supermarket chain stores, the largest black-owned retailer in the country, were broken into and two stores were gutted. Although there were 3,076 arrests for looting, the televised version of the riots and arson left an impression of the police as observers on the fringes, while the looters vented their rage at "the system."

In England, the police had enjoyed excellent relations with the public until recently. Civil in manner, unarmed with handguns, they had a good reputation until about ten years ago, when a breakdown in police-community relations began—most acutely in nonwhite neighborhoods. A governmental commission blamed police, politicians, and racial discrimination for precipitating riots in 20 cities where most of Great Britain's 2,300,000 minority group members lived. This was the worst street violence in Great Britain in this century. In the main, young blacks attacked police while engaging in looting and arson. The commission recommended a new, independent system for reviewing complaints against the police, a change in the police code to make racial prejudice a cause for dismissal, and more recruitment of minority group members into the police force. Black community leaders were criticized for increasing police-community tensions through inflammatory rhetoric.

This kind of situation in Florida or England applies to many American cities, where the excessive use of force by the police is notorious. Philadelphia has seen years of seething racial anger and accumulated tension. There are numerous cases of middle-class citizens who are reported dead of self-injury or suicide at the police station within a few hours of some minor infraction of the law. The coroner's office often fails to clarify the circumstances around the death. Just as private psychiatrists are in a role conflict in any civil disaster, so are the police constantly on the grinding edge of social conflict. Their law enforcement duties put them into role conflict in family disputes, saloon fights, street altercations or neighborhood quarrels, where there is rarely a right or a wrong side. The victim is often as blameworthy as the perpetrator, although everyone wants the police to "do" something.

THE MEDIA, MISINFORMATION, AND RUMORS

The lesson for the nation's press from the Attica Prison riots in New York State (1971) was that racism was the underlying cause of over 40 deaths. Much of the press, including the nation's most respected newspapers, at first reported as facts portions of the now discredited version of the Attica massacre originally given by police and prison officials. The most common errors were in reporting, without attribution, that prisoners slashed hostages' throats and that one hostage was castrated. The press repeatedly published erroneous official statements as facts. A preset attitude toward the prisoners, under conditions of extreme danger, engendered misperceptions, lies, and follow-the-leader conformity to official misinformation.

A prison is a community of defeated men. The atmosphere is tense with degradation, anger, rage, sexual frustration, rebellious attitudes, racism, and fantasies of revenge, escape, and gratification. The upheaval in a prison or ghetto stimulates "get-tough" attitudes for many in the public rather than in-depth analysis of the gradual accumulation of tension. To attack and kill one's guards in the guise of protecting them is a reversal of official responsibility.

There is a need for the participation of psychiatrists in studying police-community relations, police recruitment and training, juvenile offenses, domestic quarrels, recognition of the deinstitutionalized, and gang conflict.

The Role of Rumors in Civil Disaster

The media often exaggerate the disaster by repeating false information and augmenting an existing situation of near-panic and confusion. Rumors and threats of mobs, crime and rape may reflect collective projections of anxiety. I do not mean that there is a group mind in Durkheim's sense, but rather that there is a commonality in mass acceptance of rumors, which gives credibility to irrational action in situations of disaster. For many people the earthquake, tornado, flood, riot, or assassination tips their emotional balance. What emerges is their unconscious fear of attack, annihilation, invasion, pain, helplessness, castration, and death. Rumors encourage the hopes, savagery and deep fears we all possess. During the riots in Liberty City, Florida, one of the main rumors was that this was the beginning of guerrilla warfare of black Vietnam veterans against the white community. One can recall a similar appeal by Charles Manson to organize his cult family for the coming black revolution against whites.

THE APPEAL OF AUTHORITY

During periods of disaster and crisis, people turn to authority figures and protective agencies in the community for guidance and reassurance. During the Three Mile Island episode, the inconsistencies reported in the media matched the inconsistencies of the political and scientific leaders. Firm, clear, consistent, truthful, authoritative statements help to decrease anxiety in such a situation. Weak, contradictory, vacillating, untruthful statements increase the likelihood of panic. If the civil disaster continues over an extended period, unperceived fears gradually emerge as rumors. One hears of miscarriages, freak births, UFOs, strange events, and the devil incarnate stalking the land.

PROFESSIONAL ROLE CONFLICTS IN CIVIL DISASTER PLANNING

Role conflict in civil disaster planning often limits decision-making and effective response. A psychiatrist can be needed at the hospital and at the same time be a father or mother searching for his or her children. A large organization also has competing demands on its personnel, resources, facilities, time, money, and capability. Awareness of clear-cut personal priorities and obligations can prevent some ambivalence and confusion in disaster relief, but personality factors usually favor the local over the distant, the familiar over the foreign, the family and individual over the larger organization.

Most psychiatrists fulfill a number of institutional and practice roles while they maintain their nonprofessional activities and personal ties to friends and family. The professional role of the physician/psychiatrist varies with the type of practice. In an emergency, every psychiatrist is in conflict as to the best interests of the institution, the patient, and the family. The private practice of psychiatry continuously sensitizes us to how much of an impact even broken appointments, vacations, arbitrary changes in schedule, and illness may have on some patients. An acute crisis that disrupts the entire therapeutic web for many patients may become lethal if it is not handled with awareness. A civil disaster challenges one to balance the direction and intensity of one's activities between home, office, hospital and community needs.

How is one to decide how much to devote to professional responsibilities and how much to one's kinship and family? A crisis impinges on all aspects of our lives, as victims and as professionals. Therefore, one has to consider what is happening at home, or the professional may desert the institutional ship. In most human events, parent-child, husband-wife, and small-group ties usually take precedence over the more impersonal, neutral professional attachments. For all of us to be effective in civil disaster we should first look at how we will deal with our primary emotional ties. This also applies to police officers, firefighters, public health workers, politicians, nurses, social workers, and hospital and community mental health center staff. Ideally, plans for crisis management should include discussion of role conflict before activities are assigned.

Between one's professional obligations that are objective, contractual, and rationally defined and one's particularistic ties to spouse, children, relatives and friends lies a morass of psychiatric confusion. The greater the attachment, the greater the sense of obligation to rescue others. Occupational and professional ties are defined more rigidly than personal ones. Duty to a relative, spouse, child or friend versus duty to one's professional job lies behind much confusion in civil disaster planning. It is the family that takes precedence. How you and your colleagues perceive and respond to your professional obligations is variable, and depends on your pre-crisis self-awareness and role preparation for emergencies.

For the individual and institution in the pre-disaster phase, there is a time to organize, rehearse and modify a set of standard procedures and clearly defined roles. It is preventive psychiatry to develop practice drills for our institutions, establish communication centers, and rehearse fall-back evacuation procedures. This actually helps to decrease sudden anxiety and individually initiated rescue missions. Civil disaster planning which is anticipated helps to master anxiety and to prepare for the unknown. Because of the defensiveness of most psychiatrists (like everyone else) in the face of disaster, it helps to prepare. The psychiatrist in private practice is more isolated than one who already holds an institutional role. All psychiatrists and other mental health personnel are at equal risk for becoming potential victims. As psychiatrists, we may have some tendency to disregard our own vulnerability and regressive tendencies under stress while we displace our concern onto those other people who worry about earthquakes, toxins and nuclear issues.

Many physicians and psychiatrists are not aware of just how much of their identity and security is wrapped up in their role behavior. During a crisis and the consequent disruption of their daily lives, they may be just as vulnerable to psychological distress as the rest of the population. The breakdown of routine work, predictable community ties, and job-related security disrupts the identity of many physicians.

SYSTEMS PANIC

"Systems panic" refers to the collapse during disaster of supporting social services and control agencies in society. The separation of the professional psychiatrist and mental health team member from their families and the disruption in communications due to telephone and media overload are two of the main causes of emotional strain and panic during a crisis. Family preparation for a crisis far outweighs any action during a crisis. Deciding where people go, when they will meet, how they will behave in the days and weeks thereafter if they are separated is good preventive psychiatry and good civil disaster planning.

Civil disaster planning after the event shifts to another level of activity for the professional psychiatrist. Grief work, ventilation and prevention of emotional withdrawal will help victims process their experiences.

Professionals should focus after the event on populations at high risk for later breakdown. The children, parents and siblings of those who have died or who have suffered acute loss need attention.

A team role for a psychiatrist comes after recognition of community responsibility. This role in disaster planning requires preparation, 24-hour-a-day duty, cooperation with other authorities, sacrifice of one's family role, giving up private practice, loss of income, and accepting supervening goals. Emergency psychiatric assistance takes over. Psychiatric triage is acceptable in a context of disaster work, but it is unacceptable in private practice. To work on a team allows for selection of cases and for mutual support during overwhelming situations of suffering and death.

CULTURAL HOMOGENEITY AND CIVIL DISASTER

During a civil disaster, I believe there will be less panic behavior if the rescue teams are similar in language, religion and ethnicity to the victims.

Often, one may rely on the wrong indigenous leaders and organizations to distribute aid, which is then subverted into preselected channels for secondary personal and political gain. Disaster planning must take into account cultural and class differences, the status structure within a community, preexisting values about assistance and collective living arrangements, and changed patterns of male/female or child/parent authority.

HURRICANE AGNES AND THE FLOODS

On June 23, 1972, as a result of what some have termed the greatest natural disaster in American history, 80,000 persons had to evacuate their homes in northeastern Pennsylvania, many with less than 30 minutes notice. The Wilkes-Barre area was the hardest hit. Fifty persons died as a direct result of this disaster, and more than 25,000 residences were flooded. Thousands were left jobless and destitute in an already economically depressed region; over 3,000 commercial enterprises and 150 manufacturing firms with 11,000 employees were flooded and severely damaged.

A dozen temporary workers were hired immediately by the county administrator, were given crash training courses, and were assigned to multidisciplinary mental health teams already in the community. Cooperation and coordination among local, state and federal agencies led to NIMH funding for a crisis program within weeks after the disaster.

Mental health services were taken directly to the victims to prevent long-term emotional disability. Fifty additional nonprofessionals, local people who had also suffered in the disaster, were hired as human service counselors under the supervision of mental health professionals. Before entering the disaster area, the counselors underwent a five-day training program for crisis therapy. In subsequent months, further in-service training was provided. A humanistic, brief, targeted approach to emotional problems of disaster victims was emphasized. The focus was on those individuals and families who had returned to their homes. The highest-risk group for service consisted of those with known psychiatric illness or a suicidal history. The elderly and children were also high risk groups. There was an increased incidence of alcohol and drug abuse, marital problems, and symptomatic reactions during the weeks and months after the flood ebbed. During the recovery phase, many disaster victims complained of red tape, long delays, and what they felt was the "indifference" of the authorities.

Recommendations Derived from This Disaster [3]

1. Most stress reactions resolve themselves quickly. A crisis approach that focuses on specific concerns helps to turn individuals toward adaptive work. Most specific problems are nonpsychiatric in origin and are related to housing, medical care, employment and transportation. Counselors trained to reach out and pinpoint these issues, including personal losses, can help to alleviate much of the predictable suffering.
2. Ventilation of feelings helps people to face their current reality. Immediate and long-range changes in their life style due to the disaster should be discussed, not denied or avoided. The ventilation may take many weeks and may entail more than brief episodes of weeping. We tend to allow ventilation, then shut off the process too abruptly, with a pill for sedation. The acute phase of expression of feelings about the disaster mobilizes intense transference attachments to the crisis workers which, if not recognized, can lead to seductive, exploitative, and other counterproductive reactions.
3. There is often resistance to being identified as a patient in need of the services of mental health personnel. It appears preferable to identify the program of crisis intervention as a community service for all.
4. Counselors who go into the community should be motivated to deal with the fierce independence and self-reliance that many Americans feel with regard to government programs.
5. Repeated in-service sessions for the disaster workers can help to prevent burnout, frustration from inadequate assistance, and countertransference reactions aroused by the victims.

COMMUNICATIONS CENTER

A communications center, which operates as an open network, with priorities of incoming and outgoing messages, is mandatory. The police must tell the medical teams, which must tell the block captains, who must tell the families, and so on. Coordinated communication will prevent much confusion by pooling information, controlling appeals for help, and allocating resources.

Civil disaster planning also requires a disaster headquarters to coordinate individuals into an organization, provide other agencies with a communications link to the field, and coordinate between helping agencies.

Converging into the disaster area may act as a barrier to other relief activities. Masses of people get in the way, even though they may want to offer assistance. Police roadblocks and news releases can help to stop the influx. Study of the convergence problem in civil disaster suggests that inaccurate and irresponsible news reporting may increase kinship anxiety about friends and relatives in the disaster area and bring people in droves. The urgent need to know about the safety of one's family, friends and close associates underlies much of the random activity, searching, and confusion in the acute phase of civil disaster. Where the extended family unit is the center of life, many individuals cannot function in their professional roles in the larger community until the family is secure. Even hardboiled, busy practitioners caring for others eventually have to take stock of their own private worlds.

The phenomenon of civil disaster planning requires a look at humankind's worst fear—the nightmare of chaos that becomes reality. We search for a way to put the civil disaster into a meaningful frame of reference, whether psychiatric, political or religious. We will not be able to endure the pain and stay sane without substantial ties to others and the future. One of the most important tasks in civil disaster planning is convincing people that disaster is real and that reality can be modified through human cooperation.

REFERENCES

1. Baller, G.W., Chapman, D.W.: The emergency social system. In Baller, G.W., Chapman, D.W. (eds): Man and Society in Disaster. New York: Basic Books, 1962, p 222.
2. Croskey, L., Lefley, H.P.: Bestman E.W. A community mental health center's response to urban violence. Hosp Community Psychiatry (in preparation).
3. Heffron, E.F.: Project Outreach: crisis intervention following natural disaster. J Commun Psychol 5:103-111, 1977.

Special Populations and Problems

10

Emergencies Related To Alcohol:

ALEX D. POKORNY

INTRODUCTION

A very large proportion of persons seen in emergency room practice have been drinking heavily and/or are alcoholics. Alcohol may not only be a problem in its own right, as in the case of gross intoxication, coma, and withdrawal states, but it is also a very common cause, precipitant, or accompaniment of other emergency conditions. It is well known that over half of auto crash victims in most series are found to have alcohol blood levels at or above the "legally intoxicated" level. Drinking and alcoholism are very commonly associated with assaults, falls, and suicide attempts. Alcohol intoxication may also complicate or aggravate other disorders. It may overlap with psychiatric disorders such as depression. At times an episode of intoxication may represent an appeal for help, just like a suicide attempt [1]. In a series of 305 alcoholics referred to the emergency room, it was found that the following categories of presenting complaints were the most common, in order of frequency: (1) social problems such as simple drunkenness, lack of funds, need for a rest, (2) acute physical symptoms associated with alcohol. (3) anxiety or depressive symptoms, (4) danger to self or others, (5) socially unacceptable behavior [2]. I will take up the emergencies related to alcoholism in the following order: Intoxication, interaction of alcohol with other drugs, alcohol withdrawal states, alcohol psychoses, and general measures including follow-up.

INTOXICATION

Mild to Moderate Intoxication

Mild to moderate drunkenness is so common that it hardly requires any description. If one can be reasonably certain that this is the total problem, then no special treatment or management within the medical system is indicated. One might merely see to it that the person stays around long enough to sober up, or that he can be returned home without danger.

It would be uncommon, however, that an individual in our society would come to an emergency room with no other problem other than mild to moderate intoxication. There is therefore a presumption that something else must be going on. If such a person is brought in by companions, then they may be able to provide a clue. A period of watchful waiting is more reasonable in such situations than the immediate use of aggressive diagnostic measures.

Severe Intoxication

This may be present with disorientation, with assaultive behavior, with evidence of depression or crying, or with a generalized slowing which may approach stupor [3]. Persons presenting with near-stupor or disorientation need to be watched closely, preferably in a bed. Attempts should be made to obtain an accurate history, to see whether the person is a regular heavy drinker or a novice, and whether he has taken other substances. Patients who seem to be in a stupor should have their vital signs checked frequently.

Among the more difficult patients are the assaultive, aggressive, destructive, or belligerent intoxicated subjects, who are more typically males. As in the case of simple moderate drunkenness, one should ask oneself why such a person is in the emergency room. Persons who become belligerent when drunk are usually managed by relatives and associates; therefore, why is this person brought here in this specific instance? One should think of complicating psychiatric factors, such as some acute social upheaval, depression, psychosis, as well as possible complicating physical injury and ingestion of other drugs.

The management of violent or assaultive intoxicated persons is difficult. It is best done with the assistance of several persons. The intoxicated individual should be approached slowly and carefully with much explanation and a firm businesslike manner. It may be necessary to use physical restraint if the situation becomes extreme. A general sedating medication should be avoided or deferred, and if medication is required, then benzodiazepines are probably the safest [3, 4].

Alcoholic Coma

This is an emergency. A patient presenting in such a condition must be retained in the hospital and must be provided intensive care, with stress on prevention of respiratory depression. This is an extreme but typically reversible degree of alcohol intoxication, and therefore one's goal is to support the patient through the period of respiratory depression and to prevent complications.

Since the cause of the coma might not be clearly known, there must also be a thorough attempt at differential diagnosis. Historical information obtained from associates, when available, is highly valuable. Such patients typically need to have laboratory studies for other drugs and poisons, as well as x-rays, and other studies to evaluate possible head trauma.

Although it would be desirable to hasten the metabolism of alcohol, this is probably not possible. In the past, glucose and insulin have been used. It is probable that stimulant drugs such as caffeine, amphetamines, picrotoxin, etc., are not particularly useful [5, 6, 7].

Pathological Intoxication

This is an acute episode of grossly disturbed behavior occurring after ingestion of a small amount of alcohol. Patients showing this syndrome may become violent, self-destructive, or assaultive, and may have hallucinations and delusions, with subsequent amnesia for the episode. The cause of this condition is unknown, and it has been suggested that it might be related to epilepsy or that it might be an interaction of alcohol with psychiatric disorders such as mania, paranoia, and homosexual panic.

Such conditions are typically handled by security measures, possibly requiring physical restraint, with use of a sedating drug such as a benzodiazepine, and by observation of the patient until the episode has passed.

Intoxication Accompanying Other Conditions

As mentioned earlier, intoxication is present in over half of auto crashes, and is a very common accompaniment of injuries from assaults, falls, suicide attempts, etc. Alcohol intoxication is also commonly found with those disorders which are themselves complications of alcoholism, such as gastritis, esophageal varices, liver ailments, pancreatitis, and infections. All of these disorders need to be included in the differential diagnosis. For example, hepatic insufficiency with impending coma accompanied by a mild intoxication may be difficult to differentiate from simple severe intoxication [1].

Corrigan [8] has called attention to an "alcoholic trauma triad," which is characterized by the simultaneous occurrence of three lesions: fatty liver, acute pneumonia, and acute subdural hematoma. Although this syndrome was identified in a series of autopsies, Corrigan feels that there is a need to keep this triad in mind when dealing with patients who present with any one of these three component conditions.

Methyl Alcohol Intoxication

Methyl alcohol is widely used as a solvent in denatured alcohol and may occasionally be consumed for its intoxicating properties. This is commonly seen only in "down-and-out" alcoholics. It is typical for symptoms of methyl alcohol toxicity to appear only 8-36 hours after ingestion, although visual disturbances may occur within six hours [9]. The tipoff to this disorder is the presence of visual symptoms, ranging from various visual disturbances or soreness of the eyes to blindness. Such patients typically have acidosis; treatment includes oral bicarbonate or IV bicarbonate. In severe cases it may be necessary to use hemodialysis. Death occurs typically from respiratory depression.

The patient's eyes should be protected from light during the period of acute intoxication [3].

INTERACTION OF ALCOHOL WITH OTHER DRUGS

It is common for alcoholics to use other dependency-causing drugs such as barbiturates or benzodiazepines. Therefore, it is urgent that a careful history be taken either from the patient or from associates to clarify the situation as much as possible [5]. There are several groups of interacting drugs which are of special importance.

Sedatives-Hypnotics

These drugs act by depressing CNS function; therefore, the combination of these drugs with ethyl alcohol will result in the potentiation of these depressant effects. Whether or not this is a simple additive effect or whether there is a multiplicative effect is unclear. Nevertheless, the combination of such drugs, particularly the short acting barbiturates, with ethyl alcohol may be lethal.

The presence of alcohol may inhibit the activity of the enzymes which are responsible for detoxification of the barbiturates [10] without inhibiting the central action of the barbiturates, and this may make such drugs more easily fatal. The effect on enzymes also accounts for the tolerance to the depressant effects of barbiturates during the acute alcohol withdrawal period; the enzyme activity is increased and the drug is metabolized more rapidly. Whether the effect is simply additive or something more, it is commonly accepted that the sedation from the combination of alcohol and barbiturates is more profound than either drug alone [10]. The combined effects of alcohol with chloral hydrate are well known as the "Mickey Finn," which has accounted for several cases of death.

Psychotropic Drugs

When alcohol is added to phenothiazines, it may aggravate the hypotensive effects which accompany phenothiazines. There is also some additive effect in CNS depression from these two groups of substances.

Since alcoholism often leads to impaired liver function, this may interfere with the metabolic degradation of phenothiazines, which may affect the necessary dosage. There may be further confusion because the phenothiazines can produce a type of jaundice and may have to be used with caution in alcoholics with liver disease.

The butyrophenones have similar interacting properties. Both phenothiazines and butyrophenones lower the convulsive threshold, which may lead to increased likelihood of seizures during alcohol withdrawal. For this reason these are not good drugs for treatment of alcohol withdrawal syndromes.

Tricyclic antidepressants also seem to potentiate alcohol CNS depressant effects, and there are scattered reports of deaths in persons who have been using both classes of substances.

A special instance of an undesirable reaction is observed when the monoamine oxidase inhibitor antidepressants are used with certain alcoholic beverages containing tyramine, such as Chianti wines and beer. This may cause a hypertensive crisis which is quite serious.

Disulfiram (Antabuse)

Many alcoholics are placed on disulfiram therapy as a useful pharmacologic "barrier" to further drinking. In a minority of cases, such patients may unknowingly ingest alcohol or may knowingly resume drinking either out of recklessness, self-destructive urges, or disbelief that a reaction will occur. The resulting alcohol-disulfiram reactions are very serious and may be fatal, although there are also cases of mild and minor reactions which may not be seen in the emergency room. In a serious reaction the patient has a feeling of warmth in the face, his skin turns red in the upper chest, arms, and particularly in the face; the vessels of the patient's sclerae dilate; the patient feels intense pulses, headache, and a sense of constriction in the neck. Later there may be nausea, drop in blood pressure, respiratory difficulty, along with a sense of dread and blurred vision [9].

The milder reactions can be handled with a period of observation and supportive measures. The more severe reactions can be treated with intravenous antihistamine or Vitamin C, and by measures to combat hypotension.

ALCOHOL WITHDRAWAL STATES

This is a group of disorders which appear in the individual who has become physically dependent on alcohol, and who then has the alcohol withdrawn, either abruptly or relatively (i.e., the alcohol consumption is reduced). Alcohol withdrawal reactions may be seen as a presenting disorder in the emergency room. On the other hand, it is common for persons who are physically dependent on alcohol to be processed through an emergency room in relatively good condition, only to have a withdrawal syndrome appear from one to three days later in the hospital. For this reason it is important that the drinking history be evaluated in such patients while they are still in a condition to give a reliable history.

Tremulousness ("Shakes")

There are several degrees of this disorder, which represents the most common manifestation of the abstinence syndrome [6, 5]. Patients presenting with the shakes may also have nausea, vomiting, and general irritability. It usually requires several days of regular or continuous drinking to bring on this condition, and most patients with this disorder have been drinking steadily for at least two weeks. It is common for alcoholics to treat the shakes with more alcohol, which simply digs them deeper into the same pit. Quite often the drinking episode is terminated because of vomiting to a degree which makes further drinking impossible.

The outstanding feature of this condition is the generalized tremor, along with a kind of hyperalertness, startle reaction, flushed face, and tachycardia. This syndrome subsides within a few days. There is usually insomnia for a number of days.

The patient should get relief within several days of abstinence from alcohol, and he normally requires no treatment except for mild sedation, preferably with benzodiazepines for a very limited period, such as five days.

Withdrawal Convulsions ("Rum Fits")

These typically come on within eight hours to two days after cessation of drinking, most often within 13-24 hours [6]. There may be only a single seizure, but often patients have up to six and may occasionally go into status epilepticus. The seizures are grand mal in type. About a third of the patients with such seizures go on to develop delirium tremens. Rum fits are usually found in persons who have been drinking heavily for many years. They do not seem to be related to epilepsy (although, of course, epileptics may also be alcoholics). Oral phenytoin does not act sufficiently rapidly to be useful in such conditions, although intravenous phenytoin may be helpful. More commonly such patients are treated with phenobarbital or with parenteral diazepam.

Hallucinosis

About a quarter of tremulous withdrawal patients develop hallucinations. These may range from distorted sensations to clear visual or auditory hallucinations. Typically, such patients have auditory hallucinations in a clear sensorium; that is they are not confused, and this distinguishes this disorder clearly from delirium tremens. The patients, however, believe the hallucinations to be real [6]. The symptoms typically occur within a short time after cessation or marked reduction in intake of alcohol. The symptoms usually last for only a few days, but can last up to ten days. The treatment is the same as for the tremulous stage [5].

Delirium Tremens

This is the most dramatic and serious of the alcohol withdrawal reactions. It is characterized by marked confusion and disorientation, vivid hallucinations, delusions, tremor, agitation, marked anxiety, insomnia, as well as by such signs as profuse sweating, fever, tachycardia, and dilated pupils [6]. Delirium tremens typically follows a period of heavy and continuous drinking which has lasted many weeks. It may, however, be precipitated by an acute infection, injuries, surgical procedure, etc., when illness and hospitalization interfere with the patient's accustomed heavy drinking pattern.

The genuine full-blown delirium tremens, which includes profound disorientation, is a medical emergency and should be treated by hospitalization. The patient needs to be constantly attended in a well-lighted room, preferably with someone else such as a family member present. The patient should be given repeated explanations and reassurances.

Such patients should have continuous monitoring of fluid and electrolyte balance with correction of abnormalities; however, there should be no routine administration of fluids without prior determination that this is necessary.

Since delirium tremens represents a withdrawal reaction, it is logical to replace the alcohol with a cross-dependent but more readily controlled drug, such as one of the barbiturates, paraldehyde or benzodiazepines [7, 11]. The current most commonly used drug for this purpose is chlordiazepoxide (Librium). Patients with delirium tremens should also be given vitamins and other supportive measures.

It is still observed that about 15% of definitely established delirium tremens patients have a fatal outcome. However, it appears that this occurs largely in the subgroup which also has accompanying physical disorders.

Alcohol Withdrawal Reactions Accompanying Other Disorders

As mentioned earlier, it is quite common to have delirium tremens or lesser degrees of withdrawal reaction develop in patients who have been hospitalized with fractures, head injuries, pneumonia, or other disorders. Quite often such syndromes will appear only two or three days following admission to the hospital and an interruption of the usual heavy drinking schedule.

ALCOHOL PSYCHOSIS

(The conditions of pathological intoxication and delirium tremens which would both qualify as psychoses have already been mentioned.)

Wernicke's Syndrome

This may overlap the Korsakoff's Syndrome. It is believed that Wernicke's is caused by thiamine deficiency. The patients present with delirium together with ophthalmic symptoms such as nystagmus or ophthalmoplegia [1].

Korsakoff's Syndrome

This is also called Korsakoff's Psychosis. It is a cerebral organic disorder which is thought to result from Vitamin B deficiency. It is characterized by a severe disturbance in memory, with confabulation (the patient manufactures stories to fill in his memory defects). It is also characterized by polyneuropathy. It is typical for such a patient to appear superficially mentally clear and this may be quite deceptive; when the patient is tested his memory span is very brief [1].

Alcoholic Deterioration

In some patients with long-lasting and heavy alcohol abuse, there develops a gradual disintegration of personality, not unlike that found in arteriosclerosis or any other gradually developing organic brain syndrome. Such individuals show some dementia, emotional lability, and loss of the more refined aspects of personal habits and behavior.

GENERAL MEASURES—FOLLOW-UP

When a person is seen for one of the emergencies related to alcoholism and is given life-saving and other necessary treatment, this is of course a very worthwhile achievement. Nevertheless, it is common for such individuals to go in and out of emergency rooms without any attempt being made to interrupt the drinking cycle.

It is therefore important that some attempt be made regularly to involve each such patient or his family or associates in some attempt at rehabilitation and treatment of the underlying behavior disorder of alcoholism.

This engagement in rehabilitation should be initiated as part of the emergency intervention, preferably as soon as possible after the acute symptoms are under control. Without a program of comprehensive rehabilitation, even the clinician's emergency efforts will eventually not be sufficient to save the patient from the ravages of his chronic disease.

REFERENCES

1. Bridges, P.K.: Psychiatric Emergencies—Diagnosis and Management. Springfield, Illinois, C.C. Thomas, 1971, pp 47-53.
2. Schwarz, L., Field, S.P.: The alcoholic patient in the psychiatric hospital emergency room. Q J Stud Alcohol 30:104-111, 1969.
3. Ottenberg, D.J., Rosen, A., Fox, V.: Acute alcoholic emergencies, in Rosen A., Fox V. (eds): Emergency Psychiatric Care—The Management of Mental Health Crises, Bowie, Md., Charles Press, 1975, pp 63-77.
4. Shurley, J.T., Pokorny, A.D.: Handling the psychiatric emergency. Med Clin North Am 46:417-426, 1962.
5. Manual on Alcoholism, AMA, Chicago, Illinois, 1973, pp 49-62.
6. Victor, M., Adams, R.D.: Alcohol, in Harrison T (ed): Principles of Internal Medicine 7th Ed, New York, McGraw Hill, 1974, pp 671-681.
7. Hollister, L.E.: Clinical Use of Psychotherapeutic Drugs. Springfield, Illinois, CC Thomas, 1973, pp 156-159.
8. Corrigan, G.E.: Alcoholic head trauma triad. J Stud Alcohol 36:541-549, 1975.
9. Morgan, R., Cagan, E.F.: Acute alcohol intoxication, the disulfiram reaction, and methyl alcohol intoxication, in Kissin B., Begleiter H. (eds): The Biology of Alcoholism Vol 3 Clinical Pathology, New York, Plenum, 1974, pp 163-189.
10. Coleman, J.H., Evans, W.E.: Drug interactions with alcohol. Resident & Staff Physician 34-41, February 1976.
11. Moessner, H.F. Bennett, F.W., McClure, C.F.: A suggested regimen for treating the acute stage. Resident & Staff Physician 42-49, February 1976.

11

Substance Abuse in Emergency Practice

MICHAEL A. FAUMAN

A psychiatric emergency is an alteration in behavior, mood, or thought, which the patient, a friend, a relative, or a professional feels requires immediate medical/psychiatric attention [1]. In the case of substance abuse, this emergency is caused by a drug or other toxic substance which the patient usually takes voluntarily [1,2,3,4,5,6,7,]. Implicit in the usual definition of a psychiatric emergency is that it occurs in the context of an outpatient crisis service or a medical emergency department. This is an artificially limited view of the setting of a psychiatric emergency and will be broadened in this paper to include psychiatric emergencies which occur in inpatient and outpatient medical and psychiatric settings as well as a psychiatric crisis-walk-in clinic or medical emergency department.

The major diagnostic challenge presented by substance abuse in emergency medical practice is the recognition and differentiation of drug withdrawal and toxic drug reactions from functional psychiatric disorders [3]. Together, these conditions are capable of producing behavioral, affect and thought disorders which mimic most psychiatric disease. Yet, unlike most psychiatric conditions, they may rapidly become serious and potentially life threatening medical problems if not quickly treated. A third significant but less serious diagnostic challenge is the identification of drug seeking behavior in the guise of psychiatric or medical illness.

Drug withdrawal and toxic drug reactions can be considered delirium states or acute organic brain disorders [8]. Usually they are reversible with appropriate treatment, but at times they may be superimposed on irreversible brain damage caused by chronic use of a toxic agent or some other organic insult to the central nervous system. This is common for encephalopathy caused by chronic alcohol abuse. Substance abuse may produce syndromes that mimic many psychiatric disorders such as agitation, depression, paranoid delusions, auditory and visual hallucinations, and neurological symptoms such as alterations of consciousness and seizures. In addition, toxic agents may produce more subtle changes in the patient's behavior, affect and thought such as anger, irritation, mild confusion, and mild memory impairment producing repeated simple questions which annoy the medical staff and lead to a dismissal of the patient as uncooperative or hostile.

CLASSES OF ABUSED SUBSTANCES

Central Nervous System Depressants

Central nervous system depressants comprise the largest group of drugs whose abuse brings patients to hospitals. This group includes alcohol, barbiturates, opiates, sedative hypnotics, minor tranquilizers and "T's and blues" (pentazocine and pyrabenzamine). All of these substances have the capacity to produce coma in overdose and are associated with a significant withdrawal syndrome. In addition, since many of these drugs are readily available from medical facilities, substance abusers may seek medical attention in order to obtain a prescription for these agents.

The first step in the evaluation of all potential CNS depressant abuse is the evaluation of the patient's level of consciousness. Comatose patients should be treated as medical emergencies with immediate establishment of an adequate airway. Blood and urine should then be obtained for standard metabolic tests and screening for toxic agents. Patients are administered two ampules (0.8 mg total) of naloxone and 50 cc of 50% dextrose intravenously to counter opiate overdose and hypoglycemic coma. Comatose patients should then be admitted to the medical intensive care unit even if they do respond to the naloxone because of the possibility of recurrence of coma and development of pulmonary edema. Somnolent patients should be observed closely since they may be in the early stage of absorption of the toxic agent. Emesis should be induced in conscious patients to empty the stomach of the toxic agent unless emesis is contraindicated, as is the case with hydrocarbons. Patients who do become increasingly somnolent or comatose after presenting to the hospital should be admitted to the medical intensive care unit.

Narcotics

Narcotics are physiologically addicting and produce withdrawal symptoms including nausea, sweating, rhinorrea, aching bones, anxiety, mydriasis, and piloerection. None of these withdrawal symptoms are life threatening and all are influenced by the patient's psychological expectations. Treatment of opiate withdrawal is best approached by treating the patient's symptoms rather than giving the patient narcotics which may encourage the use of the medical facility as a ready source of narcotics to support the patient's addiction. However, if it is necessary to keep the patient for further observation or treatment of painful medical conditions it may be necessary to give the patient narcotics and even more than the usual dose because of his/her tolerance to opiates. Often the patient's fear of his/her impending withdrawal will produce significant anxiety, agitation, and hostility leading to additional behavioral problems.

The effects of narcotic overdose can be reversed with naloxone as indicated above. Failure to respond to a single dose of naloxone indicates that the patient either did not use a narcotic, used a narcotic in conjunction with another drug, or used a very large dose of narcotic. In these cases a second 0.4 mg dose of naloxone can be administered but it is probably not useful to administer more if there is no effect. The effects of naloxone are rapid and brief. Before administering the first dose of naloxone to the unconscious patient, restrain all four limbs since the patient may wake up with extreme agitation. Since naloxone is short acting the patient may lapse back into coma in 30-40 minutes, especially if the abused narcotic was long-acting, such as methadone.

Other CNS Depressants

Central nervous system depressants other than narcotics often have medically significant and severe withdrawal syndromes. Alcohol withdrawal may proceed to a classic delirium tremens with hyperpyrexia, tachycardia, hypertension, hyperreflexia, dehydration, severe anxiety, and auditory, visual, or tactile hallucinations. Alcoholics may also become very paranoid during withdrawal and may initially appear like paranoid schizophrenics. This may lead to their transfer to a psychiatric unit which does not have adequate medical facilities to treat alcohol withdrawal, with potential fatal consequences for the patient. Benzodiazepine and barbiturate withdrawal may produce significant psychiatric symptoms as well as seizures which can initially present as pronounced muscle twitching. Patients in barbiturate withdrawal may become delusional and attack other patients or staff because they are responding to hallucinations or paranoid ideation. Patients who abuse minor tranquilizers, barbiturates, or sedative hypnotics often under-report the amount of drugs they are taking. Therefore care must be taken to start their treatment protocol with enough medication so that the physiological addiction is actually treated rather than masked only to reappear as a severe withdrawal syndrome again after the medication is stopped.

Unlike narcotic withdrawal, which can be treated symptomatically, the withdrawal from most other CNS depressants can be life-threatening and must be treated with a drug which cross-reacts with the abused substance. Barbiturates such as phenobarbital are often used for withdrawal of minor tranquilizers, barbiturates, and sedative-hypnotics because they have a cross-tolerance with these agents. The patient is given increasing doses of phenobarbital until the agitation, muscle twitching, and psychotic symptoms subside. This dose is then repeated every six hours for the first day or two. The patient is then gradually withdrawn from this dose at a rate of 10% reduction per day. Occasionally the patient may continue to have some symptoms of sleep disturbance or thought disorder after withdrawal is completed. In these patients it is useful to investigate the possibility of a deep underlying seizure disorder which the patient has been self medicating with CNS depressants. The potentially medically serious nature of CNS depressant withdrawal makes it more appropriate to treat this disorder in an inpatient service.

Central Nervous System Stimulants

Abused stimulants include amphetamine and its various analogs, methylphenidate and cocaine. Stimulants are less likely to be taken in a suicide attempt and do not directly cause coma. Acute or chronic use of stimulants can cause an acute confusional state, paranoia, or paranoid psychosis. The patient may not openly acknowledge that he has been using street drugs. However, some of the physical signs of stimulant abuse, including needle tracks, nasal septal necrosis, increased temperature, pulse, and blood pressure, or evidence of septic emboli in the lungs, will help make the diagnosis. The patient may report sleeplessness or may appear restless or anxious. His delusional system may be so subtle and well-fixed that the physician may not even recognize it as a delusion at first. Paranoid psychosis produced by stimulant abuse is responsive to the major antipsychotic agents such as haloperidol or thiothixene and may require inpatient treatment. The paranoid delusions that develop from amphetamine abuse have been known to persist for several months after cessation of the drug. The patient may also develop a tolerance to the psychological effects of stimulant drugs taken in large doses over prolonged periods of time. Therefore the individual may increase the dose to get the desired psychological effect and eventually take enough of the drug to cause death.

The withdrawal syndrome from CNS stimulants is psychological and not physiological in the same sense as CNS depressant withdrawal. Abrupt withdrawal from these agents will not produce seizures, hallucinations, or delusions, but may produce a severe depression with subsequent suicidal ideation and attempts. Therefore, suicidal patients should be questioned about possible stimulant abuse as a possible etiology for their depression.

Psychotomimetic Agents

The psychotomimetic agents include psychedelic and hallucinogenic agents such as LSD, mescaline, and phencyclidine. Marijuana is also often included in this group. These agents have no significant physiological addiction and little if any psychological addiction. Drug overdoses producing serious medical problems are unusual with these agents, although large doses of phencyclidine may produce a serious and potentially fatal hypertensive episode. It is not clear whether this is a result of the phencyclidine itself or some other agent contaminating the drug. The vast majority of these drugs are manufactured illicitly and are often sold as some other agent. This is particulary true for phencyclidine, which is often sold as LSD, mescaline, psylocibin, or some other psychotomimetic agent.

Marijuana

It is not yet clear whether marijuana used in moderation produces significant medical or psychiatric complications. It may produce an acute anxiety syndrome, particularly in the naive user or in a more experienced user who is undergoing some stress. Marijuana use alone is unlikely to produce a psychosis. Psychosis appearing after marijuana use is probably related to the patient's underlying psychopathology or the concurrent use of other drugs. Long-term heavy use of marijuana may produce an "amotivational syndrome," with apathy and lack of interest in the future, school, or work.

Lysergic Acid Diethylamide (LSD)

LSD produces mainly visual perceptual distortions often described as objects melting and shifting with vivid color changes. The patient may also describe complicated visual hallucinations which may be associated with delusions, severe anxiety, or even psychosis. This experience is often referred to as a "bad trip." The patient is usually cared for by friends at this time and avoids seeking treatment at a hospital. If the patient is brought to a medical care facility the appropriate treatment consists of calmly and repeatedly reassuring and orienting the agitated patient, and telling him/her repeatedly that she/he is experiencing the effects of a drug, that it will wear off in time and that she/he will be protected until the effects wear off. This may take three or four hours and could be done by a friend of the patient rather than a physician. The use of major tranquilizers instead of this "talkdown" to treat a "bad trip" is perceived as brutal ("crash landing"). It may relieve the symptoms, but results in increased subsequent drug use, often with recurrent bad trips. Prolonged psychosis following LSD use is rare and is probably an example of a functional psychosis which has been unmasked. Patients who get worse instead of improving in response to a talkdown may have taken phencyclidine instead of LSD.

Phencyclidine

Phencyclidine (PCP) is a psychotomimetic drug which was originally investigated in the 1960s as a possible analgesic and preanesthetic agent for humans. Its clinical use was discontinued because of the drug's severe behavioral side effects, including psychosis. Phencyclidine first appeared as a street drug in 1967 and soon spread throughout the country. It is usually smoked after being sprinkled on marijuana or inhaled as a powder. Intravenous injection is common in heavy users. Phencyclidine does not appear to be associated with a significant withdrawal syndrome, but overdose may produce serious medical and/or psychological problems. Phencyclidine produces disturbances in body image and position sense rather than visual or tactile hallucinations. Signs of cerebellar dysfunction, including ataxia, nystagmus, and slurred speech are common. The blood pressure is often elevated and in overdoses may produce a cerebrovascular hemorrhage leading to death. The patient may appear confused and frightened, is often violent, and may appear to be completely unaware of his environment although he appears to be awake. In addition she/he is experiencing the anesthetic effects of the PCP, so that she/he may sustain serious injury without experiencing any pain.

Most PCP users do not come to hospitals for treatment of the acute effects of the drug. They may die from the consequences of their behavior while intoxicated, rather than from medical complications. They often drown because they are unable to orient themselves in water. At least one patient drowned in a shower after sticking his face in the water. Other users fall or jump out of buildings or are hit by motor vehicles because of delusions or proprioceptive distortions. Individuals who are under the influence of PCP may appear to have extraordinary strength and commit acts of extreme violence including primitive, sadistic mutilation to themselves and others. Phencyclidine may produce a toxic psychosis which lasts a few days or a more extended psychosis which lasts several weeks. The length of the psychosis does not appear to be directly related to the amount of PCP taken by the patient. The patient may initially be comatose for several days or weeks and then awake with significant psychotic ideation including paranoia. The prolonged psychosis is probably a functional psychosis precipitated by the stress of the dissociative effects of the drug. There is some indication that patients who have a prolonged psychotic episode with PCP may return to the hospital up to a year after resolution of the PCP psychosis with another psychotic episode which is hard to distinguish from a typical schizophrenic episode.

When a patient is brought to the emergency department with a probable PCP intoxication, sensory isolation is the treatment of choice. The patient should be placed in a room with minimal furniture, only dim lights, and reduced outside stimuli. Blood pressure should be closely monitored. If the patient is acutely agitated or psychotic, she/he should be given antipsychotic medication. The high-potency neuroleptics such as haloperidol or thiothixene are best for this. The patient with a prolonged psychosis may need antipsychotic medication for many days or weeks.

CLUES TO THE DIAGNOSIS OF SUBSTANCE ABUSE

There are several specific findings in the medical history and physical examination which suggest that the patient has a substance abuse problem.

1. A change in performance at work or at school
2. Abrupt change in behavior or personality
3. Multiple medical illnesses in a person under the age of forty
4. A history of overdose or prior suicide attempts
5. The patient's friends are substance abusers
6. Actual physical evidence of substance abuse
7. Altered state of consciousness
8. Involvement of several organ systems
9. Cyanosis, seizures, or shock
10. Impairment of orientation, memory, judgement or cognitive ability
11. Lateralizing neurological sign, ataxia, tremor or seizures
12. Repeated simple questions, confusion or *apparent* uncooperative behavior

Any of these findings should alert the physician to the possibility that the patient's psychiatric disorder is secondary to substance abuse.

REFERENCES

1. Fauman, B.J., Fauman, M.A.: Emergency Psychiatry for the House Officer. Baltimore, Williams & Wilkins, 1981.
2. Fauman, M.A., Fauman, B.J.: Chronic phencyclidine (PCP) abuse: A psychiatric perspective, J Psychedel Drugs 12:307-315, 1980.
3. Fauman, B.J., Fauman, M.A.: Recognition and management of drug abuse emergencies. Comp Ther 4:38-43, 1978.
4. Kline, N.S., Alexander, S.F., Chamberlain, A.: Psychotropic Drugs: Manual for Emergency Management of Overdose. Oradell, Medical Economics Co., 1974.
5. Taylor, R., Maurer, J., Tinklenberg, J.: Management of "bad trips" in an evolving drug scene. JAMA 213:422-425, 1970.
6. Wesson, D.R., Smith, D.E.: Psychoactive drug crisis intervention. Curr Psychiatr Ther 16:203-208, 1970.
7. Fauman, M.A., Fauman, B.J.: Violence associated with phencyclidine abuse. Am J Psychiatry 136:1584-1586, 1979.
8. Fauman, M.A.: Treatment of the agitated patient with an organic brain disorder. JAMA 240:380-382, 1978.

12

Crisis Intervention for the Chronic Mental Patient

DONALD G. LANGSLEY

Crisis intervention has become so popular that it is the subject of nearly 50 books and hundreds of scientific papers. It has proved its usefulness for a variety of mental disorders and for human problems which are not a psychiatric illness. For the chronic mental patient (CMP), it has a special usefulness. Effective crisis intervention designed to meet the needs of the CMP is likely to answer some of the concerns and criticisms of the deinstitutionalization movement, though it must be said from the beginning that crisis intervention is not the only service needed by that population [1].

Citizen and professional groups alike have expressed concern that the CMP has been inadequately served by the public (and private) mental health system. That we all have been inadequately responsive to the needs of that group is a message frequently heard. Knowledgeable observers call the effects of deinstitutionalization a scandal. In some areas the general hospital emergency room (presumably offering crisis intervention to the CMP) has become a substitute for the state hospital. When the emergency room offers only triage, and not definitive crisis intervention as one part of a total package of services to the CMP, it is likely to result in major deficiencies. A 1979 *New York Times* article pointed out

Yesterday the hospital was attempting to relieve its overcrowding by discharging those judged to be least sick—a form of psychiatric triage that was being performed in the emergency room, where only patients who appear to be a danger to themselves or others are admitted [2].

The crisis service when operated as a 24-hour professionally staffed psychiatric emergency service has become the interface between the community and the hospital. The shift of the CMP from state hospital to the community has been a major factor in the expansion of psychiatric emergency services, but those services must be well planned and executed, and must be only one part of a total system of care for that population [3]. The massive discharges from the state mental hospitals, often to communities unprepared to receive and rehabilitate such patients, has been the catalyst which forced the general hospitals to expand crisis intervention programs in their emergency rooms.

The history of the development of crisis intervention is well known and is attributed to the work of Lindemann and Caplan, as well as the contribution of Freud, the ego psychology and developmental theories of Hartmann and Erikson, the military psychiatrists, and social systems theorists. We define a crisis as a response to external or internal stress which cannot be managed by the usual coping mechanisms of the person stressed. When the ego cannot solve acute problems, a disequilibrium occurs and there is disorganization when the affect becomes one of extreme tension. The presence of a crisis depends on both the external hazard experienced and the susceptibility of the individual stressed. By definition, the chronic mental patient is one who is more susceptible to stress than the average person. The tension and disorganization associated with a crisis may result in decompensation and an exacerbation of the underlying mental illness [4].

Recognizing the importance of crisis as a precipitant of frank mental illness, emergency psychiatric services were mandated as one of the required services of a community mental health center, along with inpatient treatment, partial hospitalization, outpatient treatment, and consultative services. However, the regulations defining a crisis service were varied and the requirements too often met by a daytime walk-in service five days a week along with a telephone recording referring the caller to some central agency when the problem couldn't wait until the next business day. The community hospital-based or hospital-sponsored centers were more likely to operate a 24-hour professionally staffed emergency psychiatric service in the general hospital emergency room. In such a setting, the staff was often multidisciplinary, but a psychiatrist was always immediately available to personally evaluate the patient. Such services initially focused on triage to decide about admission or referral. As crisis intervention techniques were developed and as they were demonstrated to be effective alternatives to hospitalization, these emergency room programs began to undertake definitive treatment. In urban emergency rooms in community and publicly funded hospitals, the psychiatric patients soon constituted approximately 10% of the population of a busy emergency room. Of that group, it is not unusual to have a fourth of them admitted, half of them referred to outpatient treatment resources, and to have a fourth treated definitively with crisis intervention techniques of from 1 to 6 visits. The return visits are best made directly to the emergency service staff member who saw the patient initially.

THE CHRONIC MENTAL PATIENT

This model of crisis intervention was developed for both acute and chronic patients, but the chronic patients were too often simply rehospitalized instead of being treated with crisis intervention techniques. It is not unusual that health care professionals prefer to deal with acute rather than chronic illness. The chronic patient is seen as unresponsive and unrewarding, and occasionally the word "chronic" is changed to "crock" because the patient is not immediately responsive to treatment or because medicine has no treatments to alter the course of such diseases [5]. Kutner found that medical students avoid the chronically ill in their search for fulfillment as doctors who can "cure" [6]. The television shows about medicine feature the acute disorders which respond dramatically to hospital interventions—most of them surgical in nature. Yet most physicians, especially primary care physicians, are concerned with chronic rather than acute illness. The disorders of the cardiovascular system as well as diabetes and arthritis are examples of conditions which make up the bulk of the primary practitioner's work. The internist, pediatrician and family practitioner learn (usually after residency) that they will focus on helping patients with such conditions become symptomatically better and achieve better functioning. Only rarely do they achieve "cure." Alleviation of symptoms, remissions, and rehabilitation are the usual goals of treatment. In like fashion, the young psychiatrist would like to cure; if he deals with long-term illness he prefers the neurotic or personality disorder to the chronic psychotic. The term "YAVIS" (young, attractive, verbal, and insight-oriented) applies to the most popular patients in the outpatient clinic. If cure is not rapid, at least the effort with such patients is intellectually challenging, and one hopes that insight will eventually produce significant change. The chronic mental patient is viewed as difficult, unresponsive and unmotivated. All too often the chronic patient who has been thrust into the community receives a handful of pills, and any psychotherapy is done by one of the "junior" members of the mental health team (if the patient is motivated to come for treatment). These patients were to be a major priority for the community mental health center when that movement was originated. However, most centers have neglected this population [7].

A large proportion of such centers have preferred to deal with acute and less-sick patients, and have devoted their efforts to "prevention" in the hope that this yet-unproven approach will be effective. The centers have moved from a health-oriented to a social service-oriented model and many have become frankly antipsychiatric. As a result, the numbers of psychiatrists per center are often inadequate and frequently consist only of part-time psychiatrists. Since the CMP often requires medical-psychiatric skills, non-medically based centers may be unmotivated and ill-staffed to care for this population.

The term "chronic mental patient" has been defined in terms of severity of illness, the extent of disability, a history of hospitalization (usually multiple hospitalizations in a state mental hospital) [8].

The duration of the illness is not the sole criterion because personality disorders and psycho-neuroses have a long history. Neither is chronicity defined only in terms of the length of treatment since many of the less severe conditions in individuals never hospitalized may take years of psychotherapy. The CMP is diagnostically most likely to be a schizophrenic or a severe paranoid, but occasionally the affective psychoses and organic brain syndromes qualify for this label. Goldman estimates that there are at least three million chronic mental patients in the US [9].

With the advent of community treatment and efforts to avoid unnecessary hospitalization, it was hoped that patients would not become chronic. Chronicity was often defined as a consequence (in part) of institutional treatment. Recent experience suggests that we will continue to have chronics, and Caton has described a new group of chronic patients who require extensive community care [5]. Bassuk has described a group of repeaters in the psychiatric emergency room [10]. The centers which have had programs especially designed to meet the needs of the chronic patient have frequently defined this group as young adults who are schizophrenic or who have antisocial or paranoid personality disorders. They do not do well in community residence programs because of violence and serious interpersonal difficulties.

The responsibility for the chronic mental patient is almost exclusively that of the public sector. There are formidable financial disincentives which discourage private practitioners from taking responsibility for these patients. They must make their way in the public-funded mental health centers and hospitals who may find it all too easy to remand such patients to the hospital.

Problems of the Chronic Mental Patient

Bassuk has identified a group of repeaters who return to the psychiatric emergency service within six months [10]. Of the repeater population at Beth

Israel, 13% were seen 2 to 7 times within six months. This group consumed a great deal of staff time and effort. 86% of them had a history of previous inpatient psychiatric treatment, and of those, 47% had six or more prior hospitalizations while 23% were hospitalized 3 to 5 times in the past.

Caton defines the specific problems of the chronic mental patient as suicide, violence, and low compliance [5]. The suicide rate in his population (in New York City) was 4.2%, which is 210 times the suicide rate in the general population. They also have a high arrest rate (25% as compared with a 3% arrest rate for the general population in the same precincts where the study was done). In terms of compliance with medications prescribed, only 17% took medications in accordance with physicians' recommendations (according to self reports by the patients).

In the Bassuk group, the clinical symptoms which differentiated the repeaters and nonrepeaters were (1) hostility, (2) suspiciousness, (3) uncooperativeness, and (4) an absence of guilt over deviant behavior. They had high scores on psychopathology rating scales, and showed significant functional impairment. The other major characteristics were that they had a very sparse network for social supports, and that they elicited negative reactions from the staff.

A large proportion of psychiatric emergency room repeaters are in psychiatric treatment (60%) and another 22% had previously been in psychotherapy. It was felt that the use of repeat visits to the emergency room was often due to a transference bind with the therapist. In such cases, the crisis team would focus on the psychotherapy itself rather than just the symptoms of the crisis. Patients would be encouraged to talk over their complaints and concerns with their therapist. While in the emergency room, the staff would attempt to deal with the distortions of the reactions to the therapist who had been treating the patient. Frequently, the crisis service visits were seen as an opportunity to engage such patients in treatment.

THE GENERAL HOSPITAL EMERGENCY ROOM AS A SETTING FOR CRISIS INTERVENTION

Crisis intervention for the CMP is most effectively carried on in the emergency room or the general hospital. Though crisis services may operate from ambulatory centers or from mental health centers that are not hospital based, in such settings the service generally operates as a 9 to 5 business day walk-in service. The general hospital emergency room is professionally staffed 24-hours a day and is the natural setting for both physical and mental problems. The advantage of using this setting is that staff is available for comprehensive evaluation and treatment of all problems. In addition, placing the psychiatric emergency service in such a setting is a clear message that there is no difference in the attention afforded patients with mental disorder and those with physical ailment. Community emergency personnel such as police officers, life squads, fire departments, etc., are accustomed to bringing people in trouble to the hospital. It serves as a resource for all in difficulty.

There has been a phenomenal growth in the number of patients seen in hospital emergency rooms for both the general medically ill and those with psychiatric problems. Indeed, the growth has often been due to difficulty in finding adequate numbers of primary care physicians. Patients with family physicians become used to coming to the emergency room for immediate aid or for after-office-hours treatment. In like fashion, the general hospital has become the setting for the treatment of acute psychiatric disorders. In 1963 there were 465 psychiatric inpatient units in general hospitals, but by 1979 this number had grown to 1,045 [11]. The general hospital emergency room has become the only segment of the health care delivery system which can handle medical-psychiatric and psychosocial crises 24 hours a day [12, 13]. In large, public-funded and private-community hospitals alike, approximately 10% of the patients who are seen in the emergency room come specifically seeking psychiatric treatment. In the two general hospitals in which this author has been responsible for psychiatric service, the emergency room averaged about 100,000 visits per year and of those 10,000 visits were psychiatric—a population of 6,000-7,000 patients (since many were repeaters).

CRISIS INTERVENTION TECHNIQUES

The key problem among patients seen in emergency room settings relates to rapid evaluation. That evaluation should take into account: (1) the nature and availability of a support system and the patient's capacity to use it, (2) the degree of dangerousness to self and others, (3) past psychiatric history and present psychiatric symptoms, (4) ability to care for self, (5) motivation and capacity to participate in treatment, (6) the request of the family and/or the patient for a specific type of help, and (7) the physical illness status of the patient.

The crisis intervention may take place in the emergency room or on an outpatient basis. It generally means 1 to 6 visits. Some patients require more intensive observation and respite from the stresses of the environment which may have precipitated the crisis. They may be helped by the use of the overnight bed in the hospital emergency room. By holding the patient overnight, the therapist may better judge the degree of dangerousness to self or others. Most groups find that half of the patients judged to be dangerous when admitted to the overnight unit are felt to be safe to release on the following day.

Crisis intervention may also require brief hospitalization. For the patient who has no family or social support system, the severity of the crisis may require brief admission. The hospital is useful for the patient who needs the support of the 24-hour staff to aid in recompensation. Crisis intervention for this population consists of psychotherapy, medication as indicated, and the use of the hospital milieu. In deciding about hospitalization, the nature and severity of the patient's problems play an important role, but the staffing and organization of the emergency room is also an important determinant. The decision often depends upon who evaluates the patient. When a seasoned attending physician, rather than a psychiatric resident or nonmedical mental health professional, sees the patient, an outpatient or overnight bed in the emergency room is more likely to be chosen than the 24-hour inpatient service.

SPECIFIC CLINICAL PROBLEMS

In the clinical practice of crisis intervention, certain problems are common. These suggestions about management are meant to address those situations which are frequently encountered.

Physical Illness: It is essential to think about and look for physical illness. That fact alone makes it important that a psychiatrist-physician be involved in the crisis evaluation service. At times, physical illness produces symptoms of mental disorder and, when properly treated, results in remission of the mental or behavioral symptoms [14]. A number of recent studies suggest that unrecognized physical illness causes 30 to 60% of psychiatric disorders. Koryani, in reporting on 2,090 lower socioeconomic-status outpatients, found that 43% had a major medical illness [15]. Of that group, 46% had been unrecognized by the referral source. Physical illness strongly affected psychiatric symptoms in 69% of those cases and in 18% was thought to be the sole cause of the psychiatric symptoms.

Acute Psychotic Disorders: Acute psychotic symptoms may be superimposed on chronic mental illness. In the patient who is acutely psychotic, a history and complete examination are the basis for decisions about management. Because of the problems associated with acute psychosis, it is essential to obtain collaborative history when available. This may be available from family, friends or caretakers. If the illness is a diagnostic problem, or if the patient is dangerous to self or others, or if troublesome symptoms cannot be controlled by the usual psychopharmacologic agents, it may be wise to hospitalize the patient. Slaby has suggested an approach to rapid tranquilization in the emergency room [16]. He feels that haloperidol or perphenazine may be given by intramuscular route in doses of 5-10mg every hour up to five times. Fluphenazine (in nondepot form) or chlorpromazine in doses of 50 mg intramuscularly may also be used. Slaby uses antiparkinsonian medication in advance of side effects and reduces or removes it at a later date. If the patient has not improved after six hours, hospitalization is indicated.

Self-destructive Behavior: Many of the patients seen in the emergency room are suicide risks but they don't always indicate that possibility as the cause of the visit. The crisis service staff should always think about suicide and evaluate that possibility. The factors which increase suicide risk are well known. Prior attempts, especially the near-lethal ones, are associated with high risk. Other factors which should be considered are age, sex, the presence of chronic illness, and a sense of hopelessness. Those who live alone are at a higher risk. The incidence of suicide in adolescents and in black males has increased significantly. An especially dangerous group are the chronic schizophrenics who hallucinate voices telling them to kill themselves.

The Violent Patient: Patients with violent behavior are a special problem for emergency room staff. They represent a physical risk to the staff as well as those who may become victims outside the emergency room. Staff should take care to have security or police personnel nearby, thereby gaining enough confidence to do an adequate examination. Violent behavior is seen among certain chronic mental patients, including schizophrenics, severe paranoid disorders, and antisocial personality disorders. It may be precipitated by alcohol, drugs or interpersonal stress. Where violent outbursts are expected or predicted, it is important to warn and counsel family members, caretakers and potential victims.

Aged Patients: Increasing numbers of aged persons have come to the attention of psychiatric services. Instead of being sent to state mental hospitals, most of those who require institutional care have been in nursing homes. When an aged person becomes confused or behaviorally disturbed, many nursing home operators or family members (when the aged person lives with family) assume that this represents an organic senile disorder and seek mental hospital admission. In fact, many such disorders are hidden depressions. Twenty-five to thirty percent of the aged population who have been labeled senile psychotics suffer from treatable depressions. Another group have a treatable delirium which may be superimposed on a dementia.

Careful diagnostic evaluation is indicated when an aged person is brought to the psychiatric emergency service. Consultation to the nursing home operators and the availability of crisis intervention (including a mobile team) will often reassure the nursing home operator that he or she can manage the patient. The availability of short-term inpatient treatment will frequently permit the aged person to return home and avoid a long-term hospitalization.

Children and Adolescents: Increasing numbers of children and adolescents are seen in crisis services. They often come with problems of impulsive behavior disorders or suicide risk. Both situations require intervention with the family as well as with the child, and both suggest the need for contact with teachers, and even peers, to obtain an adequate history.

The Developmentally Disabled: Patients with developmental disability are another group of chronic mental patients. Just as the traditionally mentally ill have been deinstitutionalized, those with mild and moderate retardation are now more often cared for in community settings rather than institutions. Many of them have functional mental disorders as well as organic brain disorders. They appear in psychiatric emergency services when mental or behavioral symptoms are troublesome. They require careful evaluation and work with family and/or other caretakers. It is also essential for emergency service staff to have a knowledge of those community resources which are helpful to the developmentally disabled.

MOBILE TEAMS

Although crisis intervention is generally done in the emergency room or a clinic, it is advisable to have the capability to travel. In many residential settings for the CMP, crises will arise which require on-the-spot assistance. This occurs when a disturbed person will not go to the emergency room or where a caretaker will not make that trip. A visit to the residential care home may often avert a hospitalization since the caretaker will sometimes send the patient to the emergency room by ambulance and refuse to have the patient return. Nursing homes sometimes resort to this "dumping" practice when they feel they can no longer manage a patient. If the crisis team is able to send a staff member to the home, the caretaker is assured of outside help and becomes confident that the patient could be hospitalized if truly necessary. With such assurance, many caretakers of the CMP are willing to work with the patient and thereby avoid a hospitalization. In similar fashion, the patient feels that help is available when necessary.

CRISIS TEAM AS CONSULTANT

In addition to direct services to patients, the crisis intervention team may aid the CMP indirectly by acting as consultant [17, 18]. The consultation may be to agencies or to caretakers. As mentioned, many caretakers will do a better job with the CMP if aided by mental health consultants. Caretakers can be taught about the specific problems of a given patient including the management of the day-to-day crises which the CMP may experience. The social service agencies involved with the CMP may be taught techniques for the management of these crises. The purpose of this program would be to help the social service agency understand how crisis management can keep the CMP in the community and how to promote his rehabilitation. Agencies which might use such a service include welfare workers, vocational rehabilitation workers and caretaker-operators of residential care homes. When the CMP is receiving medication and treatment from a primary care physician, this consultation service may be helpful to the doctor [19].

TEACHING CRISIS INTERVENTION SKILLS

In many residency programs, the emergency room rotation is seen as a brief exposure to a setting which is concerned with rapid evaluation, triage, and making decisions about whether to admit or refer. It may occur early or late in the residency and is associated with night call—never a happy part of the residency. The resident carries on his night duty without the benefit of a senior staff member physically present, and sometimes gets to discuss cases with a faculty member the morning after the night on call. There may be a voice at the other end of the telephone, but the resident does not have the chance to see senior teachers do emergency room evaluations and treatment. In such circumstances, it is not surprising that there is no overwhelming enthusiasm for this type of professional work.

Nielsen has suggested that emergency room and clinic teaching specifically oriented to the chronic patient should follow a number of principles [20]. These include the following:

1. Such education should involve teaching hospitals and programs and not be remanded to outreach settings away from the other teaching programs. It should be taught over the total residency and not for a brief rotation.

2. Role models must be available. If the respected senior teachers don't do it, the students will regard it as a "scut" assignment to be completed and put behind them, and not a valued and respected part of psychiatric practice.
3. Emergency room time must be scheduled as part of the training program, and not simply an on-call experience for service instead of training.
4. Teaching should focus on functional evaluation, and not just clinical diagnosis or dynamic formulations.
5. Psychopharmacology skills must be well taught. The resident should become expert in this aspect of psychiatric practice.
6. The residency should teach psychotherapy techniques which will be helpful to the chronic as well as the acute patient. Residents should be taught how to work with families as well as individuals. They should learn how to be active in intervention, not just passive (as in long-term psychoanalytically oriented psychotherapy).
7. Residents should learn to work with a non-hostile multidisciplinary emergency room team. When the resident is engrafted on an existing group and only asked to sign prescriptions, the value of the experience diminishes rapidly.
8. The focus of the emergency room work with the chronic patients should be on susceptibility to stress and the management of stress.

Schwed suggests a series of specific skills which should be taught in the emergency room [21]. In terms of interviewing style, the resident should learn a crisp, direct style by which rapid evaluations can be done. He must learn to place greater emphasis on the patient's immediate life situation, precipitating events, and existing social support systems. The resident must be helped to sharpen observational skills and to be especially receptive to nonverbal cues. As a fourth principle of interviewing, the resident should become expert in and use appropriately the formal mental status. In terms of therapeutic style, the resident should learn to use a warm, friendly, concerned and supportive approach. It is important to learn about community resources, and Schwed encourages his students to develop their own resource file of names and phone numbers of persons, institutions and agencies. Residents in such settings must deal with their own stereotypes and prejudices, and he uses the example of learning to see police officers as helpful rather than authoritarian individuals likely to simply incarcerate citizens.

RESEARCH DIRECTIONS

Little research has been done which points to answers and data about the effects of community treatment of the chronic mental patient. Schulberg outlines a series of research questions including:

1. Do patients function better when there are community support services? Data should be sought on:
   (a) social adaptation
   (b) psychiatric status
   (c) environmental conditions
   (d) vocational performance
   (e) satisfaction with the treatment
2. What about the burden on the family and what crises occur there when chronic patients are managed in the community instead of institutions?
3. What effect does the CMP have on staff stability in mental health services which treat them in large numbers? This includes difficulties which arise in the treatment process and staff "burn-out."
4. What effect does the CMP have on community acceptance in terms of shelter, social relations, and the accessibility of services?
5. What interactions occur among programs for various groups within a mental health treatment system? Do the acute patients co-mingle with chronics? [22].

CONCLUSIONS

Deinstitutionalization is a fact. It is also true that there are serious problems associated with it. Many patients were discharged from mental hospitals before the community was prepared to offer treatment and were remanded to a lonely and fearful existence in run-down hotels. They were offered only a handful of pills without the psychotherapy and/or social support which would help them remain in the community. They often experience problems which could be managed by a normal person but which in a CMP may precipitate a major regression. But we are not likely to go back to the state mental hospital to warehouse these people. The courts won't permit it and mental health professionals would resist that approach. In my opinion, the general hospital's emergency psychiatric service will make an enormous difference. Such crisis intervention as they may offer represents a secondary prevention approach which can avoid unnecessary hospitalization—especially long-term institutionalization.

REFERENCES

1. Langsley, D.G., Barter, J.T., Yarvis, R.M.: Deinstitutionalization—the Sacramento story. Compr Psychiatry 19:479-490, 1978.
2. Sullivan, R.: Hospital forced to oust patients with psychoses. New York Times, November 8, 1979, p. B3.
3. Talbott, J.A. (ed): The Chronic Mental Patient: Problems, Solutions, and Recommendations for a Public Policy. Washington, D.C., American Psychiatric Association, 1978.
4. Langsley, D.G.: Crisis intervention and the avoidance of hospitalization. New Directions for Mental Health Services 6:81-90, 1980.
5. Caton, C.L.M.: The new chronic patient and the system of community care. Hosp & Community Psychiatry 32:475-478, 1981.
6. Kutner, N.G.: Medical students' orientation toward the chronically ill. J Med Educ 53:111-118, 1978.
7. Langsley, D.G.: The community mental health center: does it treat patients? Hosp & Community Psychiatry 31:815-819, 1980.
8. Minkoff, K.: A map of chronic mental patients, in The Chronic Mental Patient: Problems, Solutions, and Recommedations for a Public Policy. Edited by Talbott, J.A. Washington, DC, American Psychiatric Assn, 1978.
9. Goldman, H.H., Gattozzi, A.A., Taube, C.A.: Defining and counting the chronically mentally ill. Hosp & Community Psychiatry 32:21-27, 1981.
10. Bassuk, E.L.: The impact of deinstitutionalization on the general hospital psychiatric emergency ward. Hosp & Community Psychiatry 31:623-627, 1980.
11. Keill S.L.: The general hospital as the core of the mental health services system. Hosp & Community Psychiatry 32:776-778, 1981.
12. Pardes, H.E.: Mental health-general health interaction: opportunities and responsibilities. Hosp & Community Psychiatry 32:779-782, 1981.
13. Bachrach, L.L.: The effects of deinstitutionalization on general hospital psychiatry. Hosp & Community Psychiatry 32:786-790, 1981.
14. Johnson, D.A.W.: Evaluation of routine physical examination in psychiatric cases. Practitioner 200:686-691, 1968.
15. Koranyi, E.K.: Morbidity and rate of undiagnosed physical illness in a psychiatric clinic population. Arch Gen Psychiatry 36:414-419, 1979.
16. Slaby, A.E.: Emergency psychiatry: an update. Hosp & Community Psychiatry 32:687-698, 1981.
17. Smith, W., Kaplan, J., Siker, D.: Community mental health and the seriously disturbed patient. Arch Gen Psychiatry 30:693-696, 1974.
18. Stein, L.E. and Test, M.A. (eds): Alternatives to Mental Hospital Treatment. New York, Plenum Press, 1978.
19. Wasylenki, D.A., Plummer, E., Littman, S.: An aftercare program for problem patients. Hosp & Community Psychiatry 32:493-496, 1981.
20. Nielsen, A.C., Stein, L.I., Talbott, J.A. et al: Encouraging psychiatrists to work with chronic patients: opportunities and limitations of residency education. Hosp & Community Psychiatry 32:767-775, 1981.
21. Shwed, H.: Teaching emergency room psychiatry. Hosp & Community Psychiatry 31:558-562, 1980.
22. Schulberg, H.C., Bromet, E.: Strategies for evaluating the outcome of community services for the chronically mentally ill. Am J Psychiatry 138:930-935, 1981.

13

Child Psychiatric Emergencies

JAY D. TARNOW

Historically, a major difficulty in providing quality psychiatric care for children has been poor recognition of their special needs. The purpose of this chapter will be to underscore the uniqueness of child psychiatric emergencies. Much of crisis theory has been based on work with adults. Children present special needs and difficulties. Demographic data will be presented in order to familiarize the reader with the field. Clinical data from the author's study at the University of Colorado Medical Center will be presented. A theoretical formulation of child psychiatric emergencies also will be presented.

INCIDENCE OF CHILD PSYCHIATRIC EMERGENCIES

In 1977 five hundred and one hospitals in the United States offered psychiatric services. Forty three percent of these offered emergency psychiatric care for adults. Only a few offered specific child and adolescent emergency care. Errera et al [1] surveyed the psychiatric referrals from the Yale-New Haven Medical Center Emergency Room, and found that 11% of their patients were under 21 years of age, but less than 1% were children under the age of 15 years. Ungerleider [2] reported three hundred eighty seven psychiatric emergencies seen at the University of Cleveland Hospital during a six-month period. They found that less than 7% were under the age of 19, none were under the age of 10 years. Mattsson et al [3] reported that child and adolescent psychiatric emergencies were 0.6% of all emergency room visits as compared to adult psychiatric visits of 3% of the emergency population. Schowalter and Solnit [4] confirmed these figures in their study.

Bristol et al [5] also reviewed the psychiatric emergency room utilization of the Yale-New Haven Hospital, seventeen years after the original emergency study. They found that 20% of the psychiatric emergencies were under 21 years of age, but did not break down the ages further. Shafti et al [6] reported that nine hundred ninety four child psychiatric emergencies were seen over a five year period. However, they do not compare their population to the adult population. Thus, these studies confirm that child psychiatric emergencies do occur but indicate that they are infrequent compared to adult emergencies. It is unclear whether this is a result of the lack of the need or the lack of service provided.

As Visotsky [7] concluded in a progress report on the Task Force of the Joint Commission on Mental Health of Children, the mental health service system "tends to be oriented to the needs of professionals providing services rather than to the needs of the children being served."

DEMOGRAPHIC DATA

There have been four major studies in the literature reporting demographic data. Comparisons among the studies are difficult since they studied different patient populations, were in different types of clinical settings, used different administration routines to screen patients, and had varying visibility in the community. In addition, each study had its own purpose and therefore individual reporting criteria.

Study I Mattsson, Hawkins, Seese [3]. This study was done in a university teaching hospital where the child psychiatric emergency service was integrated with the pediatrics department. In this study the authors were interested in comparing child psychiatric emergencies to an intake control group from a child guidance clinic.

Study II Morrison & Smith [8]. This study was done in a large metropolitan community psychiatry clinic with a specific children's emergency service, which took referrals from Cincinnati General Hospital. This study focused on comparing child psychiatric emergencies from this clinic population with those of a private practice population.

Study III Shaffii, Whittinghill, Healy [6]. This study was the most comprehensive, with nine hundred ninety four cases over a five year period. It took place in a child guidance clinic strongly affiliated with a medical school.

Study IV Tarnow & Glenn [9]. This study took place in a child psychiatry clinic in a state university teaching hospital. This study had fewer patients; however, the focus of the study was on the process of emergencies and their resolution.

SYMPTOMS

Almost all children seen in emergency services present with more than one symptom; many had previous crises. Tables 1 and 2 show the symptoms precipitating referral to the emergency services in all studies. Adolescent females were the most common patients in this category. Mattson et al [3] found few children with reported suicidal thoughts in his clinic intake control group. The prevalence of suicidal behavior and ideation in adult psychiatric emergency populations was similar to the adolescent rates. Suicidal behavior in children below the age of 10 was rare. Acts of violence (including against the self) were an extremely common symptom in the emergency population (from 45%-75%). In acts of violence directed against others, males predominated in all age groups. Acts of violence were less common in the in-take control groups. An emergency room that deals with children and adolescents, therefore, must be prepared to handle this form of behavior, with appropriate security and medical backup.

Table 1. Child's Symptom or Behavior Precipitating Referral as Child Psychiatry Emergency (in Percentages)

Symptom Behavior	Clinic (n=100)	Private (n=50)
Suicide attempt or threat	34	12
School refusal (school phobia)	14 (7)	28 (12)
Assaultive behavior	5	22
Hysterical conversion (paralysis or seizures)	12	4
Acute anxiety (panic, night terrors)	9	6
Exhibitionism or voyeurism	3	8
Bizarre behavior (hallucinations, delusions, compulsions)	6	4
Delinquent behavior	2	6
Sexual Promiscuity	2	2
Fire setting	4	—
Drug intoxication	3	—
Incest	3	—
Threatened school expulsion	—	6
Acute grief (Parent's death)	1	2
Killed pets	2	—
Total	100	100
Destructive Behavior Towards Others	11	22
Violent Behavior	45	34

From: Morrison, G.C., and Smith, W.R.; Child Psychiatric Emergencies: A Comparison of Two Clinical Settings and Socio-Economic Groups. In *Emergencies in Child Psychiatry,* G.C. Morrison (ed.), Springfield, Illinois: Charles C. Thomas 1975, p. 110 (by permission of authors).

Table 2. Distribution of 994 Emergency Cases Among Children and Adolescents, 1973-1978 in Percentages*

| | AGE GROUPS | | | | | | | |
| | 1-6 Years | | 7-12 Years | | 13-18 Years | | | |
Presenting Problems	Boys (n=129)	Girls (n=74)	Boys (n=256)	Girls (n=140)	Boys (n=183)	Girls (n=212)	N	Total (percent)
Suicidal, self-destructive or marked depressive	7	12	21	12	18	39	340	34.2**
Harmful or destructive behavior to others	20	5	35	10	23	7	305	30.7**
Abuse or neglect	20	26	20	25	4	5	102	10.3
Phobic or extremely anxious behavior	9	9	32	22	18	19	102	10.3
Psychotic behavior	7	10	13	17	40	13	30	3.0
Runaways	0	0	25	10	20	45	40	4.0
Medical-psychiatric emergencies	12	9	12	12	12	43	33	3.3
Drug/alcohol abuse	9	9	9	0	36.5	36.5	11	1.1
Other	19	16	26	23	10	6	31	3.1

*Values within age/sex columns are expressed as percentages of problem category

**65% — acts of violence

From: Shafii, M., Whittinghill, R., and Healy, M.: Pediatric Psychiatric Model for Emergencies in Child Psychiatry: A Study of 994 Cases. Am J Psychiatry, Vol. 136, No. 12, December, 1979, pp. 1600, 1601 (by permission of authors).

School refusal (school phobia) was the second most common symptom in the Morrison study both in the clinic and private practice population [8]. In other studies, this was much less prevalent or not even mentioned. The author suspects the Morrison had special liaison to the school systems, whereas the other studies were more involved with the medical community. Emergency services more integrated into a medical facility received more patients with physical complaints.

Mattsson et al [3] concluded that 62% were referred because of changes in mood and behavior, such as depression often associated with suicidal behavior, somatic complaints, and fears. The remaining 38% of the referrals presented behavioral manifestations that were more outwardly directed in an impulsive, often unmanageable fashion, which indicated emotional conflicts acted out using assaultive, delinquent, or truant behavior, at times associated with suicidal gestures.

An acute conflict between the child and his parental figures was the most common event that appeared to have triggered the emergency symptom. The second most common precipitating event was the exacerbation of chronic physical illness or physical injury, including surgery. Following those were school problems; sexual conflicts related to masturbation, menstruation, or homosexual contacts; conflicts with loss of heterosexual love objects; pregnancy; grief reactions; intoxication; sexual molestation; and child abuse.

DIAGNOSIS

The study by Mattsson and colleagues [3] is the only child investigation which attempted to categorize patients by diagnosis (Table 3). They found adjustment reaction to be the most common diagnosis.

The most common diagnosis in adults was psychosis; conversely, in children this is relatively rare (9%) [16, 17, 18, 19].

AGE AND SEX OF CHILD

The majority of emergency patients were adolescent, whereas the majority of patients in a comparison intake group were in the pre-adolescent age group (55%). Morrison et al [8] and Mattsson et al [3] found girls were most commonly seen in the emergency population, being most heavily represented in the adolescent age range. Boys predominated in the 7-12 age group of the emergency referrals. However, boys (65%) were referred more often than girls (35%) in the intake group. Shafii et al [6] did not find this distribution but his population had more pre-adolescents, which usually include more males.

Table 3. Child Emergency Group: Initial Diagnosis

Diagnosis	Age Group				Totals
	0–11	*12–15*	*16–18*		
Organic Brain Syndrome	1	2	2	5	(3%)
Psychotic Reaction	0	9	7	16	(9%)
Depressive Reaction	0	7	11	18	
Anxiety Reaction	4	3	2	9	
Diss or Conv Reaction	2	5	5	12	45 (27%)
Phobic Reaction	3	1	0	4	
Obs-comp Reaction	2	0	0	2	
Personality Disorder	5	4	18	27	(16%)
Adjustment Reaction	12	27	38	77	(45%)
	29	59	82	170	(100%)

From: Mattsson, A., Hawkins, J.W., Seese, L.R.: Suicidal Behavior As Child Psychiatric Emergencies: Clinical Characteristics and Follow-Up Results. Reprinted from the Archives of General Psychiatry, 17:584-592. Copyright 1969, Am Med Assoc. p. 587, 1967 (by permission of authors).

SOURCE OF REFERRAL

Children do not come alone to emergency rooms. They usually are brought there by adults. In the author's own study only one child (age 16) in the sample of seventy referred herself for emergency service. (This child was living away from her family and had a child of her own). Mattsson et al [3] were the only other investigators to report the source of referral. Unfortunately, they combined the family and self referrals (Table 4). In adult psychiatric emergencies 26% were self-referred [10].

DURATION OF PRESENTING PROBLEM

A remarkable finding that has been recurrent in studies of child psychiatric emergencies has been the long duration of symptoms prior to the emergency visit. Smith & Morrison [11] found that two thirds of one hundred and fifty patients from a variety of socioeconomic backgrounds had a previous history of psychiatric symptomatology. Often these children experienced the problem for three to ten years prior to the emergency visit. This was as much as one third to one half of the children's lifetime. Mattsson et al [3] found that three quarters of emergencies had greater than one year history of emotional disturbance. Visotsky [7] found that in 50% of the cases the presenting problem was of more than a year's duration.

Table 4. Emergency and Intake Group: Source of Referral

	Age Group					
	0–11		12–15		16–18	
Referral Source	Emergencies (n=29)	Intakes (n=94)	Emergencies (n=59)	Intakes (n=54)	Emergencies (n=82)	Intakes (n=22)
Doctor	41%	41%	32%	50%	24%	37%
School	14%	29%	14%	24%	7%	18%
Agency	10%	11%	7%	13%	22%	18%
Family, Self	35%	19%	47%	13%	47%	27%
Total	100%	100%	100%	100%	100%	100%

From: Mattsson, A., Hawkins, J.W., Seese, L.R.: Suicidal Behavior As A Child Psychiatric Emergency: Clinical Characteristics and Follow-Up Results. Reprinted from the Archives of General Psychiatry, 20:100-109, Copyright 1969, American Medical Association, p. 102 (by permission of authors).

Smith & Morrison [11] studied this question and concluded there were four reasons for this long tolerance of psychopathology: (1) Unconscious parental participation or gratification in the child's behavior (the most common), (2) Conscious participation in the child's behavior (ego-syntonic), (3) An unrecognized psychotic or seriously inadequate parent, and (4) Severe and overwhelming deprivation.

LOSS ISSUES

In a majority of child emergencies the presenting problem was related to the recent and specific loss of a parent or caretaker. Morrison & Smith [8] report more than 60% of children seen in emergency consultation had lost a parent or near relative through illness, hospitalization, marital separation, or death within three weeks of the onset of the emergency behavior (See Table 5). If threatened separation or anniversary of the loss were added to this, four out of five of the children would be included. Tarnow and Glen [9]also showed that emergency cases had a higher incidence of loss within six months of the emergency (63%), as compared to a control intake group (17%). Loss of a parent within six months was also higher in the emergency (30%) versus the control group (11%).

The relationship of separation experiences to the precipitation of crises has been noted by many authors [12, 13, 14, 15, 16, 17]. The loss of a parent, however, is particulary devastating to a child [18]. The child not only physically loses a caretaker, but the remaining parent's coping capacity is overtaxed, which may result in a psychological loss of the survivor. In addition, children have not fully mastered their own ways of coping with loss. They depend on the adults around them to support them during this process.

Table 5. Crisis in the Family:
Emergency Consultation Occurred Within Three Weeks of the Event (in percentages)

Separations Experienced	Clinic (n=100)	Private (n=50)
Separations (significant object loss):	61	62
Serious illness of parent	22	24
Separation of parents (marital)	14	2
Death of a parent*	7	4
Separation from significant adult	7	16
Family move with school change	5	6
Breakup with boyfriend or girlfriend	4	4
Child's hospitalization (surgery or injury)	2	6
Threatened separations (anticipated or feared loss of family member, school, move, etc.):	18	24
Chronic Family Problems (with no known loss or change):	21	14
Total	100	100

*Includes four anniversary reactions

From: Morrison, G.C. and Smith, W.R.: Child Psychiatric Emergencies: A Comparison of Two Clinic Settings and Socio-Economic Groups, in Emergencies in Child Psychiatry G.C. Morrison, ed, Springfield, Illinois, Charles C. Thomas, 1975, p. 113

OUTCOME

It is extremely important for an emergency service to have access to a child and adolescent psychiatric in-patient service. Most children and their families who are referred to emergency services have a long-standing history of emotional disturbances. They already have been referred to many agencies. These families frequently do not follow through on these recommendations. Rather, an emergency must occur or be precipitated for them to receive help. Mattsson et al [3] note that only 58% of emergencies referred for follow-up out-patient treatment ever follow through. Therefore, the emergency room clinician must approach the family in a style which will engage them in the process of therapy.

Mattsson et al [3] found that 29% of their emergency population required referral to community agencies. Therefore, an emergency service should establish and maintain good working relationships with community agencies, schools, clinics and juvenile courts. Since 24% are referred to an out-patient psychiatric clinic, this should be readily available.

DISCUSSION

After reviewing the literature, the uniqueness of child psychiatric emergencies becomes clearer. A theoretical formulation which considers the special needs and problems of children will now be presented. Therapeutic implications based on the formulation will then follow. Three theoretical constructs need to be understood for treating crises with children: (1) child development, (2) family homeostasis and development, (3) coping behavior.

THEORETICAL FORMULATION OF CHILD EMERGENCIES

Children usually express their dysphoria through overt behavior rather than through verbal experience. This makes understanding of an emergency very difficult. One must look more deeply than the immediate behavioral problem responsible for the emergency referral. A comparison of adult and child emergencies shows that behavior problems are the primary reasons children are brought to these services, and someone other than the patient defines the emergency (crisis). In the author's study it was found that there was an immense difficulty in defining who was the person in crisis, the child (the identified patient), or the adults responsible for the child. Usually the adults responsible for the child were more affectively disturbed than the identified patient.

When someone other than the patient defines the emergency there is ambiguity about the true nature of the crisis. The identified patient may see the crisis as his parents' unwillingness to allow him privileges, whereas the parent may define the problem as the child's unwillingness to accept the limits they set. In child emergency work, one frequently sees the " real" problem as the parent's definition of the problem. A classic example of this problem in child psychiatry is that of a parent complaining that a child is hyperactive. Hyperactive is a relative term. A child who is hyperactive in one family may be normo-active in another. A two-year old whose mother is eight months pregnant may be defined by mother as hyperactive, not by the total amount of activity, but relative to her ability to tolerate the child's behavior.

Children are developing organisms whose ego mechanisms are in the process of being formed. Thus, the very mechanisms by which they cope with life's stresses are being developed. Parad & Caplan [16] define a crisis as a situation in which "a person cannot solve quickly a problem of basic importance by means of his normal range of commonly used problem-solving techniques, but must employ novel patterns of solution." Thus, one way of viewing child development is as a series of crises, each of which the child resolves by developing a new coping mechanism (novel pattern of solution). The first day of school is a life stress which requires a certain level of developmental competence and also demands new behaviors. Not every first day of school will precipitate a psychiatric emergency. However, stress will be felt by the child and his family. How the child in the context of his system manages the stress will determine whether the child reaches a higher, equivalent, or lower level of adjustment.

Children have different developmental needs and capabilities at different stages of their lives. Therefore, behavior that may be appropriate at one stage may be totally inappropriate at another stage. Adult crisis theorists have defined a crisis as a disruption of the steady state, and the resolution of crisis occurs when the patient returns to the same, higher or lower level of adaptation [16, 17]. Returning a child to a previous level of adaptation may not be desirable as a child's maturation needs to forge ahead, reaching higher levels of adaptation. Thus, restoring a steady state in children may be regressive.

All families seek homeostasis, adjusting to and synthesizing the conflicts and stresses of their members. Solomon [19] defines family homeostasis as "the result of the operation of mechanisms which define, delimit, and enforce the norms for the relationships which exist within the family. Once there is a stabilized homeostasis for a given family, the range of behavior for family members as they relate to one another is relatively circumscribed and well defined."

A child's coping style is a characteristic way of responding to stress. It is determined by the interaction of the child's constitutional makeup and his family's homeostasis. Since each developmental stage teaches a child new coping mechanisms, the family unconsciously will negotiate with the child which styles are tolerated. Thus, the child must fulfill the needs of the family system as well as maintain his or her own growth and development. A crisis can be seen as a situation in which there is a crucial change in the demands placed on the system, which prevents the homeostasis from providing for the basic needs of its members and requires the disruption of the old patterns of gratification. When a child is stressed, he will turn to his family for support and aid. This will put stress on the family system. If this stress is "poorly" or incompletely mastered by the parents, it will disturb the family's homeostasis. This will create a disequilibrium (crisis). The family may try to rework the problem and come up with a new solution or will reject the source of tension—the individual who most feels the stress or represents the stress. This rejection may be expressed by sending the child for psychiatric help.

Thus, this author agrees with Morrison & Smith's definition of a child psychiatric emergency "as that situation in which the significant adults around the child can no longer help him master his anxiety and can no longer provide temporary ego support and controls" [20]. All crises provide an apportunity for growth for both the child and the rest of his family.

CASE HISTORY

The following is a case example which provoked much of the thinking expressed in this theoretical formulation.

Kay was an eight year old girl brought to the emergency service by her parents with a chief complaint of stealing. Kay had been stealing from her family for about two years—since she started attending school full time. Kay usually stole food and hid the remains in her brother's drawers and closets. She would also take glasses, plates, liquor, etc and after using them hide them in the backyard or in her brother's room. Kay also had stolen money from her parents and used it to buy candy, chewing tobacco, etc.—always leaving the remains in clear view.

In an attempt to deal with the problem themselves, the parents began to lock Kay in her room at night and put a lock on their bedroom door. However, Kay continued to steal and they had to watch her every move. Someone would be with her at every moment while at home.

A couple of weeks before we were contacted Kay stole some of her mother's Darvon pills. She also stole her father's rifle and assembled it. The parents then increased their vigilance, and when they left the home they would tie Kay to her seventeen year old cousin with a rope.

These events led to the family's first contact with the clinic. They stated that they did not need crisis therapy as yet and were put on the waiting list for evaluation. The intake secretary reported that mother seemed to have almost no affect.

About three weeks later, the family called back in crisis, noting that things had gotten much worse. Kay had started to steal from outside the family. She got a ride from another mother to the 7-11 and took some pop, leaving the money on the display counter. Kay had also stolen a bee bee gun from a neighbor and lied to her parents about where she got it. Her parents went from one neighbor to another at Kay's direction until most of the neighborhood knew she had a problem with stealing. Her mother was particularly embarrassed by this.

Kay's mother talked to her until late that night to find out why she was stealing. Kay finally confided that stealing makes her "happy, glad, happy inside." This upset her parents considerably, since they felt they had given Kay "everything." The mother was conflicted about tying Kay to her cousin, but didn't know what else to do. At the time of the second phone call to the clinic, the mother noted that she was on the verge of a nervous breakdown and desperately wanted some help with her daughter.

Kay was adopted at about five months of age. Her mother felt that she was still somewhat attached to her first foster mother, who was a gray-haired lady. As an infant, Kay could only be comforted by her paternal grandmother, who supposedly resembled the foster mother. Her mother noted that Kay cried from the time she came to live with them until she went to school full-time.

The parents were married for twenty years. They had another child of thirteen who was also adopted, before the age of one month. The mother reported no problems with his care.

In late December of 1975 the mother's seventeen-year-old niece came to live with the family. The circumstances of this were not known at the time of contact.

Assesment of Crisis

Mother was the person in distress in the family. Here was a family that complained of behavior that had been going on for two years. The precipitant for first contacting our clinic was the increase in stealing life-threatening items (i.e., Darvon and rifle), and having two adolescents in the family, one who was on the verge of emancipation. It is interesting how the oldest child (17-year-old niece) became literally tied to the youngest member of the family.

We can begin to see a developing theme of separation-individuation. The precipitant of the crisis call however was Kay's sudden stealing from outside the family and her confession that the stealing was a result of an internal feeling—needing to steal to make herself feel happy. Thus, we saw a major stress on the homeostasis of the family—their old definition of the problem, Kay's stealing, which was an externalization, was confronted by the symptom carrier of the family and noted to be symbolic of internal feeling. Before Kay stole from outside, the problem was circumscribed within the family, not evident to the world at large.

Two rules of the family were being challenged:
1. That problems be externalized and solutions acted out
2. That problems be played out only within the family sphere.

We felt mother was most distressed by Kay's stealing from outside the family because it made her question her own adequacy as a woman and mother. This hypothesis was based on the fact that mother came from an Italian-Catholic background and had only two adopted children.

THERAPEUTIC IMPLICATIONS

Since child psychiatric emergencies are now understood as systems crises, all significant family members should be interviewed together as close to the crisis as possible. People in crisis often experience confusion and forget important resources. At times the clinician will need to interview individuals or sub-groups of the family.

The early family sessions should focus on the "here and now", attempting to define the problem as clearly as possible. Each member of the family should be urged to express his or her view of the problem, since the truth is greater than the sum of the parts. The clinician should attempt to help the family clarify significant factors which provoked the emergency behavior (see Figure 1 for an outline for evaluation of family in crisis).

Figure I   Outline for Evaluation of Family in Crisis*

I.   Each family member's view of the crisis (what's wrong, who is involved, what should be done).

II. Why did they call just when they did? (historical account of precipitant to calling)

III. History of attempted solutions.
   A.   How has the family tried to solve this crisis? (exactly what have they tried and why didn't it work)
   B.   What past issues are triggered by the crisis and how were these situations dealt with?
   C.   What is the family's past experience with seeking outside help?

IV. Therapist's assessment of the crisis.
   A.   What is the crisis? (temporary or permanent, internal or external)
   B.   Who is expressing it and who is excluded?
   C.   What underlying issues does the crisis symbolize for the family? (unresolved developmental issue, past trauma revived, etc.)
   D.   What are the precipitating stresses? (financial, job or school, loss of support of family or social system)

V.   Who is in the system and how are they involved in the crisis?
   A.   Evaluate the different levels of the system and how they may support or exacerbate the crisis.
   B.   Where are the cut offs?
   C.   How does the system function when not under stress?
   D.   What are their rules and who plays what role?
   E.   How have they reacted to past stresses?
   F.   Levels of the system.
      1.   Nuclear family
      2.   Extended family
      3.   Interface with other systems (schools, church, friends, social agencies, etc.)

VI. Family's goals and expectations from seeking help now.

VII. Therapist's evaluation of:
   A.   Family's strengths and weaknesses, their potential for positive crisis resolution. Can they keep things open enough to work toward change without being overwhelmed? Who is motivated for what and where are the family resistances?
   B.   Who needs to be involved in the crisis resolution? Should extended family be mobilized or informed? Do outside resources need to be brought in?
   C.   Problems of intervention
      1.   To what extent does family need outsider to mobilize supports and to what extent should therapist help family to mobilize support for themselves?
      2.   What are the hazards for therapist? (discouragement, over-responsibility, under-responsibility, side taking, etc.)
      3.   What resources will therapist need in order to intervene effectively? (support of colleagues, aid of consultant, aid of other institutional supports, time to think and gain perspective)
   D.   Game plan
      1.   Information to get
      2.   Approaches to elicit crisis
      3.   Hypothesized resistances
      4.   Techniques

*Tarnow, J., Gutstein, S., "Intervention with Children, Adolescents, and Their Families in Situational and Developmental Crisis." Presented at the American Orthopsychiatric Association for the 56th Annual Meeting, 1979.

An assessment of the family's ability to protect their child and give adequate ego support and external control should be made early in the evaluation. Protection of the patient's biologic integrity and life should be the highest priority. Therefore, access to a child and adolescent psychiatric inpatient service is imperative. If none is available, adolescents can sometimes be admitted to an adult unit in emergency situations. However, children under the age of thirteen are best admitted by a psychiatrist to a cooperating pediatric medical unit.

If none of these options is available, an emergency psychiatric service is futile. The service must have appropriate resources and backup to allow its professionals to feel comfortable enough to deal with the difficult patients and families referred.

Maximizing the potential for the patient's continued growth and development is the second priority. This may necessitate inviting a teacher, welfare worker, visiting nurse, family physician, attorney, probation officer, or clergymen to sessions. Inviting representatives of the child and family social network can be an extremely powerful intervention. These people participate with the family in developing a plan to resolve the crisis or to continue to foster the child's ongoing development. These sessions should be goal oriented. Good working relationships with community agencies, schools, clinics and juvenile courts is extremely important.

As noted in the data section, children and their families who are referred to emergency services usually have a long-standing history of emotional disturbances and frequently do not follow through on recommendations. Therefore, every attempt should be made to utilize the sense of urgency, disorganization, and regression to help the family seek psychotherapy as a "novel solution" to their crisis.

The clinician should use the sense of crisis to develop an alliance. The family must feel that they have been heard. The greater the similarity between the patient's request and the patient's perception of the physician's goal, the more likely it is that the emergency psychiatric patient will follow through on recommendations. In child and adolescent emergencies the patient is the family.

Wherever possible, the emergency room clinician should make plans to follow the patients until they are engaged with another therapist. Some families will benefit greatly from time-limited crisis intervention with the emergency clinician. Referral to another service is very difficult for these families. It can be very helpful to meet the family with the new referral resource for their first appointment. This style of intervention requires an emergency service which is flexible, especially in its schedules.

An especially good relationship should be established with a child psychiatric clinic. It is useful for the workers in an emergency service also to work in an out-patient clinic. This maximizes continuity of care and minimizes patients being lost in the "cracks."

Some of the families seen by emergency services have recurring crises. They cannot tolerate long term therapy and ignore the recommendations for continued treatment. However, when allowed to, these families are willing to return P.R.N., when future crises occur. These families can benefit from brief intensive contacts during crises over several years. The service must be flexible and must provide continuity for these difficult patients. This author has found that, given this opportunity, families can utilize this style and will return to the service for help earlier in each successive crisis.

Follow-up phone calls are also helpful to these chaotic families. They demonstrate interest, provide an object constancy, encourage follow up, and give the families an opportunity to report problems as they develop before a crisis occurs.

The staff of a child emergency service should have training in both family and child diagnosis and treatment. They sould have a good understanding of crisis therapy. The staff must be tolerant toward difficult families and willing to develop interventions appropriate to their special needs. The service should also be set up to allow flexibility in schedules, as well as mobility to make community visits.

A child psychiatrist and social worker are vital to an emergency service. Psychologists are extremely helpful. The availability of educational specialists, psychiatric nurses, and medical backup provide important resources as well.

REFERENCES

1. Errera P, Schwartz M: Psychiatric care in a general hospital emergency room. Arch Gen Psychiatry 9:113-121, 1963
2. Ungerleider JT: The psychiatric emergency analysis of six months experience of a university hospital's consultation service. Arch Gen Psychiatry 3:593-601, 1960
3. Mattsson A, Hawkins JW, Seese, LR: Child psychiatric emergencies: clinical characteristics and follow-up results. Arch Gen Psychiatry 17:584-592, 1967
4. Schowalter JE, Solnit AJ: Child psychiatry consultation in a general hospital emergency room, J Amer Acad Child Psychiatry 5:534-551, 1966
5. Bristol J, Giller E, Docherty J: Trends in emergency psychiatry in the last two decades. Am J Psychiatry 138:623-628, 1981
6. Shafii M, Whittinghill R, Healy M: Pediatric psychiatric model for emergencies in child psychiatry: a study of 994 cases. Am J Psychiatry 136:1600-1601, 1979
7. Visotsky, HM: The Joint Commission on Mental Health of Children: progress report, Psychiatric Ann 5:11-20, 1975
8. Morrison, GC, Smith, WR: A comparison of two clinic settings and socioeconomic groups, in Emergencies in Child Psychiatry. Edited by Morrison GC. Springfield, Charles C. Thomas, 1975
9. Tarnow J, Clifford G: The uniqueness of children's emergencies. unpublished data, 1977
10. Trier T, Levy RJ: Emergent, urgent & elective admissions. Arch Gen Psychiatry 21:423-429, 1969
11. Smith WR, Morrison GC: Family tolerance for chronic severe, neurotic, or deviant behavior in children referred for child psychiatry emergency consultation, in Emergencies in Child Psychiatry. Edited by Morrison GC. Springfield, Charles, C. Thomas, 1975

12. Caplan G: Prevention of Mental Disorders in Children. New York, Basic Books, 1961
13. Levi LD, Fales, CH, Stein, M, et al: Separation and attempted suicide. Arch Gen Psychiatry 15:158-164, 1966
14. Lindemann, E: Symptomatology and management of acute grief, in Crisis Intervention: Selected Readings. Edited by Parad, HJ. New York, Family Service Association, 1965
15. Hill R: Families Under Stress. New York, Harper Brothers, 1949
16. Parad HJ, & Caplan G: A framework for studying families in crisis, in Crisis Intervention: Selected Readings. Edited by Parad HJ. New York, Family Service Association, 1965
17. Rapoport R: The state of crisis: some theoretical consideration, in Crisis Intervention: Selected Readings. Edited by Parad HJ. New York Family Service Association, 1965
18. Furman, E: A Child's Parent Dies: Studies in Childhood Bereavement. New Haven, Yale University Press, 1974
19. Solomon, MA: Typologies of family homeostasis: implications for diagnosis and treatment. Family Therapy, 1:9-18, 1974, p. 9
20. Morrison, GC, Smith, WR: Emergencies in child psychiatry: a definition, in Emergencies in Child Psychiatry. Edited by Morrison GC. Springfield, Charles C. Thomas, 1975, p. 17

14

Psychiatric Emergencies of Older Persons

CHARLES M. GAITZ

Although chronological age cannot be used to differentiate psychiatric emergencies, knowledge about aging and the aged does give practitioners in general, and psychiatrists in particular, the basis for applying special principles and approaches. We know, for example, that psychotropic drugs can be helpful in treating patients with affective disorders and psychoses. We also know that when these medications are given to old people the dosage has to be monitored closely. Consequently, it seems relevant to call attention to some of the characteristics of old people and to the nuances and modifications in treatment that may be applied to achieve reasonable therapeutic goals for elderly persons, especially those in crisis.

PSYCHIATRIC EMERGENCIES AND CRISES

Experienced clinicians know that elderly persons have psychiatric emergencies and experience crises, yet only one of three recently published monographs on psychiatric emergencies [1,2,3] refers to aging, the aged, or geriatrics in its index. One should not be too critical, because even the most recent and comprehensive handbook on geriatric psychiatry does not have any references to emergencies or crises [4]. Whether by intent or oversight, these omissions reflect attitudes toward and about the aged. Geriatric psychiatrists have been concerned more with issues of long-term care than emergency care, and psychiatrists concerned with emergencies have been occupied with issues that take precedence over the chronological age of their patients. Intellectually, and upon reflection, we all agree that certain conditions manifested by elderly persons constitute emergencies, but the focus of our attention has been on features other than age-related characteristics of patients in crisis.

This may be a hidden blessing. Psychiatrists who evaluate emergency situations probably share the prevailing attitude that therapy for old people is not effective or beneficial, and is certainly time-consuming. The consequence of this is a less than enthusiastic and aggressive approach to treatment. If, on the other hand, physicians pay more attention to the patient's condition than to stereotypes of age, the treatment plan will be more optimistic and ambitious. The ideal approach is to consider the emergency patient's chronological age without using it as a contraindication for treatment.

Soreff [1] has written that "the potential for a psychiatric emergency exists when a change in a person caused by intrapsychic, interpersonal, or biologic alterations can no longer be tolerated by that person or by significant others in the environment," and that "the potential emergency becomes an actual emergency when either the person or the significant others seek immediate assistance." Alvin Goldfarb [5] used similar terms to describe a crisis. "It is not always easy to define who the patient is, or whose suffering or complaint is to be dealt with as primary," Goldfarb wrote. "Even when there is no obvious immediate danger to the person or those around him, the patient, as viewed by himself or his concerned family, friends, or neighbors, may appear to have lost control of himself as an effective, adaptive person. He can no longer master the routine physical, psychological, and emotional challenges of everyday life." These broad definitions are shared by Slaby et al. [2], who preface their *Handbook of Psychiatric Emergencies* saying, "A psychiatric emergency is defined by an individual, or by his family or community, as an event requiring immediate attention for a psychiatric or psychosocial problem." We are fortunate to have such broad definitions; strict and probably artificial criteria of what does or does not constitute an emergency or a crisis create more problems than solutions.

SOME CHARACTERISTICS ASSOCIATED WITH AGING

Certain characteristics associated with aging have implications for treatment. As persons age, they are likely to become increasingly dependent on others or, to state it in another way, to become less self-reliant and resilient.

Elderly persons are likely to have a multiplicity of physical health, psychological, and social problems. Ideally, every person presenting with a psychiatric emergency should have a comprehensive evaluation, but the benefit increases dramatically when the patient is old. Evaluating potential interaction of factors before undertaking treatment is critical. Various physical disorders may appear to be symptoms of a psychiatric illness and, in turn, some social factors, especially isolation, may influence symptom formation and mimic dementia. A patient's mood and behavior associated with chronic physical illness may be difficult to differentiate from primary depression. Inadequate housing may be a factor in recurrent respiratory infections. Complaints of physical abuse may or may not represent paranoid ideation. The high risk of physical assault may be more important than disengagement or psychopathologic social withdrawal to explain why an elderly person does not leave his home. Physical impairments may be the reason for an aged patient's not keeping an appointment; poverty may have much to do with a person's noncompliance with a diet and the resulting metabolic imbalance and nutritional deficiencies. One could go on and on with examples of the interaction of physical health with psychological and social factors that affect the well-being of elderly persons.

Recognizing the interaction of elderly persons with the "significant others" in their lives is equally important. A spouse, other relatives, family surrogates, and the resources we now label informal and formal support systems can be of immeasurable benefit to needy elderly persons. That they must be not only available but also willing cannot be overemphasized; one cannot assume that availability and capability are the same. An elderly parent, for example, could be cared for at home by his daughter if she did not work full-time or were not otherwise fully occupied by her children and husband. An elderly recluse might survive in what others consider substandard conditions until these become a risk to others. An old alcoholic living alone might be exercising his rights, but when he grows careless and there is the possibility that he might set fire to his apartment, intervention may be necessary. An elderly widow might choose to share her meager social security income with a young man who has been attentive, but when her children discover that she has not paid the rent or has no money left for food, they may declare the situation an emergency. The attempt to maintain self-esteem and independence may cause some elderly persons to drive a car well past the time when their eyesight and reflexes make this safe. An aged wife may be able to provide adequate care for her handicapped husband until she becomes ill herself.

These are but a few examples of situations in which crises arise. An appeal for help may come from an individual, the family, friends, neighbors and, in other instances, social and legal agencies. When given the opportunity, elderly persons often acknowledge that they face a crisis. They may be unable to seek help directly; the process can be eased by compassionate and empathic caregivers. In the future we may recognize cohort differences between the generation we consider aged in 1984 and later generations, but those in the present generation of elderly persons are more likely to use somatic complaints to communicate their need for help than to make straightforward statements about loneliness, hopelessness, and helplessness. Reluctant to admit weakness and decline, elderly people in our society minimize the consequences of changes associated with retirement and role reversal, and the cumulative effects of losses by death of close relatives and friends. Some patients are fortunate to have therapists who can help them explore the effects of stresses peculiar to the late stages of life. Sharing their inner feelings without fear or regret can help many elderly people when these stresses precipitate a crisis.

Who really is the patient and who the complainant, who is suffering most, and whose rights should be given first attention are questions that arise quite often when one deals with older persons. The therapists' answers are value judgments, influenced by their culture and personal experiences.

A corollary of the points made about elderly persons and their significant others is that these relationships have important implications for treatment. Treatment may be direct or indirect. Giving some attention to the needs of a spouse or child may enable them to continue caring for an elderly person. Just as enabling a young mother to have some time away from her young child helps both mother and child, we can also help middle-aged and older caregivers by giving them some relief. This may come in the form of day care or hiring a housekeeper, or even the temporary institutional placement we call ''respite'' care. We can help also by not putting undue responsibility or pressure on relatives, and we must be reasonable in our expectations of social agencies. Balancing capability with willingness is essential, and the two are not always the same.

Elderly persons can and should be included in treatment planning. Information from collateral informants and inclusion of others in the treatment plan, however, provide the basis for effective intervention in a crisis and sometimes avoid the need for long-term care.

PATIENT EVALUATION

Older people require a comprehensive evaluation in crisis as well as nonemergency situations. The objective is to determine the nature and cause of various impairments, with an emphasis on uncovering conditions that are correctable. The evaluation process not only clarifies what is wrong but reveals the patient's inner resources and the help potentially available from family and others. Age-related phenomena cannot be ignored but chronological age per se is rarely a factor that determines or severely limits therapeutic possibilities.

Little purpose would be served here by a long list of conditions that might explain behavioral disorders or cognitive impairment. The handbooks on psychiatric emergencies [1,2,3] describe many conditions that can be treated effectively. When a careful evaluation leads to the conclusion that little remedial treatment is available, therapists still must consider management options they would ignore if they believed that the goal of treatment is cure. Helping patients and families attain a reasonable level of functioning, without unreasonable demands and stresses, is the essence of evaluation-treatment planning for elderly persons. The manifestations of a disorder may be medical, psychological, or social, and these three broad fields should be explored. The patient may present with what appears to be a clear-cut psychiatric disorder, but spending a few minutes in a symptom review and obtaining a past medical history may be very helpful. Similarly, the possibility of physical or mental illness cannot be ignored when one deals with what appears to be only a social problem.

Sometimes treatment must be started before a thorough evaluation can be done. A patient who presents with behavioral changes has to be treated medically or surgically for such conditions as an infection, subdural hematoma, stroke, coronary thrombosis, or electrolyte imbalance before one worries too much about the patient's housing, income, marital status, and family relationships that might have contributed to onset of illness and may influence the outcome of treatment. A decision to hospitalize a psychotic elderly person found wandering in the streets may be made before one knows all the details about his physical condition and family relationships. Obviously then, therapists will establish a priority for problems that need attention, but the value of a comprehensive diagnostic approach designed for the individual patient is quite clear to those of us who have worked with elderly persons. Aged persons are not a homogeneous group likely to respond to plans based on unsubstantiated concepts one may have about elderly persons as a group. Temporary hospitalization may be reasonable in some crisis situations, but in other cases community support may enable a family member to provide services at home while other steps are taken to resolve the problems. Evaluation has to precede decisions about treatment. Ensuring adequate nutrition and providing transportation are often a challenge, and solutions that work for some people, in some settings, may not help others. The solution will depend on the mental and physical status of the elderly person, the availability of transportation facilities, and whether or not someone can shop and prepare food, if and when money is available.

Elderly persons in crisis situations may need a variety of caregivers: a minister for spiritual guidance, a physician and nurse for health care, a psychiatrist for resolution of emotional conflicts, a social worker for living arrangements. Even within one professional discipline the delivery of care gets complicated, and elderly persons, with their multiplicity of problems, often cannot go to a social agency for one type of assistance, to several clinics or specialists for medical care, and to still other agencies for other services. Fragmentation of diagnostic and service elements is typical of most communities. Disagreements surface about who is in charge, who is responsible legally or morally to intervene, and which problems are to be given priority. A case manager or, perhaps, a responsible family member has to coordinate the caregivers' efforts. Communication among physicians, for example, is essential if the damaging effects of polypharmacy are to be avoided. One should not expect an elderly person to know the potential danger of drug interactions and to keep several physicians informed about what the others are doing and prescribing. Understandably, the patient thinks of treatment for high blood pressure with a diuretic as unrelated to treatment of an affective disorder with lithium, but physicians know the potential risks and must know all the medications being prescribed.

ATTITUDES OF CARE-GIVERS

Value judgments are made in the evaluation and treatment of all patients. Physicians, culturally bound to the belief that disability, dependence, and death are associated with aging and the aged, may well be cynical about therapeutic intervention [5]. Stereotyped views of the aged will lead psychiatrists and other care-givers into selecting patients and therapeutic interventions that may preclude elderly persons. The likelihood that chronic disease and disability are common features of elderly patients is overemphasized in evaluating prognosis. Conceivably, then, an awareness of these attitudes becomes even more important in emergency situations in which caregivers are pressed to make hasty decisions.

On reflection, psychiatrists and other care-givers will see that working with older people can be quite rewarding. Mature physicians will accept responsibility for what is possible and to recognize limitations, of which age rarely is the single differentiating or determining factor. Many elderly persons have a remarkable capacity to adapt and to cope: they have survived years of stress and they respond to minimal supportive efforts. Their requirements for help are not inevitably overwhelming. Yet, it is only from personal experience with aged patients and possibly with aged persons in their own families that physicians come to accept the fact that advanced age does not preclude aggressive therapeutic intervention.

Physicians must guard against condescension, an attitude that may be communicated in many ways. Sometimes we assume that an elderly person is not competent enough to participate in the evaluation and development of the treatment plan. The importance of obtaining information from an informant sometimes leads to excluding the patient. Surprising as it may be to many caregivers, elderly persons are usually quite capable of giving a history and discussing the treatment objectives. Simply interviewing an elderly patient *before* talking with informants goes a long way toward establishing a therapeutic cooperative relationship.

An elderly person's multiplicity of problems and complaints makes it desirable that services be provided by a multidisciplinary team. Although each member of the team has to respect and acknowledge the contributions of colleagues, it is often the psychiatrist who is best qualified to provide comprehensive care. In this age of specialization, we are inclined to constrict our interests and responsibilities, but we are the ones best trained to recognize the interaction of social, medical, and psychological factors. While respecting the ability of social workers to solve certain problems, psychiatrists can explain the medical and psychological needs of elderly persons who also require help with housing and transportation. In treating elderly persons, in crisis or not, the psychiatrist's unique contribution is to coordinate and correlate the efforts of others.

TREATMENT

Although we stress here the relative unimportance of age, there are instances (prescription of medications is one) in which the age of the patient should alert the psychiatrist to certain possibilities. The older person is likely to be taking a number of drugs whose cumulative effect may be devastating. A detailed history of medications a patient has taken — or failed to take — may be all that is necessary to understand an otherwise puzzling delirium or abnormality manifested by disturbed and disturbing patients. Medications may be effective regardless of the patient's age, but physicians are advised to use small dosages and to increase them slowly for elderly persons. Sometimes this caveat results in inadequate treatment if one assumes, before a medication is given a reasonable trial, that it is ineffective. The knowledge that physiological changes associated with aging may be the basis for differences in drug metabolism and tolerance should not preclude the use of medications. The patient's overall situation, his or her ability to follow instructions, the caregiver's ability to supervise, and similar factors influence decisions about giving a medication in one form or another and whether or not it is safe to give a drug that is efficacious but requires adherence to a rigid regimen.

TYPICAL GERIATRIC PSYCHIATRIC EMERGENCIES

The following case histories illustrate some emergencies and crises that have come to the attention of the geriatric service of the Texas Research Institute of Mental Sciences. TRIMS serves patients of all ages, and its geriatric outpatient clinic is coupled with a senior information and outreach service. In addition, elderly persons are treated in a small inpatient service (49 beds) for adults of all ages.

Obviously no one history can be given in sufficient detail to answer all questions. These cases highlight some problems that constitute emergencies and show aspects that may or may not be related to chronological age. Not selected randomly — many of our patients are older than the ones described here — the case histories do represent psychiatric problems of the "young old" which, at least to some extent, differ from those presented by persons 75 years old and older. The histories include some follow-up, because the handling of an immediate crisis is only part of the picture. Generally, many crises can be treated without hospitalization, but we have found also that short-term hospitalization enables us to conduct a thorough evaluation and to mobilize resources, while protecting the patient who is alone or who has only limited family and social supports.

CASE HISTORY #1

L.M., a 72-year-old widow, was seen as an emergency case by the TRIMS geriatric outpatient clinic after being referred by a nursing home. She had been screaming periodically for two months, disturbed other residents, and demanded much attention from the staff. She was disoriented and agitated, showing a poor memory. She had pulled out her in-dwelling Foley catheter several times, had gotten out of vest restraints and fallen, and needed constant supervision because of her destructive behavior.

Mrs. M. could not be seen immediately at TRIMS and instead was taken to a general hospital emergency room where she remained unattended for eight hours. Her family then took her to another hospital, where the examining physician decided there was no physical reason to hospitalize her, and sent her back to the nursing home. She was eventually seen at TRIMS, and it was learned that in spite of taking various medications, including amitriptyline, trihexyphenidyl, hydroxyzine pamoate, thioridazine, haloperidol, and chloral hydrate, her behavior had not improved. She took other medications for the physical conditions previously mentioned and there seemed to be no evidence of drug interaction. She had been treated for a stroke two years earlier, and also for arteriosclerotic heart disease, angina pectoris, high blood pressure, arthritis, and diverticulitis of the colon. She had a history of diabetes but was not being treated for this at the time she was seen in the clinic.

A psychiatrist at the TRIMS outpatient clinic concluded that Mrs. M. was getting lost in the health-care-system shuffle, and was suffering from dementia and severe agitation. He prescribed haloperidol in a dosage to be titrated according to her needs. Returning to the clinic a few days later, she was calm, friendly, pleasant, and communicating well, but she still had evidence of dementia. Arrangements had been made for a daughter to stay with Mrs. M., and her behavior improved and she was able to feed herself. The immediate crisis had passed, but the daughter was considering moving Mrs. M. to another nursing home. The daughter failed to call our clinic during at least a two-month interval; about four months after the patient's initial evaluation at TRIMS, we called the daughter and learned that Mrs. M. had been transferred to another nursing home. There was little change in her behavior; she still screamed at times but the nursing home staff was not upset. Her daughter had had other problems which had taken precedence over reporting her mother's progress to TRIMS.

Comment

This case illustrates the breakdown of a nursing home's efforts to manage a patient with senile agitation; her family had been given an ultimatum to take Mrs. M. out of the nursing home. As more or less a last resort, psychiatric consultation was requested. The emergency room staff of one general hospital ignored Mrs. M. and in another they failed to take into account the seriousness of psychological problems. When this patient was finally evaluated at TRIMS, there was enough discussion with her family and nursing home personnel to establish a reasonable plan of treatment; the nursing home staff was reassured and probably more supportive, knowing that help was available if the problems arose again. A guarantee of follow-up care provided both the family and nursing home personnel much support, and the "emergency" aspect tended to evaporate once continuity of follow-up was assured. In spite of this, however, the daughter decided to move her mother to another nursing home and did not return to TRIMS for services that had been offered.

CASE HISTORY #2

B.D. is a 65-year old retired carpenter referred to the TRIMS outpatient clinic after his wife had applied for his commitment to a mental institution. This had been recommended by a neighborhood justice center and a community mental health center after a hearing regarding a complaint of aggravated assault against the patient's wife. Mr. D. had a history of extreme jealousy for 40 years, a pattern he had apparently learned from his parents. He had retired two years ago because he could not run his cabinetmaking business any longer, especially money management and job estimates. His wife went to work because of financial need; his father died at about the same time, and since then he had beome even more paranoid about his wife's activities. Anger was also directed toward his children, grandchildren, and mother-in-law, and there were several incidents of aggression against his daughter.

Mr. D. and his wife had been married 40 years and had five children; a divorced daughter and 17-year-old grandson were living with them. Mr. D. had constantly accused his wife of not caring and not being affectionate, but when he was interviewed at the clinic he denied any difficulties, claiming no memory of hitting his wife and laughing when he was asked about an earlier episode in which he had stomped his daughter's foot, causing three fractures. His recent and remote memory were impaired. He had not considered divorce because his wife was a good woman even though she had "refused sex for two years." His family physician had prescribed thioridazine, but Mr. D. stopped taking it after a short time. When his wife took an aspirin tablet he would accuse her of taking birth control pills. When she was late he would scream at her about infidelities, and he had deflated the tires on her car so that she could not go to work. He felt neglected and wanted her "to be more loving and caring." Though his wife claimed to hate him, she wanted to keep Mr. D. at home and not place him in a nursing home. The application for commitment had been dropped.

Born in a northern state, Mr. D. had two brothers and three sisters. His parents were described as jealous and inclined to anger. His father spent the late years of his life in a nursing home because he had "become so mean" toward his grandchildren.

Mr. D. was admitted to the TRIMS inpatient service for further evaluation the same day he was examined in the clinic. An aggravation of paranoid tendencies and assaultive behavior had occurred during the two years of Mr. D.'s retirement, and his memory had declined. Physical evaluation confirmed pulmonary emphysema; he had bilateral cataracts; the electroencephalogram was within normal limits. A diagnosis of organic brain syndrome was made, and tests for possible remediable conditions were done but none found.

After about six weeks of hospitalization, Mr. D. was discharged. Since then, he and his wife had been seen at approximately one-month intervals. She continued having problems coping with her role as a working wife and trying to keep the family together. Mr. D. continued having problems controlling his anger, and he was taking thioridazine, 25 mg three times a day. The couple sometimes missed appointments. It was unclear whether he was actually taking his medication as prescribed. Three months after discharge, his wife called to say that Mr. D. was threatening, trying to get access to a gun, and she didn't know what to do. When Mr. D. was seen, he could not understand why people were so concerned about him and claimed not to remember why he had been hospitalized. Evidence of memory and other cognitive impairments were noted but his wife refused to take any steps, such as following up on a recommendation that she obtain a power of attorney. Six or seven months after discharge, Mr. D. was reported to be less suspicious and more easily managed. By then he was taking 100mg of thioridazine at bedtime, and he was rarely upset, aggressive, or combative. Nine months after discharge, his wife reported that Mr. D. had started soiling himself, his memory seemed to be worse, and he would occasionally threaten. When seen ten months after his discharge from the hospital, he was said still to be aggressive, had pushed his wife off a chair, and his memory impairment was quite severe.

Comment

This case illustrates the problems of a spouse who is working and also trying to maintain home management of a demented person as long as possible. Long-term marital problems were aggravated by Mr. D.'s dementia. His wife's dependence and ambivalence about separation were clear also. The therapist had to work with a patient whose mental decline was obvious and with a spouse who was reluctant to be assertive. Personality traits had become even more accentuated when Mr. D. had to adapt to such changes as retirement. Mrs. D., after 40 years of marriage, was more reluctant to place her husband in an institution than perhaps would be a younger woman who still had other responsibilities. The progression of changes such as incontinence associated with organic mental disorder may finally provide an acceptable reason for separation, more so than paranoid ideation or assaultive behavior. Therapists must have reasonable goals in working with such couples — a younger couple may be more likely to work through emotional conflicts than is an elderly couple with an increasingly demented spouse; nevertheless, offering the healthier spouse an opportunity to explore feelings and attitudes may be beneficial.

CASE HISTORY #3

G.D. is a 69-year-old married male who was seen in the geriatric outpatient clinic because he had become severely depressed, cried often, and was socially withdrawn. He was having insomnia, awakening early in the morning; his appetite was poor, and he felt hopeless and apathetic. He often thought it would be good if he were dead, but there was no definite suicidal ideation. He attributed his depression to worry about his 20-year-old retarded son. Mr. D. and his wife had found it increasingly difficult to care for the son at home but were having conflicts about placing him in an institution. Mr. D. had retired some five years earlier from a job as a machinist, then worked part-time as a maintenance worker at his church, but had stopped working completely a year earlier. He continued playing golf twice a week until six or seven months before he was first examined. He had given it up and didn't feel like doing much of anything.

On examination, Mr. D. was noted to look younger than his stated age but was quite depressed and was found to have no evidence of organic mental disorder or a thought disorder.

He had been married 40 years and had eight children, all of whom lived in Houston and were quite supportive. The youngest child, now 20, can do little more than feed himself. Mr. D.'s family physician had treated him with tranquilizers and antidepressants but his depression had not been relieved, and it had reached an intensity that required psychiatric intervention.

Following initial evaluation, and clarifying that Mr. D. had no serious physical health problems, a decision was made to undertake a combined psychotherapeutic and pharmacotherapeutic approach. Sometimes Mr. D. was seen individually and sometimes he and his wife were seen together. They were able to agree on respite care and also arranged for the son to attend a day school for retarded persons. When the son would no longer be eligible for day care because of his age, Mr. and Mrs. D. had agreed reluctantly to accept institutionalization for their son because they found it harder and harder to care for him. This chronic stress became more critical as they grew older. Mr. D. was aware that his own attitudes were related to having spent several years in an orphanage as a young child, and he recalled feeling abandoned and unloved because his widowed mother had placed him in an orphanage while keeping some of the other children at home. Mr. and Mrs. D. recognized that they displaced anger toward their son onto each other since nothing would be accomplished in getting angry with the son. The couple had never been able to communicate adequately and to empathize with each other. Mrs. D. had wanted to keep her son at home because she feared that her marriage would not improve under any circumstances and then she would have no one. Caring for the retarded son kept her busy and feeling needed. Mr. D. became more aware of his impoverished coping resources and not having anything especially meaningful to do with his time. His depression often seemed to have a manipulative quality, and he used it against his wife when he felt she was winning a struggle for control. After about 16 months of treatment, it was clear that Mr. D. would need close supervision to make certain that he continued taking medications as prescribed; he had been titrating levels without consulting his psychiatrist. He also needed to become more aware that he could do things differently and that this would improve the marital relationship. He wanted his wife to be more giving but he was unwilling to be more giving himself, explaining that he was the one having problems, not she.

Comment

Mr. D.'s history could have been presented by a person ten or twenty years younger, but the cumulative effects of stress perhaps had even more impact on him at age 65 than on his wife who was ten years younger. On the other hand, his psychotherapy was based on problems and interactions, and his age was not an important factor. This case illustrates also that early-life experiences may have little impact until problems arise quite late in life, to be magnified when a combination of events or stresses coalesce.

Elderly couples may have denied their conflicts and focused attention on rearing children and other responsibilities until these no longer mask their underlying conflicts. When this occurs, a sensitive psychotherapist can help spouses face feelings and conflicts and find better ways of relating to each other. Chronological age is not a contraindication to insight psychotherapy.

One might question whether a slow onset of depression such as Mr. D.'s should be considered an emergency. When he was first seen in our clinic, he was upset. A strong, clear statement had to be made regarding disposition and the need for treatment. The age of the patient was not a determining factor, but it seems to help older people to be told firmly that psychotherapy can be beneficial. Initially medication may have to be closely monitored, making certain that the therapist's opinions about frequency of treatment and other details confirm for the patient that the therapist is sincerely interested in the patient's well-being.

CASE HISTORY #4

Mrs. A.D., 58-year-old divorced woman, was admitted as an emergency case to the TRIMS inpatient unit for treatment of depression and possible dementia. Mrs. D. had contacted TRIMS several months earlier to volunteer for gerontological research on depression and memory. The research team had recognized that Mrs. D. needed treatment and referred her to the TRIMS adult outpatient clinic because our geriatric service ordinarily does not accept patients below age 60. She was accepted for follow-up by the geriatric clinic when, after three or four months, the major treatment attention shifted from depression to dementia. She did not follow through and was not seen for about two months, but after telephone contact she was referred to a neurologist for evaluation. She was then examined in the geriatric clinic, where arrangements were made for hospitalization because of the uncertain diagnosis and the patient's failure to cooperate as an outpatient. She had no one who offered support or supervision.

Seen in the adult outpatient clinic several months before her hospitalization, Mrs. D. had had typical depressive symptoms. She had also complained that her memory was impaired and attributed her inability to work to this condition. She had been taking propranolol for hypertension and was referred to a local clinic for follow-up.

A psychological evaluation given during her hospital stay was not able to clarify whether she had an organic or a functional disorder. Some of the data suggested a frontal lobe involvement but there was also evidence of depressed affect, mounting ambivalence and confusion, and possibly paranoid features. Her electroencephalogram was considered abnormal; it showed disturbances involving both temporal regions and possibly a moderate, generalized disturbance. Physical evaluation confirmed elevated blood pressure. A computed tomography scan revealed diffuse loss of cortical mass.

Mrs. D. and her husband had immigrated to the United States from a South American country many years before. The marriage had been prearranged by her wealthy father, who was described as domineering and dictatorial. After longstanding marital conflicts and abuse, Mrs. D. obtained a divorce and custody of their child. Later her husband kidnapped the child. Acquaintances would ask her about the child's whereabouts, and this would upset her; she had moved to Houston from another city 12 years before she was seen at TRIMS. She continued to feel frightened and alone and had had three psychiatric hospitalizations in general hospitals and received electroconvulsive therapy at least once.

At the time of her hospitalization at TRIMS, Mrs. D. complained of restlessness, depressed mood, sleep disturbance, poor appetite, and suspiciousness—symptoms which had become more severe during the past several months. She had been living on social security disability payments for a few months, but before that her only income had been a small food stamp allowance. She may have had some financial assistance from a friend. She had not been employed for at least six months. She had little interest in socializing or dating and did not consider marriage because her marriage had not been annulled by the Roman Catholic Church (to which she belonged and attended regularly). For a number of years she had done office work, but memory problems had begun to interfere with this. She had had much difficulty maintaining friendships. She had no history of drug or alcohol dependence.

In the hospital Mrs. D. became less anxious and depressed but her memory deficit persisted. She continued taking propranolol for hypertension, nortriptyline as an antidepressant, and hydrogenated ergot alkaloids for memory problems. She has returned to the clinic for monthly follow-up visits, but questions remain about her diagnosis. She has not returned to the neurologist, ostensibly because she cannot afford to do so. Monitoring and close supervision are necessary to make certain that she obtains care for hypertension and continues psychiatric treatment.

Comment

This case presents some of the difficulties encountered in diagnosis. Mental disorders manifested early in life may continue into old age, but determining whether organic factors begin to affect the clinical picture is not always a simple matter. In this instance, a woman who had been known to psychiatrists for many years began at about age 55 to complain of memory impairment, and, after several years of observation and a recent evaluation, it is still difficult to determine whether organic changes are affecting her clinical course significantly. This case also illustrates the difficulty in treating persons who have little support from family or others in the community and the difficulty one encounters in looking for such resources. This obviously ill woman is being followed in our clinic while living alone, and there has been little or no evidence of interest on the part of anyone other than clinic personnel in monitoring and supporting her during a time when she needs medical, psychological, and social services. The reluctance of our own adult outpatient clinic to continue treating her reflects a rather prevalent belief that aging people are likely to have organic brain syndrome and should be referred or relegated to a geriatric clinic. The geriatric clinic can, of course, be a positive rather than a pessimistic step, insuring that patients receive necessary multidisciplinary support. Even under these circumstances, patients such as this one may not comply and cooperate, and instead fall back to a pattern of seeking treatment only when a crisis arises.

CASE HISTORY #5

Mrs. E.F. is a 67-year-old divorced woman who was admitted to the TRIMS inpatient service as an emergency case on the day she had been examined in the geriatric outpatient clinic. She had been hit by a car the day before but examination had revealed no serious injury. Her memory was grossly impaired, and she was disoriented for time and place, was extremely dirty and somewhat malnourished. A 75-year-old sister was contacted but could give little information. Other relatively uninformed sources reported that Mrs. F. had been literally living in the streets for six to nine months, eating out of trash cans and sleeping in the open.

In the hospital, Mrs. F. offered no complaints except that she was hungry. A niece was contacted who knew little about the patient's history. Repeated efforts were made but little information could be obtained. Mrs. F. had been observed picking through debris along the streets in her neighborhood, and she was alleged to have bought a car in which she slept, ate, and traveled, until she brought the car to a shop for repair and could not recall where she had left it. She allegedly had a bank account into which a man who had bought a house from her was depositing mortgage payments, and from which she was paying a furniture bill, but no one knew where the furniture was. Details were unknown, but social agencies had in the past made some attempt to help Mrs. F. She would run away if she thought people were looking at her. She had taught school for eight years, ending three years before this hospitalization.

Mrs. F. appeared older than her chronological age and walked with a shuffling gait. Her affect was appropriate. She denied having any problems or knowledge about why she was hospitalized. She seemed remote, her memory and orientation were grossly impaired, and she confabulated. No psychotic ideation was elicited, and she denied a history of alcohol or drug abuse.

Psychological tests placed her in a low borderline range of intelligence; memory impairment was confirmed but there was no evidence of agraphia, acalculia, or aphasia. Projective tests suggested a person who was in conflict with a confusing, anxiety-provoking world around her. Her responses, though flavored with confabulations, were more representative of an organic process than a functional one. Reality testing was poor, and her ability to maintain control was consistently tenuous. She was marginal in her capacity to justify percepts, and her sometimes bizarre responses indicated a lack of critical judgment. Depression was not a predominant feature.

Early treatment consisted of a mild sedative and vitamin supplements. A careful physical evaluation showed no significant abnormalities. A computered tomography scan showed moderate ventricular dilatation and mild cortical atrophy but no evidence of tumor, infarct, or hemorrhage. An electroencephalogram was within the range of normal variation.

Mrs. F. was hospitalized for 147 days before she was admitted to a nursing home. Her discharge was delayed because no one was available to pursue certain matters. She could not be placed in a nursing home until her financial condition could be established, and the family members were unwilling or unable to help. Social agencies were equally reluctant.

During her hospital stay, she had wandered away from the office where the CT scan was to be done. Several days later someone observed her wandering in her old neighborhood. The police were called; they refused to search for Mrs. F. but were willing to return her to the hospital if someone would hold her until she could be picked up. She was returned to the hospital after a TRIMS social worker arranged for it. Mrs. F. reported that she had walked to her neighborhood some eight or nine miles away because she was afraid to ride with anyone. She had come to the attention of many people, but apparently no one was willing to intervene. She was pleased to be back in the hospital and spoke of being home again.

Mrs. F. was seen as an outpatient a month after her discharge. She was neatly dressed and showing appropriate behavior but was still disoriented. She was unaware that she had been living in a nursing home. An attendant who came with her reported that Mrs. F. was still a management problem in the sense that she wandered away at times and had been found across the street at a shopping center. She was continued on haloperidol, 1.0 mg twice a day, and vitamin supplements.

A later follow-up, about five months after her discharge from the hospital, revealed that Mrs. F. was doing well in the nursing home and was no longer wandering away. She is being followed by a physician at the nursing home and does not need to return to TRIMS for treatment.

Comment

The emergency in this case arose because no one would intervene or take responsibility for the elderly woman who could no longer take care of herself. Family members, acquaintances, social institutions, and other potential resources were unwilling, or unable, to intervene. One can understand the reluctance of a health or social agency to get involved, and this is demonstrated by the prolonged hospitalization and difficulty of placing Mrs. F. in a protective setting because of social and legal constraints. Perhaps some observers attributed Mrs. F.'s behavior to eccentricities associated with aging and did not see intervention as feasible or necessary. Though Mrs. F. had resisted help and had literally run away from potential caregivers, she accepted prolonged hospitalization without any serious complaints and wandered away only when she was taken away from the hospital for special testing. Similarly, she has adjusted to being in a nursing home and, though she wandered for the first few weeks, has stopped doing this after being a nursing home resident for several months and realizing that her needs are being met. Working with older people sensitizes therapists to the importance of satisfying dependency needs and providing protective environments. This is especially clear when working with very old people, but, as this case illustrates, it may be necessary for relatively young but seriously impaired persons.

CASE #6

Mrs. S.B. is a 64-year-old widow. She was referred to the TRIMS geriatric outpatient clinic by her psychiatrist, who treated her in a local private general hospital. She refused to come to the clinic until repeated contacts by an outreach worker were finally successful. When first interviewed, she complained of sleeplessness, despondency, poor appetite, and frequent headaches. She thought that airplanes put chemicals into her lungs and other organs. She had considered killing herself but had no gun or other weapon available. She was afraid of being alone, had few friends, and her symptoms had increased in severity before she finally agreed to come to the clinic. She had stopped taking an antidepressant prescribed for her.

Hospitalization was recommended after initial examination, and she agreed to enter the TRIMS inpatient service. Examination and tests in the hospital disclosed no significant physical disorders, nor did she have evidence of organic mental disorder. A diagnosis of chronic paranoid schizophrenia was made, and she was treated with chlorprothixene. Her symptoms improved. We made contact with her family and they became more interested and supportive.

A few weeks after her discharge from the hospital, Mrs. B. fell and fractured her right hand and collarbone. Arrangements had to be made for her transportation to our clinic and to the physician who was treating her fractures. Later she seemed to be getting along fairly well but began complaining of loneliness. She wanted one of her sons to live with her, but he preferred to live alone. Her medication dosage had been reduced a few months after her hospitalization, but Mrs. B. called to report that she was becoming more depressed, had difficulty sleeping, and was quite discouraged. When she failed to keep an appointment she was called and the appointment rescheduled, but she did not come in. Still later it was learned that she had been hospitalized for eight weeks in a private hospital because she had taken an overdose of tranquilizers. Two weeks after being discharged she reported being in good spirits with no depression or suicidal ideation. She said she would return to the clinic when she could arrange transportation. A TRIMS outreach worker is staying in contact with Mrs. B., but there is no assurance that she will return to the clinic until another crisis arises.

Mrs. B., the sixth of seven siblings, was born in the South. After marrying a laborer, she had moved to Houston about 43 years ago. Her two sons had offered little support in the months before she was seen in our clinic. She had worked for more than twenty years in the central service of a local general hospital, retiring several years earlier because of her nervous condition. Her husband had died ten years before. She reported having periods of the "blues" after delivering her babies. She had a history of several psychiatric hospitalizations dating back some 30 years but could not give details. She recalled fearing that she would be killed and being told that her diagnosis was paranoid schizophrenia. She also thought that something had been done to her brain, possibly referring to the electroconvulsive therapy she had undergone during some of these hospital stays.

Comment

Emergencies are likely to arise for elderly persons who do not have good social supports, especially in urban settings where the extended family is scattered. Follow-up of chronically ill patients is often difficult once the emergency or crisis situation is over. Continual monitoring and supervision are necessary to maintain contact, and special efforts should be made to stay in touch as the patients get older and have more trouble obtaining transportation. Caregivers may need to demonstrate their interest and commitment even more clearly to keep up the patient's motivation and participation in treatment. Perhaps caregivers can turn the patients' increasing dependence to the patients' advantage. Finding transportation, making phone contacts, and being understanding when patients do not comply may strengthen the caregivers' rapport with elderly patient.

SUMMARY

Chronological age of the patient may or may not be a critical factor in the development or manifestations of a psychiatric emergency. Nevertheless, persons dealing with elderly persons who have psychiatric emergencies will be more effective when they consider characteristics of aging and the aged and also attributes of caregivers toward elderly persons and their problems. Such knowledge is essential to achieve appropriate and adequate evaluation and treatment. Data obtained from patients' records have been presented to confirm that special information about aging and the aged should be utilized in managing geriatric psychiatric emergencies.

REFERENCES

1. Soreff, S.M.: Management of the Psychiatric Emergency. New York, John Wiley & Sons, 1981, pp 89, 126, 130.
2. Slaby, A.E., Lieb, J., Tancredi, L.R.: Handbook of Psychiatric Emergencies. Garden City NY, Medical Examination Publishing Co, 1981, p 149.
3. Glick, R.A., Meyerson, A.T., Robbins, E., Talbott, J.A. (eds).: Psychiatric Emergencies. New York, Grune & Stratton, 1976.
4. Busse, E.W., Blazer, D.G. (eds). Handbook of Geriatric Psychiatry. New York, Van Nostrand Reinhold Co, 1980.
5. Goldfarb, A.I.: The aged in crisis. In Psychiatric Emergencies. Edited by R.A. Glick et al. New York, Grune & Stratton, 1976, pp 241-257.
6. Gaitz, C.M.: Aged patients, their families and physicians, in Aging: The Process and the People. Edited by G. Usdin & C. Hofling. New York, Brunner/Mazel, 1978, pp 206-239.

15

Problems in Treating Abused Children

MARTIN J. DRELL

Since Kempe's pioneering article in 1962 [1] on the battered child syndrome, there has been an increasing focus on the various aspects of child abuse. According to Carolyn Okell Jones, the first decade of child abuse work drew attention to the associated brain injury and the high mortality rate [2]. The response to this focus was "to protect the child from lethal physical harm [3]." Work in that first decade was basic: description of the syndrome, diagnosis, legal ramifications, and beginning efforts to address the needs of the abusing parent. The children were usually stereotyped on the basis of early anecdotal data and theoretical generalizations concerning their development. Despite clinical observations indicating considerable emotional damage to the children, direct work with them was largely neglected [4]. The subtler nuances of the problem, i.e., the emotional effects of abuse, were less of a priority than the more urgent, life threatening issues of physical abuse.

Although there was little doubt that the abused child was compromised emotionally by his situation, it was not until the end of the first decade that this became a serious focus for the researchers. As the ever-increasing population of abused children was identified and hopefully physically protected, the issues of treatment and follow-up slowly emerged. The first follow-up studies confirmed all too clearly what was already suspected — that these children were at increased risk for emotional and/or developmental problems [5,6,7]. Research was then conducted to elaborate on the seriousness and pervasiveness of their problems. Pioneering efforts at treatment began.

Much was learned in the second decade, the 1970s, about the etiology and extent of the emotional effects of child abuse [8,9,10,11,12,13]. Unfortunately, less has been done with regard to treatment to address these specific emotional and developmental difficulties. Ann Harris Cohn, in her paper describing 11 demonstration child abuse and neglect programs established in 1974, states that "only 3 developed and operated treatment programs for the abused and neglected child [14]."

In this article I should like to briefly highlight what is known of the emotional effects of abuse and neglect and to establish that treatment can indeed be helpful in ameliorating some of these emotional difficulties. With that accomplished, I will end with some speculations as to why the child victim does not receive the needed psychological treatment more often.

ARE THERE EMOTIONAL SEQUELAE WHICH NEED TREATMENT?*

Because of the numerous factors involved in child abuse and neglect, it would be simplistic and misleading to assume that there is any one psychological profile for these children. It is helpful, however, to strive for some useful grouping of behaviors that may aid the help-giver. The literature provides a number of such useful groupings.

Starting with the broadest of these groupings, several researchers have noted a dichotomy of reactions [15,16,17,18]. This dichotomy includes those children who respond to situations with an introverted style and those who respond with an extroverted style. Although these response styles do not seem to be fixed, the evidence suggests that they may leave an indelible mark on the personalities of these children. Jones describes these two groupings from the perspective of having participated in a treatment program for 25 of these children:

> The introverts were children who, at the time of referral, have seemed withdrawn, controlled, wary and generally lacking in energy and interest. Now they appeared healthy but delicate,

---

*By treatment I refer to those modalities aimed at addressing the specific individual needs of the abused child. I make this distinction to separate these modalities from those that aim at changing the environment, e.g., placement or treatment of the abusing parent/s. Although intensive, individual psychoanalytically-influenced psychotherapy represents to me the prototype of individual treatment, I speak here of a range of treatment modalities which would include crisis and supportive work, group therapy, family therapy, infant stimulation programs, pre-school projects, etc. This paper will focus on those modalities specifically aimed at the emotional life of children and is not meant to minimize the importance of work with the parents, or ancillary therapies such as speech therapy and physical therapy.

fairly sprightly and spontaneous, aware of themselves and sensitive to their surroundings and other people. Some of these children showed traits of obsessive neatness in their behavior, wariness of their parents and perhaps an over-eager compliance and willingness to please others. They seemed to be holding in their feelings, but the appearance of recurrent problems such as enuresis, food refusal and sleeplessness suggested that these are highly sensitive and anxious children.

The extrovert group consisted of robust, hyperactive and clumsy children, careless of personal danger in the environment and prone to accidents. Some were aggressive or destructive, uncontrollable and liable to temper tantrums. They were easily frustrated and distracted and unable to involve themselves with others. Interaction with groups of children or their parents tended to trigger this reckless, violent behavior, which seemed imitative of their parents or siblings. Though many of these children had shown similar characteristics at the time of referral, a few developed them at a later stage [19].

Galdston elaborates on the violence of this latter group by saying that the children have an "automatic, stereotyped and repetitive quality; it is without discernible signs of mounting inner tension before it erupts into an assault, so that the observer usually cannot anticipate it and intercede, even though she might be right next to the child [20]."

Martin and Beezley, in their evaluation of 58 abused children (ages 2-13 years) noted several problem areas:

1. Impaired capacity to enjoy life (66%)
2. Psychiatric symptoms e.g., enuresis, temper tantrums, hyperactivity, bizarre behavior (62%)
3. Low self esteem (52%)
4. School learning problems (38%)
5. Withdrawal (24%)
6. Opposition (24%)
7. Hypervigilance (22%)
8. Compulsivity (22%)
9. Pseudomaturity (20%)   [21]

Arthur Green [13] describes a group of twenty children who were seen in individual psychotherapy over a three year period. From his psychodynamic viewpoint, Green found several prominent areas of disturbance. An outline of these would include:

1. Overall impairment in ego functioning associated with intellectual and cognitive deficits.
2. Traumatic reactions with acute anxiety states.
3. Pathological object relations characterized by the failure to develop "basic trust."
4. Excessive use of primitive defenses such as denial, projection, introjection and splitting.

5. Impaired impulse control.
6. Impaired self concept.
7. Masochistic and self-destructive behavior.
8. Difficulties with separation.
9. Problems in school adjustment.   [22]

It is interesting to note that all these authors, despite differing orientations, locations and population groups have identified similar emotional sequelae. This point underscores the fact that abuse and neglect definitely affect the emotional life of children. There still remains the question of whether treatment is necessary for these children.

When considering the need for treatment of the child, we enter, for the most part, uncharted territory. Despite national concern about child abuse, there is a paucity of research on treatment needs [23,24,25,26,27,28,29]. Those studies that do exist often consist of small samples, are poorly controlled and rarely have extended follow-up. Few of these studies delve into the specifics of individual treatment. In addition, there are remarkably few case studies [30,31,32]. Criticism aside, the researchers have often come to the same conclusion, that treatment is needed:

> We feel that early psychiatric involvement in cases of child abuse is necessary in determining the child's role in producing the abuse and his reaction to it and in recommending appropriate comprehensive treatment for the child, including psychotherapy in many cases. [33]

> Some children who have endured misplaced abuse are so emotionally disturbed by the time they come to the attention of the protective agency that psychiatric treatment is clearly indicated. [34]

> Direct and active intervention must be considered with each mistreated child. [35]

DOES TREATMENT WORK?

Still fewer studies give details about their results. The ones that do feel that there is improvement in the abused children they have tried to help [36,37,38,39,40,41,42].

Green states that "15 of 16 children remaining in treatment at least 9 months exhibited significant improvement" as judged by the therapist, the treatment team, home observations and reports from parents and teachers [43]. Galdston concurs and felt that he found "improvement in the rate of growth and development [44]" of the children in his project. He also felt that these children showed an increased ability to "endure stress without regression [45]." Beezely, Martin, and Kempe report that their interventions yielded:

1. Increased ability to trust adults.
2. Increased ability to delay gratification.
3. Increased self esteem.
4. Increased ability to verbalize feelings.
5. Increased capacity for pleasure.   [46]

Cohn [47] summarizes work done with 70 children from three treatment programs across the United States (as judged by caseworkers).

	% with problem	% improved
1. Ability to give and receive attention	51.5	79
2. General happiness	50.0	66.7
3. Attention span	50.0	57.0
4. Sense of self	54.0	57.1
5. Reaction to frustration	51.4	50.0
6. Interaction with adults	57.1	65.8
7. Interaction with peers	70.0	58.8

These studies imply that not all the children were equally helped by the interventions. The complexity of variables involved makes it difficult to compare these studies. The feeling is that many of these children are significantly aided in the short run. There is also the sense that these interventions help to prevent secondary complications of abuse such as problematic school performances and difficulties with authority figures. The authors hesitantly predict that treatment tailored to the specific needs of the child can be helpful in altering the long term emotional sequelae of abuse. They all join in calling for efforts at well designed follow-up studies.

ARE CHILDREN BEING TREATED?

If we agree that abuse does have emotional sequelae and that treatment of the child can be helpful in ameliorating those problems, then our next question perhaps should be whether or not these services are in fact being rendered. A study which best illustrates the answer to this question is written by Anne Harris Cohn [48]. She surveys eleven 3-year demonstration child abuse and neglect service projects that were established in 1974 to address the needs of abused children and their families. These projects, which were initially funded for three years, included cities throughout the U.S. and in Puerto Rico. She found that only three of the 11 projects developed treatment programs specifically for children and that these three projects treated only a few children at any one time.

A poignant answer to the question at hand, whether or not treatment services are being given to the children, lies in the inequitable statistics of these treatment programs: the total population of parents treated was 1,724 while the population of abused children who were treated was only 70.

WHY ARE ABUSED CHILDREN NOT TREATED?

As in most aspects of child abuse, the answer to this question is complex and involves issues on many levels. For clarity I will divide the issues into three broad groups: (1) societal and historical issues, (2) treatment issues, and (3) definition issues.

The concept of child abuse and neglect is woven into the fabric of each society to the extent that what is considered abuse varies from culture to culture [49].

What is considered abuse in a society can tell us about that society. If so, it would seem that the vast number of cases of abuse and neglect in the U.S. should tell us something about our society. Gil hypothesized just this point and has expounded on a sociologic model of child abuse which focuses on the society, its cultures and its communities. He feels that there is a cultural acceptance of violence in the U.S. as well as certain socio-economic factors that lead ultimately to child abuse [50]. In keeping with his sociological model he has proposed sociologic methods for dealing with child abuse. But implementation involves changing society over a period of years, and does not assist the child who is presently in an abusive situation.

Gil's theory is not the only one. In their comprehensive article entitled "Child Abuse: An Interdisciplinary Analysis," Parke and Collmer list three approaches to understanding child abuse [51]:

1. The psychiatric model of child abuse which has tended to focus on the personality characteristics of the abusing parent (not the child).
2. The sociological model of child abuse, which is well represented in Gil's work [52].
3. The social-situational model of child abuse, which focuses on the social situation and tries to figure out how those involved in abuse are interconnected in the process of perpetuating an abusive system.

Only the third model allows a careful scrutiny of the part played by the child in the system of abuse. Only the third model allows for treatment of the child. Only under this model or one like it can legitimate research be allowed to look at the part the child brings to the situation of abuse.

When we speak of models we are dealing with definitions. At this level, we find further difficulties. These involve such issues as how to define abuse and who will be empowered to define. It is easy to define abuse when one is confronted with multiple fractured bones, but when we deal with the less definitive signs of physical abuse there is more difficulty. At what point is corporal punishment termed abuse as opposed to part of the normal prerogative of the parent in disciplining his child? The lines traversed in these questions make it difficult to define abuse, and it must be defined before it will be reported and before it can be treated.

If there are troubles in defining physical abuse, the concept of emotional abuse is more troublesome. How is one to define that? In this area we aren't even lucky enough to have x-rays.

The issue of definitions pervades all aspects of child abuse. One of the most fundamental problems is that those professionals involved in identifying and treating abuse cannot agree upon a system of definitions. Giovannoni and Beccera, in their book *Defining Child Abuse* approach this issue from a sociological standpoint [53]. Their study sought to investigate the similarities and differences in the views of four professional groups who determine policy and practice concerning child abuse. The four groups, including lawyers, social workers, pediatricians, and police were found to differ considerably in their definitions and the courses of action they recommended. These differences involved perceptions as to the seriousness of the consequences of certain acts, the seriousness of specific incidents, and the balance between parental and child rights. The area of most conflict was emotional care. As might be expected, there was more difficulty when dealing with less than extreme examples. The authors also compared these four professional groups with a lay group in the community. The study shows that this community sample has its own definitions. Furthermore, the community must in turn be broken down into smaller subgroups with respect to cultural background. The definitions proliferate. One can quickly see how unclear definition of abuse might affect its reporting, investigation, and treatment. The end result is often a paralyzing confusion that obscures rather than promotes treatment.

The tendency, in the case of such differences in definition, is to use the strictest definition, i.e., that which describes the abuse in objective, measureable terms. This might be the most reasonable thing to do under the circumstances, but many cases in which the damage is not assessable on these parameters are left unreported and therefore untreated. This process, in turn, skews the population considered "abused" and focuses attention on the group of recognized abuse cases for research purposes. This research is needed, but the focus of attention away from those not defined as abused may prove costly. Such a narrowness of definition has slowed the research into the emotional effects of abuse and its treatment. Ultimately the planning of strategies to help these unfortunate children is also affected.

In a political vein, society is culpable for lack of commitment to child welfare by virtue of its funding priorities. During their time in office, elected officials have to balance the short term satisfaction of their voting constituents with the long term issues, the present and future lives of abused children. These long term issues often lose out when it comes to funding.

The cost/benefit ratio is always present. Cohn reduces one aspect of care for abused children to dollars and cents when she writes:

> Working with parents is also less expensive and less time consuming (e.g., the annual cost of a basic treatment package for a parent is about $1800 as contrasted with $3500 a year or more for one common mode of treatment, therapeutic day care, for a child. [54]

It is difficult to make treatment decisions, especially when they are compounded by such issues as politics, definition, and incomplete research.

The shortage of psychiatrists is yet another societal issue which has been surfacing slowly [55,56,57]. It follows then that child psychiatry is also suffering a shortage of new clinicians. At present, there are not enough child psychiatrists and there will be a shortage for many years to come [58]. This, plus the distribution inequities which leave most child psychiatrists in the highly populated cities, can't help but affect the quality and quantity of care for the abused child [59].

Eveoleen Rexford [60] addressed society's reluctance to commit national resources to the welfare of children. She feels that despite areas of consensus as to what is needed, there is little action taken to remedy the situation. Rexford poignantly illustrates her case with data concerning funds allocated to the care of children. Although her figures are now dated, today's statistics do not suggest that matters have changed significantly.

Rexford makes the point that this lack of commitment stems from society's ambivalent attitudes towards children. She states that

> . . . we cannot as a society act upon our modern knowledge of children's needs because many of us become stalemated by the effects of our unresolved conflicts about children. We do not free ourselves sufficiently from our personal past to act upon our mature wishes to care for children as our times demand.

She goes on to say that the areas of conflict often involve: (1) Sibling issues, with the child representing the hated rival who all too often usurps one's need gratifications. (2) "Oedipal fantasies . . . [which] could be aroused in many of us to produce continued guilt, anxiety, and ambivalence." (3) Envy, in its own right, of the child. (4) Use of the child for projection of the uncomfortable impulses of the adult.* (5) Unconscious denial of the child's aggression and sexuality.** (6) Fears of regression.

All these issues fit into an historical framework. Several recent articles speak to this point [61,62,63]. Lloyd DeMause writes:

> The history of childhood is a nightmare from which we have only recently begun to awaken. The further back in history one goes, the lower the level of child care, and the more likely children are to be killed, abandoned, beaten, terrorized and sexually abused . . . If today in America there are less than a million abused children, there would be a point back in history where most of the children were what we would consider abused. [64]

DeMause has noted the same trends throughout history that Rexford pointed out in present times. He expounds a theory of evolution which he feels is still going on. According to DeMause "the evolution of parent-child relations constitutes an independent source of historical change" which lies in "the ability of successive generations of parents to regress to the psychic age of their children and work through the anxieties of the age in a better manner the second time they encounter them. It involves regression and a second chance [65]."

In thoughts reminiscent of Rexford, DeMause further explains that even from an historical perspective, adults have responded in one of three different ways when confronted with the needs of children. These are: (1) a projective reaction towards the child (2) a reversal reaction, in which the child is used as a substitute for an adult figure in the parent's own childhood (3) an empathetic reaction, where the adult adequately assesses the needs of the child and provides "good enough" mothering. [66]

DeMause's search of history leads him to believe that the first two reactions have predominated throughout history and are seen today in the abuse of children. He states that these two reactions create a "double image" in which "the child is loved and hated, rewarded and punished, bad and loving all at once. . . . It is the child's function to reduce the adult's pressing anxieties: the child acts as the adult's defense." He clarifies however, that the problem is not one of love for the child, but "rather the emotional maturity needed to see the child as a person separate from himself" [67].

---

*She feels that projection plays an important part in the notorious "generation gap" seen with adolescence and is the underpinning of the concept of original sin.

**This denial is the underpinning of the concept of "original innocence." She feels that both the concept of original sin and original innocence obscure the actual needs of children and therefore add to the delay in the meeting of their needs.

Kanner, in his history of child psychiatry which encompasses the first four decades of the 20th century [68], elucidates what he feels has been the evolution of child psychiatry:

First decade: Cultural focus on thinking about children (psychometry, dynamic psychiatry, juvenile courts, the mental hygiene movement).

Second decade: Community focus on doing things to children (special classes, probation, organized foster care).

Third decade: Family and school focus on doing things for children (Child Guidance clinics study family relationships and work with parents and teachers).

Fourth decade: Child focus on working with children (including having the child in a therapeutic program).

Time and again we note that the needs of children are directly met only after an evolutionary process which indirectly meets their needs by efforts aimed at other sectors of society. In the short history of child abuse (considering Kempe's 1962 article as the beginning) I believe we are seeing an evolution similar to the one that Kanner proposed for child psychiatry in general:

(A) Thinking about abused children, i.e., defining the syndrome and establishing reporting laws.

(B) Doing to abused children, i.e., placing them.

(C) Doing for abused children, i.e., treating their parents.

(D) Working with abused children, i.e., therapy for the children.

We see then that there are many factors that impede the emotional treatment of children. Even when a child is seen in therapy, these impeding factors (society, definitions, politics, funding, manpower, and history) often continue to obviate effective treatment.

A formidable deterrent to adequate treatment is the fact that these cases include a sizeable number of children of pre-school age. These children, who are "non-verbal" (in the adult sense of being able to communicate) have presented a problem to professionals throughout the years. These problems are clearly illustrated in this 1976 quote pertaining to child psychiatry:

> One must also consider how much exposure and training child psychiatrists have had with pre-school children. Few programs funded in the last five years by the National Institute of Mental Health have emphasized the first three years of life as an area of training for child psychiatrists. In a recent review of 97 training programs in child psychiatry, 34% mentioned a comprehensive study of child development, while only 12% emphasized clinical work with children under the age of 5 years . . . there is clearly a need for more training of child psychiatrists in the areas of early child care and child development [69].

This statement highlights Kanner's feeling that true efforts to understand the child are a recent phenomenon [70].

Extensive study of the emotional life of the infant has for the most part been even more recent. The literature on infancy seems to be in the beginning of its own evolution. Technology to study the infant is being developed and efforts to define areas of pathology and normality are just now being attempted. Recent, pioneering articles look objectively at the abused infant and find that there are significant differences in their approach, avoidance, aggressive [71] and affective behaviors [72]. The abused infants are characterized by increased withdrawal, lack of pleasure, more inconsistency, shallowness, ambiguity in affective communications, and more negative affects [73]. Clinicians are busy trying to integrate this new data. At present, only tentative answers exist as to what might be adequate treatment for these infants [74]. The treatment programs that exist can't possibly meet the demand. The difficulty in dealing with pre-school children often affects the treatment they receive. In many cases, the treatment focuses on the parents because they are "more accessible, generally more verbal, and certainly more mobile [75]."

Even with these factors put aside, there are problems inherent in the treatment of children themselves. Berta Bornstein [76] foreshadowed Rexford when she referred to these problems as barriers which include "those irrational reactions which in our society are so inherent in adult's relationships to children." She writes that these reactions are founded in a "fear of children" because of their unpredictability, their highly charged emotions, their narcissism, and their closeness to the unconscious. She goes on to elaborate on how these fears permeate the treatment efforts with children by triggering emotional reactions (such as regression) in the therapist and subsequent defensive stances. One stance is that of establishing superiority over the child and assuming the child's emotional life is one of simplicity. This leads the therapist to set up unrealistic treatment goals. When these goals are not met, the therapist often becomes frustrated and/or guilty. These conditions can further impede treatment.

Bornstein also notes attitudes towards development which are problematic. These include the opposing attitudes that the child will grow out of his problem and that any problem will enlarge as development progresses. Both attitudes lead to a feeling of powerlessness in the therapist, while the latter also leads to a feeling of fear; neither emotion is conducive to meeting the child's needs [77].

To further complicate matters, the types of emotional disturbances seen in abused children (see section on emotional sequelae) often lead to quite difficult treatments. Therapists traditionally prefer cases with fewer problems in the areas of ego functioning, impulse control, basic trust, object relations, and self esteem.

Work with the parents of the abused child also presents barriers to the child's treatment. Bornstein speaks to this issue and states that the parents are prey to the same resistances to children as the therapist. She notes that the parents often unconsciously interfere with their child's therapy by not relinquishing them as vehicles for dealing with their unconscious conflicts [78]. Green focuses specifically on this issue involving parents of abused children when he writes that their resistances "are more formidable and extensive than those exhibited by non-abusing parents whose children are referred for psychiatric assistance." He says that these parents have: poor motivation, specific denial of the psychological deviation of the child, fear of relinquishing their special relationships with their child, competition with the child for dependency gratification, and fear of the child's improvement.

Green emphasizes the necessity of working with the parents despite the powerful emotional reactions they engender in the therapist [79].

Still another difficulty in treating abused children is the necessity of working with a multitude of professionals in other disciplines. These difficulties in numbers are compounded by the aforementioned differences in training and attitudes of different professional groups [80].

CONCLUSION

In this paper I have attempted to apprise the reader of some of the research that has accumulated concerning child abuse, its effects and its treatment. Notwithstanding the research, the critical issue appears to be the fact that many abused children are not being treated or are receiving inadequate treatment. Although the reasons for this neglect are formidable, hopefully, we can enter the third decade of child abuse studies with the goal of timely and sufficient treatment as the next step in psychiatric understanding of the child abuse syndrome.

REFERENCES

1. Kempe, C.H., Silverman, F.N., et al: The battered child syndrome. JAMA 181:17-24, 1962.
2. Jones, C.O.: The Fate of Abused Children. In: The Challenge of Child Abuse. White (ed). London Academic Press p. 108-265, 1977.
3. Jones, C.O.: The Fate of Abused Children. In: The Challenge of Child Abuse. White (ed). London Academic Press p. 108-265, 1977.
4. Kempe, C.H., Silverman, F.N., et al.: The battered child syndrome. JAMA 181:17-24, 1962.
5. Elmer, E., Gregg, S.: Developmental characteristics of abused children. Pediatrics. vol. 40, no. 4:152-155, Oct., 1969.
6. Morse, W.C. Sahler, A.O.J. et al.: A three-year follow-up study of abused and neglected children. Amer J Dis Child 120:439-446, Nov., 1970.
7. Silver, B.L., Dublin, C.C., et al.: Does violence breed violence? Am J Psychiatry 126:3:152-155, Sept., 1969.
8. Jones, C.O.: Development of Children from Abusive Families. In: Child Abuse. Edited by Franklin Alfred White. Edinburgh, London, New York Churchill Livingston, 1977.

9. Galdston, A.R.: Observations on children who have been physically abused and their parents. Am J Psychiatry 1965:440-443.

10. Jones, C.O.: The Fate of Abused Children. In: The Challenge of Child Abuse. Edited by Franklin Alfred White. London Academic Press p. 108-121, 1977

11. Martin, P.H., Beezley, P.: Prevention and the consequences of child abuse. J. of Operational Psychiatry. vol. 6, no. 1 p 68-77 Nov. 1974.

12. Martin, P.H.: The Consequences of Being Abused and Neglected: How the Child Fares. Edited by C Henry Kempe, Ray E. Helfer. Chicago, London University of Chicago Press 3rd edition p. 347-365, 1980.

13. Green, A.: Psychopathology of abused children. JAACP 17:92-103, 1978.

14. Cohn, A.J.: An evaluation of three demonstration child abuse and neglect treatment programs. JAACP vol. 18, no. 2, p. 283-291, Spring 1979.

15. Galdston, R: Preventing the abuse of little children.Am J Orthopsychiatry vol. 45, no. 3, p. 372-381, April 1975.

16. Gray J, Kempe R.: The Abused Child at Time of Injury. In: The Abused Child. H.P. Martin (ed). Cambridge Ballinger, 1976.

17. Pringle, M.K.: The Needs of Children. In The Maltreatment of Children. S.M. Smith (ed). Baltimore University Park Press, 1978.

18. Jones, C.O.: Development of Children from Abusive Families. In: Child Abuse. F.A. White(ed). Edinburgh, London, New York Churchill Livingston, 1977.

19. Jones, C.O.: Development of Children from Abusive Families. In: Child Abuse. F.A. White (ed). Edinburgh, London, New York Churchill Livingston, 1977.

20. Galdston, R.: Preventing the abuse of little children. Am J Orthopsychiatry vol. 45, no. 3, p. 372-381, April 1975.

21. Martin, P.H., Beezley, P.: The Personality of Abused Children. In: The Abused Child. Edited by Harold P Martin. Cambridge Ballinger, 1976.

22. Green, H.A.: Psychopathology of abused children. JAACP 17:92-103, 1978.

23. Martin, P.J.: Treatment of the Abused Child. In: The At Risk Infant. S. Harel (ed). Amsterdam, Oxford, Princeton Excerpts Medica p. 257-261, 1980.

24. Galdston, R.: Preventing the abuse of little children. Am J Orthopsychiatry. vol. 45, no. 3, p. 372-381, April 1985.

25. Jones, C.O.: Development of Children From Abusive Families. In: Child Abuse. F.A. White (ed). Edinburgh, London, New York Churchill Livingston, 1977.

26. Jones, C.O.: Development of Children From Abusive Families. In: Child Abuse. Edited by Franklin Alfred White. Edinburgh, London, New York Churchill Livingston, 1977.

27. In: Peter A., McDermott, G.J. Jr: The treatment of child abuse. JAACP vol. 15, no. 4, p. 430-440, Winter 1976.

28. McQuiston, M., Kempe, S.R.: Treatment of the Child. In: The Battered Child. Edited by Henry C Kempe, Ray E. Helfer, Chicago, London University of Chicago Press 3rd edition p. 379-390, 1980.

29. Green, H.A.: Psychopathology of abused children. JAACP 17:92-103, 1978.

30. In: Peter A., McDermott, G.J. Jr: The treatment of child abuse. JAACP vol. 15, no. 4, p. 430-440, Winter 1976.

31. Green, H.A.: Psychopathology of abused children. JAACP 17:92-103. 1978.

32. Green, H.A.: Psychopathology of abused children. JAACP 17:92-103, 1978.

33. In A. Peter, McDermott, G.J. Jr.: The treatment of child abuse. JAACP vol. 15, no. 4, p. 430-440, Winter 1976.

34. Jones, C.O.: Development of Children from Abusive Families. In: Child Abuse. Edited by Franklin Alfred White. Edinburgh, London, New York Churchill Livingston, 1977.

35. Martin, P.H.: Treatment of the Abused Child. In The At Risk Infant. Edited by Shaul Harel. Amsterdam, Oxford, Princeton Excerpts Medica p. 257-261, 1980.
36. Jones, C.O.: Development of Children from Abusive Families. In: Child Abuse. Edited by Franklin Alfred White. Edinburgh, London, New York Churchill Livingston, 1977.
37. Beezley, P., Martin, P.H., Kempe, R.: Psychotherapy. In: The Abused Child. Edited by Harold P. Martin. Cambridge Ballinger, 1976.
38. Baker, E., Hyman, C., et al.: A Psychological Study of Abused Children. In: At Risk. Edited by Routledge Direct. London Routledge & Kegan p. 198-209, 1976.
39. Martin, P.H.: Treatment of the Abused Child. In: The At Risk Infant. Edited by Shaul Harel. Amsterdam, Oxford, Princeton Excerpts Medica p. 257-261, 1980.
40. Gladston, R.: Preventing the abuse of little children. Am I Orthopsychiatry vol. 45, no. 3, p. 372-381, April 1975.
41. Cohn, A.J.: An evaluation of three demonstration child abuse and neglect treatment programs. JAACP vol. 18, no. 2, p. 283-291, Spring 1979.
42. Green, A.: Psychiatric treatment of abused children. JAACP 17:356-371.
43. Green, A.: Psychiatric treatment of abused children. JAACP 17:356-371.
44. Galdston, R.: Preventing the abuse of little children. Am J Orthopsychiatry. vol. 45, no. 3, p. 372-381, April 1975.
45. Galdston, R.: Preventing the abuse of little children. Am J Orthopsychiatry. vol. 45, no. 3, p. 372-381, April 1975.
46. Jones, C.O.: Development of Children from Abusive Families. In: Child Abuse. Edited by Franklin Alfred White. Edinburgh, London, New York Churchill Livingston, 1977.
47. Cohn, A.H.: An evaluation of three demonstration child abuse and neglect treatment programs. JAACP vol. 18, no. 2, p. 283-291, Spring 1979.
48. Cohn, A.H.: An evaluation of three demonstration child abuse and neglect treatment programs. JAACP vol. 18, no. 2, p. 283-291, Spring 1979.
49. Taylor, L., Newberger, H.E.: Child abuse in the international year of the child. NEJM vol. 301, no. 22, p. 1205-1212, Nov. 29, 1979.
50. Gil, D.G.: Violence Against Children: Physical Abuse in the United States. Cambridge Harvard University Press, 1970.
51. Parke, D.R., Colliner, W.C.: Child Abuse: An Interdisciplinary Analysis. In: The Review of Child Development Research. Edited by Mavis E Hetherington. Chicago, London University of Chicago Press p. 509-590, 1975.
52. Parke, D.R., Colliner W.C.: Child Abuse: An Interdisciplinary Analysis. In The Review of Child Development Research. Edited by Mavis E. Hetherington. Chicago, London University of Chicago Press p. 509-590, 1975.
53. Giovannoni, M.J., Becerra, M.R.: Defining Child Abuse. New York Free Press, 1979.
54. Cohn, A.H.: An evaluation of three demonstration child abuse and neglect treatment programs. JAACP vol. 18, no. 2, p. 283-291, Spring 1979.
55. Nielsen, C.A.: Psychiatric recruitment: why they like us, but don't join us. Psychosomatics. vol. 22, no. 4, p. 343-348, April 1968.
56. Nielsen, C.A.: The Magnitude of declining psychiatric career choice. J Med Education 54:632-637, 1979.
57. Langsley, G.D., Robinowitz, B.C.: Psychiatric manpower; an overview. Hosp Community Psychiatry 30:749-755, 1979.
58. Doyle, B.B.: Working assumptions: American psychiatry in 1990. Report to GMENAC, March 1978.
59. Crowly, E.A.: Graduate medical education in the United States. JAMA vol. 246, no. 25, p. 2938-2944, Dec. 25, 1981.

60. Rexford, N.E.: Children, child psychiatry and our brave new world. Arch Gen Psychiatry 20:25-37, Jan, 1969.
61. Demause, L.: The Evolution of Childhood. In: the History of Childhood. Edited by Lloyd Demause. New York The Psychohistory Press p. 503-606, 1974.
62. Radbill, X.S.: Children in a World of Violence: A History of Child Abuse. In: The Battered Child. Edited by Henry C. Kempe, Ray E. Helfer Chicago, London University of Chicago Press 3rd edition p. 3-20, 1980.
63. Giovannoni, M.J., Becerra, M.R.: Child Mistreatment: A Historical Perspective. In: Defining Child Abuse. New York Free Press p. 31-75, 1979.
64. Demause, L.: The Evolution of Childhood. In: The History of Childhood. Edited by Lloyd Demause. New York The Psychohistory Press p. 503-606, 1974.
65. Demause, L.: The Evolution of Childhood. In: The History of Childhood. Edited by Lloyd Demause. New York The Psychohistory Press p. 503-606, 1974.
66. Davis, M., Wallbridge, D.: In: Boundary and Space: An Introduction to the Work of D.W. Winnicott. New York Brunner/Mazel, 1981.
67. Demause, L.: The Evolution of Childhood. In: The History of Childhood. Edited by Lloyd Demause. New York The Psychohistory Press p. 503-606, 1974.
68. Kanner, L.: Outline of the History of Child Psychiatry. In: Child Psychiatry. Springfield Charles C Thomas 4th edition p. 5-17, 1972.
69. Greenspan, I.S. Nover, A. Robert, et al: The Child Psychiatrist and Day Care. JAACP vol. 15, no. 1, p. 108-130, Winter, 1976.
70. Kanner, L.: Outline of the History of Child Psychiatry. In: Child Psychiatry. Springfield Charles C Thomas 4th edition p. 5-17, 1972.
71. George, C., Main, M: Social interactions of young abused children: approach, avoidance, and aggression. Child Development 50:306-318, 1979.
72. Gaensbauer, J.T., Mrazek, D: Differences in the patterning of affective expression in infants. JAACP vol. 20, no. 4, p. 673-691, Autumn 1981.
73. Gaensbauer, J.T., Sands, K.: Distorted affective communications in abused/neglected infants and their potential impact on caregivers. JAACP vol. 18, no. 2, p. 236-250, Spring 1979.
74. Minde, K., Minde, R.: Psychiatric intervention in infancy: a review. JAACP vol. 20, no. 2, p. 217-238, Spring 1981.
75. Cohn, A.: An evolution of three demonstration child abuse and neglect treatment programs. JAACP vol. 18, no. 2, Spring 1979.
76. Borstein, B.: Emotional barriers in the understanding and treatment of young children. J of Orthopsychiatry 18:691-97, 1948.
77. Borstein, B.: Emotional barriers in the understanding and treatment of young children. J of Orthopsychiatry 18:691-97, 1948.
78. Borstein, B.: Emotional barriers in the understanding and treatment of young children. J of Orthopsychiatry 18:691-97, 1948.
79. Green, H.A.: Psychiatric treatment of abused children. JAACP vol. 17, no. 2, p. 356-371, Spring 1978.
80. Giovannoni, M.J., Becerra, M.R.: Child Mistreatment: A Historical Perspective. In Defining Child Abuse New York Free Press p. 31-75, 1979.

16

Emergency Psychiatric Services to Minorities

PEDRO RUIZ AND EDWARD G. SILVERMAN

INTRODUCTION

Since the Community Mental Health Centers Act of 1963, there has been a rapid increase in the availability and utilization of psychiatric emergency services [1,2,3]. This expansion is one manifestation of a basic change in philosophy regarding the delivery of mental health services from confinement of the severely mentally ill in large state hospitals to treatment in less restrictive community mental health centers. The census of patients in mental hospitals across the nation has declined steadily from a peak of 559,000 in 1955 to 193,000 in 1978 [4]. However, this decrease has not been accompanied by adequate alternative sources of treatment [5], and many formerly institutionalized patients require rehospitalization during periods of decompensation. As a result, emergency psychiatric facilities have assumed a more important role in the management of severely disturbed patients and often serve as the "revolving door" through which such patients are repeatedly channeled into other segments of the community's mental health resources [6].

The Community Mental Health Centers Act of 1963, by legislating that emergency psychiatric treatment be included as one of five essential services in all federally funded community mental health centers, also made psychiatric emergency services more accessible to people in lower socioeconomic groups. Indeed, Coleman and Errera's [7] notion of the general hospital emergency room as the "poor man's doctor" is a reality which cannot be ignored. Within the public sector in particular, the patient population in psychiatric emergency rooms represents, for the most part, underserved and underprivileged segments of our society. Social and cultural variables become extremely relevant and important when providing services to minorities, the poor and special religious groups. And, in the emotionally charged atmosphere of the emergency room where emphasis is on rapid assessment, rapid intervention, and rapid disposition, the impact of value judgements on the decision-making process becomes a matter of critical importance.

Unfortunately, as the process of emergency psychiatric intervention becomes increasingly important as a service, training, and research area, social and cultural considerations continue to go relatively unnoticed. This is not to minimize the importance of the biological and psychological approaches in treating the mentally ill. After all, psychopathology is universal and all ethnic groups are affected by syndromes in which biological and/or psychological factors are relevant. However, the successful treatment of any minority group (class, race or religion) requires a careful understanding of the sociocultural setting. Psychopathologic signs and symptoms differ from culture to culture, culture-bound syndromes exist, and even the most common and cross-culturally prevalent syndromes have basic expressive differences among minority groups [8]. Nevertheless, mental health specialists still tend to use one value frame of reference in perceiving the behavior of a patient [9] and attempt to reduce all explanations of psychopathology to some psychobiological reality [10]. Significant advances in emergency psychiatric intervention have emerged within the last decade in psychological (e.g., crisis intervention techniques, stress reduction, coping strategies) and biological (e.g., rapid tranquilization) approaches to treatment with relatively little attention paid to social and cultural influences. In this paper, we would like to focus on a number of such issues which are relevant to the provision of emergency psychiatric services to minority groups.

INCIDENCE, PREVALENCE, AND DIAGNOSIS OF PSYCHOPATHOLOGY

One important area in the literature has been the relative distribution of psychopathology within given societies and cultures as a function of various social variables, including age, sex, race, religion, social class, and specific social parameters. The majority of the research is focused on the relationship between ethnicity, social class, and psychopathology. Although it is beyond the scope of this paper to present the results of this research in detail, some major trends are suggested which introduce important questions regarding value judgements in providing services to minorities.

With regard to ethnicity, the group most frequently studied has been blacks. Simon et al [11] conducted a study in which patients in nine New York state mental hospitals were diagnosed by research psychiatrists, as well as hospital clinicians. The hospital diagnosticians, using their routine methods, gave blacks the diagnosis of schizophrenia rather than affective illness more often than whites. The research psychiatrist, using a structured mental status interview, found no significant relationship between race and diagnosis. The structured mental status examination, more likely to extract more complete information, completely corrected for the apparent racial bias of the hospital clinicians.

In another study, Raskin et al [12] compared 159 black and 555 white depressed patients on a wide variety of rating scales. These investigators matched patients by age, sex, and socioeconomic status. Two psychiatrists, or one psychiatrist and one psychologist, independently rated the patients using the same instruments. The results revealed an absence of significant differences between the two groups on clinical features that would be necessary for a diagnosis of schizophrenia. However, in making pretreatment clinical diagnosis, white patients were more often given a diagnosis of psychotic depression, especially involutional psychotic reaction, and black patients were more often given a diagnosis of schizophrenic reaction, schizo-affective type. Thirty-nine percent of the black men were diagnosed as schizophrenic compared with twenty-three percent of the black women and only eighteen percent of the white men.

Gross et al [13] investigated the diagnosis and disposition of 2279 patients in a psychiatric emergency room and found that white females were more likely than non-white females to be diagnosed neurotic and referred for outpatient treatment. Nonwhite females were more likely to be treated in the emergency room proper and diagnosed schizophrenic.

These studies are consistent with others in which blacks appear more disturbed and receive more pathological diagnoses than whites who show the same behavior [14,15,16]. Although less frequently studied, some similar trends have been noted regarding the incidence and prevalence of mental illness among Hispanics. In reviewing current research in the epidemiology of mental illness among Hispanic people, Ruiz [17] concluded that the number of psychiatric hospitalizations for Puerto Ricans in the state of New York is higher than that of any other ethnic group within the state and that Puerto Rican males were twice as likely to be diagnosed as schizophrenic on their first hospitalization than other male patients. These findings are considered to be a rough approximation of the overall hospitalization trends among other Hispanic groups in the country.

Research regarding the incidence, prevalence, diagnosis, and treatment of mental illness as a function of socioeconomic class is equally enlightening. Hollinghead and Redlich [18] reported that lower class patients were more frequently hospitalized and received less psychotherapy than upper class patients in the same diagnostic groups. Numerous other studies have reported a higher incidence and prevalence of mental illness among those patients in the lower socioeconomic class [19,20,21,22]. Baldwin et al [23] and Wilkinson [24] found support for the hypothesis that patients with ascribed low status are more likely to be diagnosed psychotic rather than neurotic or healthy. A classic debate tends to emerge regarding the interpretation of such data. One might argue that the stresses and pressures associated with limited social and economic resources precipitate increased psychopathology. On the other hand, inherent (often presumed genetic) psychopathology may sufficiently interfere with social and occupational functioning so as to produce a "downward drift" in socioeconomic status. Both explanations, however, assume that the reported class differences in psychopathology accurately reflect real differences in population. There are some studies that suggest these base rates are really the expression of expectancies and biases among mental health professionals.

CLINICAL ISSUES

The data seem rather clear in suggesting that value judgements play a significant factor in the provision of emergency psychiatric services to minority groups. We would now like to focus on some of the major clinical issues which must be taken into consideration when providing services to such groups and which may be responsible for some of the biases which apparently exist in clinical decision-making.

The Language Barrier

Effective verbal communication is an important element in any interpersonal situation, but it becomes critical when the context is the assessment of a psychiatric emergency. In assessing minority patients, language variables may directly or indirectly affect our ability to make accurate diagnoses and appropriate treatment decisions. Several studies suggest that the bilingual patient appears different when examined in English than when examined in his native tongue. DelCastillo [32] suggested that the bilingual patient may show less psychotic symptomatology when examined in English than when examined in his native tongue. He speculated that the mental effort required to speak in a second language puts the patient in better contact with reality and masks the psychosis that is apparent when the patient is interviewed in his native language. However, Marcos et al [33] concluded that Hispanic patients are consistently seen to have increased psychopathology when interviewed using the English language than when interviewed in their native tongue. These patients exhibited significant speech disturbances generally associated with the anxiety produced by the interview. In general, these patients tended to speak more slowly and use longer periods of silence, thereby showing characteristics frequently associated with depression.

The studies cited above reach contrasting conclusions; however, they both emphasize that the bilingual patient appears different when examined in English than when examined in his native tongue. Similarly, within certain subcultures of our English speaking society, a language barrier may exist between the clinician who uses standard English and the patient for whom nonstandard English is the norm. For example, black patients from predominantly lower class backgrounds may use words and phrases that may not be entirely understandable to the white middle class clinician. These patients tend to use shorter sentences and less grammatical elaboration than white patients in middle and upper classes [34]. These differences in the use of language may lead not only to misunderstanding, but to the conclusion that blacks are inferior with regard to various aspects of cognitive functioning.

There are obvious clinical and programatic implications, particularly for the emergency psychiatric unit that treats a preponderance of minority patients. Obviously, it would be desirable to employ mental health professionals who both literally and metaphorically "speak the same language" as their patients. Unfortunately, what is desirable is not always possible and there is a definite need for adequately and appropriately trained interpreters. The qualities of a good interpreter include a familiarity with psychiatric terminology, a thorough knowledge of the languages used, and the ability to understand the culture of both the clinician and the patient [35].

At the same time, Sabin [36] emphasizes the potential risks and need for caution when using even the most competently trained interpreter. This author reviewed two cases of suicide by Spanish speaking patients who were evaluated and treated by English speaking psychiatrists using a translator. He concluded that while there was an abundance of data on life history and behavior collected, facilitating the diagnosis of psychosis, the interpersonal distance inherently involved in translation did not facilitate adequate appreciation of the patient's affective state. There is an important relationship between emotions and the words available to communicate these emotions, and the use of a translator does not provide the necessary intimate linguistic contact between patient and clinician.

Cultural Barriers

The major element in the delivery of emergency psychiatric services is differential diagnosis. Diagnostic errors may lead to inappropriate decisions regarding treatment and disposition. The potential for such error is exacerbated in the psychiatric emergency room where a high premium is placed on rapid assessment and rapid disposition. This demand for brief evaluations and brief interventions results from an interaction among a variety of factors including the urgency of the patient's problem, inadequate staffing ratios, space limitations and the tremendous volume of patients waiting to be seen. In this atmosphere, clinicians tend to pay attention to highly visible, overt symptoms that are pathognomonic indicators of certain disorders and ignore more subtle culturally related nuances in the patient's mood, thought and behavior. The result is the exclusive use of a diagnostic classification system which reflects western psychopathology and western values and puts little or no emphasis on the social or cultural context.

The definition, conception and expression of psychopathology differs from culture to culture. Rabkin [37], in a review of public attitudes towards mental illness, found that in the West there was a tendency toward more congruency between public and professional attitudes consistent with a medical model. This appears to be in contrast to the nonwestern attitude, with less emphasis on a medical model, less congruency between professional and public attitudes and less willingness to label deviance. Ruiz [38] emphasizes the importance of this issue when dealing with Hispanic patients. In many instances, Hispanic patients perceive mental illness as being caused by "supernatural" phenomena, while, on the other hand, therapists trained in the western hemisphere perceive such illness as a "natural" phenomena. Clinicians tend to perceive symptoms in negative terms, whereas Hispanic patients tend to see certain symptoms as a gift or quality. For example, hallucinatory experiences may be perceived as a sign of mediumship, that is, a special religious quality which could be developed in such a way that the person afflicted with the hallucinatory symptoms can become a "healer" in his own right and assist people in need of healing practices. Although the symptoms may still be a manifestation of psychopathology, a lack of awareness of the patient's understanding of and attitude towards these symptoms may lead to a rejection of psychiatric services or a complete failure in the treatment compliance. In addition, there are instances in which the same "symptoms" should not even be considered evidence of psychopathology. For example, in large segments of African societies, visions, hallucinations, and spirits are shared and accepted as legitimate expectations within the belief system [39,40].

Objective diagnoses should take into consideration the fact that people with different backgrounds and experiences express distress differently and that the same signs may have different meanings depending upon the cultural context. Draguns [39] found that in Argentina, as opposed to the United States, there is a tendency towards passive as opposed to active symptomatology and a greater concern with social relations in the symptomatology. He suggests that Hispanics feel less socially isolated, less ideationally active, and experience psychopathology as a suspension of cognitive effort and not a severing of interpersonal ties. Abad and Boyce [41] reported that Puerto Ricans complain little about depression per se, but rather complain about symptoms of insomnia, eating problems, fatigue, headaches, body aches, and feelings of weakness and exhaustion. Similarly, they reported that Puerto Ricans, in general, do not recognize anxiety in and of itself but rather in terms of heart palpitations, dizziness, and fainting.

Fernandez Marina [42] described a unique manifestation among Puerto Ricans which he termed "the Puerto Rican syndrome." This syndrome expresses itself as an "ataque de nervios" and tends to be viewed by clinicians either as a conversion reaction with a series of hyperkinetic manifestations or as epilepsy due to its seizure-like behavior. While it is important to rule out any neurological or psychiatric disorders which could be masked by this syndrome, it is also important to be aware that such a syndrome is accepted as "normal" within the Puerto Rican culture.

Binitie [43] conducted a factor analytic study of depression across cultures in an attempt to determine whether depressives in African cultures show typical signs of sin and guilt and whether these depressives showed suicidal tendencies. The results indicate that depression in the African cultures studied emerged principally as depressed mood, somatic symptoms and motor retardation. In the European cultures studied, depressive symptoms included guilt, suicidal ideation, and anxiety, but less somatic symptoms. Both groups lost interest in work and in the social setting. Guilt and suicidal ideas or acts were uncommon in African subjects, which suggests that guilt and suicide to a large extent are culturally determined.

The different personal and social environments of blacks also results in different personality structures, defense mechanisms and expressions of psychopathology. In many settings, considerable guardedness and/or hyperalertness is necessary for blacks' survival and the notion of adaptive paranoia among black patients is an important consideration [44,45]. The distinctions between hypersensitivity, paranoid ideation, and paranoid psychosis may be especially difficult to determine in an emergency setting, particularly when accompanied by a deliberate blunting of affect as a further defensive posture. This may account for the high proportion of paranoid schizophrenia diagnoses reported for black patients seen in emergency and in inpatient settings [46]. Black patients can also develop special signs and symptoms of psychological distress. For example, while the incidence and prevalence of depression in blacks appears to parallel that observed in society as a whole, the expressions and intensity of these symptoms may be quite different. Black patients are more likely to be active and self-destructive in their expressions of depression [47]. Black patients are also less likely to show depression by loss of appetite (the opposite is more likely) and crying is also a less frequent symptom of depression. Activity or agitated depression is more common and at times can mask the depressed mood even to the patient. There is also a general tendency for blacks to express sadness and depression through anger.

Prediction of dangerousness—the likelihood of harming oneself or others—is perhaps the most important decision made in the psychiatric emergency setting. Therefore, it is important to note that although there has been a recent rise in the suicide rate among black adolescents, black patients as a whole are still less likely to express suicidal ideation in a therapeutic situation. However, once they do, they have a higher probability of being serious in intent rather than manipulative and should be treated with more caution [48]. This author points out that although idle threats of suicide are not yet common in the black culture, threats of homicide are frequently expressed. Mothers and fathers use such threats to instill fear for disciplinary purposes and men often use them with each other as methods of engendering self-protection and respect. Thus, expressions of homicide (e.g., "I'm going to kill so and so") may be more an expression of anger than an intent to kill. In addition, the concept of victim-precipitated homicide among blacks has been offered as an explanation for the relatively low suicide rates among blacks [47,49].

Special Religious Considerations

Religion is one possible biasing influence on psychodiagnosis that has not been adequately addressed in the literature. Some studies have shown that patient religion is significantly related to diagnosis when diagnosis is considered in terms of a broad spectrum of diagnostic categories [50] or in terms of fine diagnostic discriminations [51]. However, because these studies were correlational, it is impossible to determine whether this relationship reflects real differences in the incidence of psychopathology across various religious groups or whether the findings reflect a religious bias in psychodiagnosis. Nevertheless, religion is undeniably a cultural manifestation that strongly influences one's definition of mental health and expression of, and attitude towards, psychopathology. In this regard, it is important to discuss some of the special religious beliefs which are likely to lead to diagnostic errors and therefore have an important impact on the provision of emergency psychiatric services.

With regard to the Hispanic patients, particularly Puerto Ricans, Ruiz [52] emphasizes the importance of understanding the existence of spiritism and its application to the mental health care system. The majority of the Hispanic population, although professing the Catholic religion, also makes use of other religious resources such as spiritism, witchcraft, and black magic. For example, it is estimated that between 31 and 80 percent of the Catholic Puerto Rican population of New York City also practice spiritism as a parallel religion [53,54,55]. Spiritism is defined as the science or doctrine of the inner relationship between the material world and the spirits of the invisible world [56]. Spiritists base their beliefs on the existence of spirits and their communication with the visible world. They believe that the soul is individualistic, nonmaterial and resides in a person's body only temporarily during his lifespan [57]. Thus, an Anglo therapist whose patient speaks of being in contact with a dead relative, or of having heard the voice of a dead relative, may consider this to be a sign of psychosis without recognizing it as a common and culturally accepted occurrence among Hispanics from the Caribbean area. In the high pressure of an emergency room setting, a patient reporting such "hallucinatory experiences" may all too quickly be hospitalized, treated with neuroleptic medication, and eventually receive a label of schizophreniform disorder.

This is not to imply that hallucinatory experiences in Puerto Rican patients should always be considered a manifestation of spiritism. In fact, Griffith and Ruiz [58] discuss a case of "possession" in a 29-year-old Puerto Rican female in which the patient's own family, who were also followers of spiritism, considered the patient's behavior to be abnormal. These authors state that a "possession" becomes abnormal when the experience lasts more than a few hours, when there is no perceived stimulus (e.g., the existence of a ceremony), when the phenomenon occurs in the presence of people who do not adhere to the belief, and when the associated behavior is negative or harmful. These criteria permit the differentiation between ritual possession and sickness possession. Similarly, Mars [59] described different situations in which followers of Haitian voodoo became "possessed", as well as situations in which "possession" was viewed as abnormal even by devout followers of voodoo.

The important point to emphasize is that in order to make such a distinction, and in order to avoid diagnostic and treatment errors, mental health professionals must be aware of these and other cultural phenomena. Glossolalia ("speaking in tongues") is another intense religious experience which has often been explained as a symptom of mental illness. Glossolalia is one of the distinctive aspects of Pentacostalism which is a rapidly growing religious sect in the United States. Hine [60] reported that Pentacostal glossolalics in the United States appeared to be well integrated and productive members of society. A psychological explanation of a religious experience represents a value judgement and a religious bias, particularly when these experiences become common in a certain sect or subculture. When considering such explanations for intense religious experiences, one has to be conscious again of the social factors involved. When an unusual experience becomes normative in a certain religious group, trying to explain its appearance on the basis of individual psychodynamics or psychopathology becomes very difficult [61].

This discussion raises some important implications regarding the provision of emergency psychiatric services to certain minority groups. Certain patients may hear voices, express delusions of control, or behave in other ways, permissible within their culture, which require no psychiatric intervention whatsoever. Even when such symptoms are a manifestation of a serious psychiatric disorder, classical psychiatric treatment may be an insufficient and ineffective approach due to the lack of attention regarding other belief systems concerning the etiology and manifestation of psychopathology. Several papers have focused on the importance of folk healers in providing psychiatric services to specific minority groups [38,52,58,62,63,64]. Ruiz and Langrod [62] offer an excellent comparison between classical mental health personnel and indigenous folk healers with emphasis on terminology, means of communication, diagnostic techniques and the utilization of social behavior and moral values. Folk healers communicate in the same terminology that their clients use, psychiatrists do not. Classically trained mental health professionals treat phenomena believed to be supernatural by natural means and approaches, whereas folk healers use methods more closely related to the patient's perception of causative factors. Folk healers see patients in their own homes, listen to so-called unscientific material and permit some forms of acting out. All this provides the folk healer with a better understanding of the patient's problems, thus offering a better opportunity for arriving at a correct diagnosis and treatment strategy. In addition, folk healers often understand their patient's frustrations better than traditional therapists do, because the folk healers live in the same neighborhood and know it well. Western trained psychiatrists adhere to a different ethnocentric culture and often ignore or are unaware of the way of life of communities that do not fit in the mold with which they are familiar. Finally, folk healers tend to use the patient's symptomatology in a positive way. They do not consider symptom removal as an indispensable precondition for healing the patient. On the contrary, they view the patient's symptoms as a gift or a quality. The patient is viewed as someone who can control or reduce the symptomatology by relying primarily on his inner-strength. This offers him hope of achieving greater autonomy in life.

A closer alliance between professional mental health workers and folk healers is strongly recommended in areas where the practitioners are likely to be treating a significant number of patients whose cultural and religious beliefs with regard to mental health and mental illness are incongruent with classical Western training. Folk healers can serve as "cultural consultants" to broaden our understanding of relevant cultural and religious phenomena and may serve as a treatment alternative to hospitalization. Although some mental health professionals are skeptical of those "primitive healers" who operate outside of the traditional medical system, a reframing of traditional psychiatric approaches narrows the gap considerably. As Jerome Frank points out in his 1973 book entitled *Persuasion and Healing* [65], there are three elements common to all mental healing: (1) a trained socially-sanctioned healer, (2) a sufferer seeking help with anything from minor daily distresses to acute crises, and (3) a ritualized series of contacts between healer and sufferer.

A CASE PRESENTATION

A case seen in Houston, Texas, during the summer of 1981 illustrates some of the barriers involved in provision of emergency mental health services to cultural minorities.

R.M. was a 14-year-old Cambodian male seen in the Psychiatric Emergency Service of Ben Taub General Hospital on the evening of August 24th, 1981, with the following history. He arrived in the United States in the spring of 1981 with his parents and four siblings. He was placed through the Cambodian refugee program in an apartment in Houston. They shared the space with another Cambodian family, thus making 12 the total number of persons living in the house-shelter. No one in the family was currently working, and they were living under the Social Assistance Program, food stamps, and the like. The patient was receiving irregular English classes; however, at the time of the interview, he spoke no English at all. While in Cambodia, the patient was exposed to atrocities, physical violence, and death. On occasion, he and his family were forced to dig graves for family acquaintances who were killed by the political regime there. Since his arrival in this country, the patient has suffered horrible nightmares in which he saw people being killed; concomitantly he began to speak with political overtones and frequently stated that he wanted to lead a rebellion against the communist government of Cambodia. His parents on occasion tied him to his bed for fear of their getting into political trouble in this country as a result of the patient's political statements. When the patient was five years old, he fell from a tree in Cambodia and injured his head, requiring several surgical sutures. At that time his family doctor told his parents that by age 10 he would be either dead or crazy as a result of this accident. Shortly after his arrival in this country, he attempted suicide by trying to jump out of a window; on July 12th, 1981, he again jumped out of a second story window, resulting in bruises all over his body, but no serious trauma. He was treated at a small private hospital in Houston and transferred from there to Ben Taub General Hospital for psychiatric consultation. On that day, he was admitted to the Psychiatric Service for evaluation and treatment with an initial diagnosis of acute psychotic reaction.

Upon admission, he was confused, with insomnia of several days duration, aggressive attitude towards his family and neighbors lasting several days, and an obsession with the political situation in Cambodia. Physical examination on that day revealed no abnormalities. Complete mental status examination could not be done as a result of the language barrier. The next day, that is 7/13/81, he was calmer and appeared more at ease. On 7/14/81, a complete mental status exam was performed through the assistance of an interpreter from a local Cambodian Assistance Program. At that time it was found that he was the oldest of the siblings, that he was professing Buddhism as a religion and that he felt at times possessed by a "spirit" who told him on occasions to behave well and help other people while on other occasions to hurt others and fight. He could not understand how he did not get killed while in Cambodia and felt that perhaps he was "invisible" to other people while there. He admitted hearing the voice of the "spirit" who at times possessed him. He was alert, fully oriented, cooperative and displayed appropriate affect. His associations were intact and he was able to abstract well in accordance with the interpreter. He also did well in similarities. He denied suicidal thoughts at this time and had a good appetite. Occasionally he felt like crying, particularly when angry. On this day he was placed on loxapine succinate 10 mg. three times a day orally. On 7/15/81 he was very cooperative and relaxed, and tried to communicate with others in the ward. He also built a model plane and a boat on that day. On 7/18/81 he became agitated every time the ward became noisy. On that day, his blood pressure was low and the loxapine succinate was discontinued. He was then placed on thiothixene hydrochloride 10 mg three times a day orally. On 7/18/81 he developed sore throat and difficulties in swallowing; since this was felt to be an extrapyramidal reaction, he was prescribed concomitant benztropine mesylate 1 mg twice a day orally. On 7/20/81 he was again interviewed through an interpreter and felt to be improving, although he still admitted hearing the "spirit's" voices. On 7/21/81 an unsuccessful attempt was made to find a Cambodian or Vietnamese psychiatrist in Houston to whom he could be referred for aftercare treatment. On that day the thiothixene hydrochloride was increased to 40 mg a day orally. On 7/24/81 he was discharged to the care of his family and referred to the Psychiatric Clinic at Ben Taub General Hospital for follow-up care. He was also referred to a local Cambodian family practitioner for a neurological work up. During this hospitalization period, an orthopedic consultation was done which showed no abnormalities. Laboratory tests showed a urinalysis negative for drugs; hematology negative on two occasions except for elevated eosinophiles (20 and 21), chemistry negative except for alkaline phosphatose at 163 and cholesterol 103. CT scan of the head was normal and chest x-ray was also normal. T-L spine x-rays showed minimal anterior wedging of T11 and T12. Electroencephalogram was within normal limits.

On 8/21/81 he was seen in the Psychiatric Clinic and even though there was no interpreter available at that time he was found to be doing better and was anxious to start school in September. A 30-day refill of thiothixene hydrochloride and benztropine mesylate was provided and he was told to return to the Psychiatric Clinic in one month. On 8/24/81 he was seen in the Pediatric Emergency Room of Ben Taub General Hospital with the complaint that he was unable to urinate for one day and defecate for four days. He was also shaking all day long. At that time, it was felt that he was suffering from an extrapyramidal reaction and he was given 25 mg of diphenhydramine hydrochloride intravenously and was referred to the Psychiatric Clinic the same day since there was no interpreter available in the Emergency Room to complete the evaluation. From there he was referred to the Psychiatric Emergency Room for emergency evaluation since there was no interpreter available in the Psychiatric Clinic either. That evening he was seen in the Psychiatric Emergency Room. Both he and his father were very frightened, anxious, and totally confused as to what to do and where to go from here. In French, the examiner instructed both to stop all medications and return to the Psychiatric Emergency room with an interpreter the next day. They did so and the patient was fully reevaluated on 8/26/81 and told not to take any other medications and to start school as planned. On 9/1/81 he was again seen in the Pediatric Clinic of Ben Taub General Hospital but no evaluation of him was done since he was felt to be too old for this clinic. On 9/2/81 he was seen in the Psychiatric Clinic and it was felt that he was doing fine and was told to return in two weeks. On 9/16/81 he was seen again in the Psychiatric Clinic and found to be doing well; however, he was still suffering from nightmares.

CONCLUSIONS

The most important component in the delivery of emergency psychiatric services is diagnosis; however, the diagnosis of mental illness is not an objective procedure. Psychodiagnosis always involves some element of subjective judgement in the selection and interpretation of information. For this reason, diagnostic errors are quite likely, particularly in the emotionally charged atmosphere of a psychiatric emergency room. Szasz [66] suggests that when clinicians assess psychopathology in patients they essentially compare the patient's behavior with their conceptions of normality, which in turn are influenced by the values of the culture in which they live and work. In other words, the subjective element in diagnostic labeling is primarily a value judgement based on sociocultural norms. Members of minority groups, whose behavior is more likely to deviate from mainstream cultural values, are more likely to suffer the detrimental effects of misdiagnosis. This may lead to inappropriate treatment, stigmatizing labels, and psychopathology induced by self-fulfilling prophecies [67]. For this reason, clinicians *must* pay very close attention to sociocultural, as well as biological and psychological, factors when providing emergency psychiatric services to minorities, the poor, and special religious groups. An ideal but unrealistic solution would be for patients and clinicians to always be from the same social, ethnic and cultural background [68]. Since this is not possible, mental health professionals should make every effort to acquire a knowledge and understanding of a patient's background. Research regarding biological and psychological approaches to treatment should integrate social and cultural variables. Training programs should not just offer, but require, courses in transcultural psychiatry. Nontraditional treatment resources should be investigated, cultivated, and supported. Finally, as individual clinicians, we must confront our own values and examine the attitudes we hold towards our patients and others with whom we work.

REFERENCES

1. Bartolucci, G. and Drayer, C.S.: An overview of crisis intervention in the emergency rooms of general hospitals, Am J Psychiatry, 130:953-960, 1973.
2. Gerson, S. and Bassuk, E.: Psychiatric emergencies: an overview, Am J Psychiatry, 137(1):1-11, 1980.
3. Jacobson, G.: Emergency services in community mental health, Am J Public Health, 64:124-128, 1974.
4. Bassuk, E. and Gerson, S.: Deinstitutionalization and mental health services, Scientific American, 238:46-53, 1978.
5. Slovenko, R. and Luby, E.: From moral treatment to railroading out of the mental hospital, Bull Am Acad Psychiatry and the Law, 2:223-236, 1974.
6. Johnson, J.: Psychiatric emergencies in the community, Comprehensive Psychiatry, 10:275-284, 1969.
7. Coleman, J.V. and Errera, P.: The general hospital emergency room and its psychiatric problems, Am J Pub Health, 53:1294-1301, 1963.
8. King, L.: Social and cultural influences on psychopathology, Annual Review of Psychology, 29:405-433, 1978.
9. Lorion, R.: Ethnicity and mental health: An empirical obstacle course, Int J Ment Health, 5:16-25, 1976.
10. King, L.M.: Culture and class issues in community mental health, Fannon Center Quarterly, 1:1-22, 1976.
11. Simon, R.J., Fleiss, J.L., Gurland, B.J., Stiller, P.R., Sharpe, L.: Depression and schizophrenia in Black and White mental patients, Arch Gen Psychiatry, 28:509-512, 1973.
12. Raskin, A., Crook, T.H., Herman, K.D.: Psychiatric history and symptom differences in Black and White depressed inpatients, J Consult Clin Psychology, 43:73-80, 1975.
13. Gross, H.S., Herberg, M.R., Knatterud, G.L., Donner, L.: The effect of race and sex on the variation of diagnosis and disposition in a psychiatric emergency room, J Nerv Ment Disease, 148:638-642, 1969.

14. Cole, J. and Pilisuk, M.: Differences in the provision of mental health services by race, Am J Orthopsychiatry, 46:510-525, 1976.
15. Rabkin, J.G. and Struening, E.L.: Ethnicity, Social Class, and Mental Illness, New York: Institute on Pluralism and Group Identity, 1976.
16. Warheit, G.J., Holzer, C.E. III, Arey, S.A.: Race and mental illness: an epidemiological update, J Health and Soc Behavior, 16:243-256, 1975.
17. Ruiz, P: Psychiatric research and Hispanic culture: needs and directions, World Journal of Psychosynthesis, 11:32-35, 1979.
18. Hollingshead, A. and Redlich, F.: Social Class and Mental Illness, New York: John Wiley & Sons, 1958.
19. Derogatis, L.R., Yevzeroff, H., Wittelsberg, B.: Social class, psychological disorder, and the nature of the psychopathologic indicator, J Consult Clin Psychology, 43:183-191, 1975.
20. Dohrenwend, B.P. & Dohrenwend, B.S.: Social and cultural influences on psycho-pathology, Annual Review of Psychology, 25:417-452, 1974.
21. Dunham, H.W.: Society, culture and mental disorder, Arch Gen Psychiatry, 33:147-156, 1976.
22. Srole, L.: Measurement and classification in sociopsychiatric epidemiology: midtown Manhattan study (1954) and midtown restudy II (1974), J Health Soc Behavior, 16:347-364, 1975.
23. Baldwin, B.A., Floyd, H.H., McSeveny, D.R.: Status inconsistency and psychiatric diagnosis: a structural approach to labeling theory, J Health Soc Behavior, 16:275-261, 1975.
24. Wilkinson, G.S.: Patient-audience social status and the social construction of psychiatric disorders: toward a different frame of reference hypothesis, J Health Soc Behavior, 16:28-38, 1975.
25. DiNardo, P.: Social class and diagnostic suggestion as variables in clinical judgement, J Consult Clin Psychology, 43:363-368, 1975.
26. Umbenhauer, S., and DeWitte, L.: Patient race and social class: attitudes and decisions among three groups of mental health professionals, Comprehensive Psychiatry, 19:509-515, 1978.
27. Baxter, S., Chodorkoff, B., Underhill, R.: Psychiatric emergencies: dispositional determinants and the validity of the decision to admit, Am J Psychiatry, 124:1542-1546, 1968.
28. Errera, P., Wyshak, G., Jarecki, H.: Psychiatric care in a general hospital emergency room, Arch Gen Psychiatry, 9:105-112, 1963.
29. Hansen, G. and Bibigian, H.: Reasons for hospitalization from a psychiatric emergency service, Psychiatric Quarterly, 3:336-351, 1974.
30. Tischler, G.: Decision making processes in the emergency room. Archives of General Psychiatry, 14:69-78, 1966.
31. Shader, R., Binstock, W., Ohly, J., Scott, D.: Biasing factors in diagnosis and disposition, Comprehensive Psychiatry, 2:81-89, 1969.
32. Del Castillo, J.C.: The influence of language upon symptomatology in foreign born patients, Am J Psychiatry, 127:242-244, 1970.
33. Marcos, L.R., Alpert, M., Urcuyo, L., Kesselman, M.: The effect of interview language on the evaluation of psychopathology in Spanish-American schizophrenic patients, Am J Psychiatry, 130:549-553, 1973.
34. Sue, D.W. and Sue, D.: Barriers to effective cross-cultural counseling, J Counseling Psychology, 24:420-429, 1977.
35. Cox, J.L.: Psychiatry assessment of the immigrant patient, Br J Hosp Med 16:38-40, 1976.
36. Sabin, J.E.: Translating despair, Am J Psychiatry, 132:197-199, 1975.
37. Rabkin, J.G.: Public attitudes toward mental illness: a review of the literature, Schizophrenia Bulletin, 10:9-33, 1974.
38. Ruiz, P.: For the Hispanic patient: a socio-cultural approach. In The Hispanic Mental Health Issues and Strategies, M. Karno and J.I. Escobar (eds.), New York: Grune & Stratton, Inc. (in press).

39. Draguns, J.G.: Values reflected in psychopathology: the case of the Protestant ethic, Ethos, 2:115-136, 1974.
40. Rin, H., Schooler, C., Caudill, W.A.: Culture, social structure, and pathology in Taiwan and Japan, J Nerv Ment Disease, 157:296-312, 1973.
41. Abad, V. and Boyce, G.: Issues in psychiatric evaluation of Puerto Ricans: a socio-cultural perspective, Journal of Operational Psychiatry, 8(2):52-63, 1977.
42. Fernandez Marina, R.: The Puerto Rican Syndrome: Its dynamics and cultural determinants, Psychiatry, 24:79-82, 1961.
43. Binitie, A.: A factor-analytic study of depression across cultures (African and European), Br J Psychiatry, 127:559-563, 1975.
44. Grier, W.H. & Cobs, P.M.: Black Rage, New York: Basic Books, 1968.
45. Griffith, M.S. and Jones, E.E.: Race and psychotherapy: Changing perspectives, Current Psychiatric Therapies, 18:225-235, 1979.
46. Steinberg, M.D., Pardes, H., Bjork, D., and Sporty, L.: Demographic and clinical characteristics of Black psychiatric patients in a private general hospital, Hosp Commun Psychiatry, 28(2):128-132, 1977.
47. Poussaint, A.F.: Why Blacks kill Blacks, New York: Emerson Hall, 1972.
48. Block, C.B.: Black Americans and the cross-cultural counseling and psychotherapy experience. In Cross-cultural counseling and Psychotherapy. A. Marsella and P. Pedersen (eds.), New York: Pergamon Press, 1961, pp. 177-194.
49. Bush, J.A.: Suicide and Blacks: a conceptual framework, Suicide Lifethreatening Behavior, 6(4):216-222, 1976.
50. Roberts, B.H. and Myers, J.K.: Religion, national origin, immigration, and mental illness, in The mental patient: studies in the sociology of deviance, S.P. Spitzer and N.K. Denzin (Eds.), New York: McGraw-Hill, 1968.
51. Weintraub, W. and Aranson, H.: Patients in psychoanalysis: some findings related to sex and religion, Am J Orthopsychiatry, 44:102-108, 1974.
52. Ruiz, P.: Spiritism, mental health and the Puerto Ricans: an overview, Transcultural Psychiatric Research, Volume XVI:28-43, 1979.
53. Garrison, V.: The Puerto Rican Syndrome in psychiatry and spiritism, in Case Studies in Spirit Possession, V. Crapanzano and V. Garrison (Eds.), New York: John Wiley & Sons, Inc., 1977, pp 383-449.
54. Lubchansky, I., Egri, G., and Stokes, J.: Puerto Rican spiritualists view of mental illness: the faith healer as a paraprofessional, Am J Psychiatry, 127:88-97, 1970.
55. Rogler, L.H. and Hollingshead, A.B.: Trapped: Families and Schizophrenia, New York: John Wiley and Sons, Inc., 1965.
56. Kardec, A.: El libro de los espiritos, Mexico: Editorial Diana, 1963.
57. Kardec, A.: El libro de los espiritos, Mexico: Editoria Latino Americana, S.A., 1967.
58. Ruiz, P. and Langrod, J.: The ancient art of folk healing: African influence in a New York City community mental health center, in Traditional healing: new science or new colonialism?, P. Singer (Ed.), New York: Conch Magazine Limited, 1977, pp 80-95.
59. Mars, L.: Phenomena of "possession", Tomorrow: World's Digest of the Psychic and Occult, 3(1):61-73, 1954.
60. Hine, V.H.: Pentecostal glossolalia: toward a functional interpretation, Journal for the Scientific Study of Religion, 8:211-226, 1969.
61. Beit-Hallahmi, B. and Argyle, M.: Religious ideas and psychiatric disorders, Int J Soc Psychiatry, 23:26-30, 1977.
62. Ruiz, P. and Langrod, J.: The role of folk healers in community mental health services, Commun Ment Health Journal, 12:392-398, 1976.

63. Griffith, E. and Ruiz, P.: Cultural factors in the training of psychiatric residents in an Hispanic urban community, Psychiatric Quarterly, 49:29-37, 1977.

64. Youcha, G.: Psychiatrists and folk magic, Science Digest, June, 1981.

65. Frank, J.: Persuasion and Healing; a Comparative Study of Psychotherapy, Baltimore: Johns Hopkins University Press, 1973.

66. Szasz, T.S.: The myth of mental illness, In The Mental Patient: Studies in the Sociology of Deviance, S.P. Spitzes and N.K. Denzin (eds.), New York: McGraw Hill, 1968.

67. Rosenthal, R. and Jacobsen, L.: Pygmalion in the Classroom: Teacher Expectation and Pupils' Intellectual Development, New York: Holt, Rinehart and Winston, 1968.

68. Shapiro, E.T. And Pinsker, H.: Shared ethnic scotoma, Am J Psychiatry, 130:1338-1341, 1973.

Index

Abuse, adult
  identification of, 58-61
  medical presentations suggestive of,
    56-57
  perpetrator of, treatment for,
    68-69
  psychological issues of, 63-64
  societal attitudes towards, 61-62
  treatment for, 65-68
    motivation for, 55-56, 64-65
    short-term, 66-68
Abuse, child
  behavioral effects of, 93-95,
    200-202
  causes of, 95-97
  definition of, 90, 205
  differential diagnosis of, 94-95
  efficacy of treatment for,
    202-203
  emotional sequelae to, 200-202
  evaluation of, 91-92
  funding for treatment of, 206
  history of, 89, 207
  incidence of, 90-91
  in infancy, 209
  interventions for, 97-98
  lack of treatment for, 204-210
  medical presentations suggestive
    of, 57

[Abuse, child]
  perpetrator of, characteristics of,
    92-93
  personality changes from, 200-201
  physical, 89-98
  problems in treating, 199-210
  psychiatric model of, 204
  psychological issues of, 63, 64
  psychotherapy for, 65
  sexual, 99-111
    behavioral effects from, 102-104
    definition of, 99-101
    family reactions and role in,
      104-105
    from incest, 106-108
    incidence of, 100-101
    interventions for, 108-111
    perpetrator of, 101-104
    physical examination for, 110
    types of, 100
  social-situational model of, 204
  societal attitudes towards, 204
  sociological model of, 204
  violent behavior resulting from, 201
Abuse, substance
  with central nervous system de-
    pressants, 142-144
  with central nervous system stimu-
    lants, 144-145